Study Abroad FOR DUMMIES®

Study Abroad FOR DUMMIES®

by Erin E. Sullivan

WILEY

Wiley Publishing, Inc.

Study Abroad For Dummies®

Published by
Wiley Publishing, Inc.
111 River Street
Hoboken, NJ 07030-5774
www.wiley.com

Copyright © 2004 by Wiley Publishing, Inc., Indianapolis, Indiana

Published by Wiley Publishing, Inc., Indianapolis, Indiana

Published simultaneously in Canada

For general information on our other products and services or to obtain technical support, please contact our Customer Care Department within the U.S. at 800-762-2974, outside the U.S. at 317-572-3993, or fax 317-572-4002.

Wiley also publishes its books in a variety of electronic formats. Some content that appears in print may not be available in electronic books.

Library of Congress Control Number: 2003113600

ISBN: 07645-5457-3

Manufactured in the United States of America

10 9 8 7 6 5 4 3 2 1

1B/RU/RQ/QT/IN

 WILEY   is a trademark of Wiley Publishing, Inc.

About the Author

Erin E. Sullivan graduated from Wellesley College, where she worked as a Peer Adviser in the study abroad office her senior year. She spent her junior year in Dublin, Ireland, at Trinity College and is returning to Dublin to begin her postgraduate work in International Business. Erin is originally from Duxbury, Massachusetts, but currently lives in Boston and is a Research Associate at Harvard Business School.

Dedication

For Gram and Bailey.

Author's Acknowledgments

Thanks to everyone at Wiley for their enthusiasm and hard work on this book: Jennifer Bingham, Traci Cumbay, Natasha Graf, Marcia Johnson, Neil Johnson, Laura Peterson, and Elizabeth Rea. Thanks also to Kathy Walden from Butler University for the insight she provided as technical editor. I am indebted to Sylvia Hiestand and Harriet Cole at the Wellesley College study abroad office for teaching me much of what I know about studying abroad. And, of course, thanks to my superstar agent, Megan Buckley, for introducing me to the *For Dummies* people and for many, many motivational e-mails and phone calls.

Thank you to everyone who made suggestions for the book. Just because I may not have used them does not mean they weren't great! To Camila Alarcon, Liz Johnson, Meike Sommer, Allie Speier, and Harumi Supit for your expertise on different countries. Also, to my co-workers at HBS: Laura Feldman, Debbie Freier, Jenny Illes, James Quinn, and Emily J. Thompson for various tidbits of advice along the way. To all my Irish friends who made my year abroad memorable and acted as cheerleaders by e-mail as I wrote this book: John McKeown, Dr. Saoirse O'Sullivan, and Dr. Emily Vereker.

To all my friends and family, thanks for your support and for always taking the time to ask how this book project was going. Thanks to both of my sisters: Lau for being a guinea pig while making her plans to study abroad, and to Kait for always being willing to help with the latest and greatest in procrastination techniques. And, finally, to my parents: thanks to Dad for reviewing book contracts and to Mom for assisting with the health chapter and for the snacks while I spent hours glued to the computer. Thanks for giving me both roots and wings: I would be lost without your unconditional love and support.

Publisher's Acknowledgments

We're proud of this book; please send us your comments through our Dummies online registration form located at www.dummies.com/register/.

Some of the people who helped bring this book to market include the following:

Acquisitions, Editorial, and Media Development

Project Editor: Marcia L. Johnson

Acquisitions Editor: Natasha Graf

Copy Editor: E. Neil Johnson, Laura Peterson

Editorial Program Assistant: Holly Gastineau-Grimes

Technical Editor: Kathleen Walden

Editorial Manager: Jennifer Ehrlich

Editorial Assistant: Elizabeth Rea

Cover Photos: © A & L Sinibaldi/Getty Images/The Image Bank

Cartoons: Rich Tennant, www.the5thwave.com

Production

Project Coordinator: April Farling

Layout and Graphics: Joyce Haughey, Shae Lynn Wilson

Proofreaders: John Tyler Connoley, John Greenough, Andy Hollandbeck, Carl William Pierce, TECHBOOKS Production Services

Indexer: TECHBOOKS Production Services

Special Help: Melissa S. Bennett, Jennifer Bingham, Traci Cumbay

Publishing and Editorial for Consumer Dummies

Diane Graves Steele, Vice President and Publisher, Consumer Dummies

Joyce Pepple, Acquisitions Director, Consumer Dummies

Kristin A. Cocks, Product Development Director, Consumer Dummies

Michael Spring, Vice President and Publisher, Travel

Brice Gosnell, Associate Publisher, Travel

Kelly Regan, Editorial Director, Travel

Publishing for Technology Dummies

Andy Cummings, Vice President and Publisher, Dummies Technology/General User

Composition Services

Gerry Fahey, Vice President of Production Services

Debbie Stailey, Director of Composition Services

Contents at a Glance

Table of Contents

Introduction

"It was the best year of my life!" "I wish I could go back tomorrow." "I learned so much about myself." "I made lots of great friends!" "I speak French fluently now!" "Once I graduate from college, I'm moving there!"

Studying abroad can be the most memorable semester or year of your undergraduate college experience. What can be more exciting, but at the same time equally terrifying, as packing up and moving to another country? And don't worry if you don't know anyone or fluently speak the language or know how to find your way around the place you're going! You can make friends and discover everything you need to manage in your abroad destination quickly enough. Think of it as a one big, exciting, and educational adventure.

Now, more than ever, students are heightening their awareness of the world outside of the U.S. The terms "international education" and "globalization" frequently roll off the tongues of college presidents and deans. Some schools have even gone so far as to require students to spend time abroad in order to graduate! In a way, going abroad is becoming "trendy."

The Institute for International Education (IIE) releases an annual Open Doors report each November that provides data on international students, scholars in the U.S., and American students who study abroad. A grant from the Bureau of Education and Cultural Affairs at the U.S. Department of State partially supports IIE's production of this report. According to the Open Doors 2002 Report, a record number of 154,164 U.S. college students received credit for studying abroad in 2000/01, up 7.4 percent from the previous year. While Europe continues to be the most popular destination for U.S. students studying abroad (63 percent), more students are opting to explore places such as Latin America, Oceania, Africa, and Asia. The top five most popular countries for U.S. students headed abroad are the United Kingdom, Italy, Spain, France, and Mexico.

In *Study Abroad For Dummies*, I give you all the information you could possibly need to plan and spend a successful semester or year abroad. Going abroad isn't rocket science. There are just lots of details to remember and coordinate. If you approach this experience with the right attitude — curious, adventurous, responsible, willing to learn, enthusiastic and energetic — you'll be well on your way to having the time of your life!

Who Needs This Book

I wrote this book primarily with the undergraduate study abroad experience in mind because college is when most students take advantage of the opportunity to live and study outside of the U.S. It is not unusual, however, for high school students to spend some time abroad or for graduate students to opt to do a semester away, too. This book also provides a considerable amount of insight for those of you trying to help students get ready to study abroad, whether you're a parent, professor, or study abroad director.

How to Use This Book

You can use *Study Abroad For Dummies* as a how-to manual for your study abroad experience from start to finish. You can also use it as a reference for looking up information as the need arises, whether you're in the middle of packing your bags to go abroad or have been abroad for months already. Like all *For Dummies* books, this book is designed so that you do not have to sit down and read it from the beginning to the end. You can pick it up and read only the information you need to know, when you need to know it, regardless of whether you've read all the pages that come before. Just use the detailed table of contents or the index to find the topic you're interested in. However, if you want to understand the entire study abroad experience, you can dive in and read the book from cover to cover.

Conventions Used in This Book

Here in the U.S., we tend to use the words *college* and *university* interchangeably. Students go on to colleges or universities after completing high school. Generally, a university is made up of an undergraduate division (bachelor's degrees) and a graduate division (master's and doctorate degrees). A college is either a smaller part of a university or an independent institution offering bachelor's degrees only (for example, liberal arts colleges). In other countries around the world, the term *college* connotes high school and the term *university* is reserved for institutions of higher learning that grant bachelor's, master's, and doctorate degrees. Thus, to keep all of this from getting too confusing, I invented the term "home university" to describe the undergraduate school you're going to now, regardless of whether it has the word college or university in its title.

How This Book Is Organized

Study Abroad For Dummies is organized into six parts, each of which is divided into several chapters that cover specific topics. Each chapter contains all the information you need to know about any given topic — no further reading required!

Part I: Study Abroad Basics

This first section gets you started on your study abroad journey — and you don't even have to leave the comfort of your dorm room. If you're wondering why you should go abroad or whether you have the time to go away, this is where you can get some answers! Use this section to think through your entire academic program and determine exactly how studying abroad fits into your plans.

Part II: Finding a Program That Is Right for You

You'd be surprised at the number of options you have for studying abroad. There's hundreds! Although you can narrow down your choices based on your major, which languages you speak, which part of the world you want to explore, and which programs your home university will let you participate in, chances are that you still have quite a few programs to choose from. In this part, I give you the details on what's out there and how to ultimately choose what is best for you.

Part III: Applying to Schools and Programs Abroad

Perhaps the word "application" elicits nightmarish flashbacks of staying up until all hours during your senior year of high school finishing endless college applications. Applying to study abroad, however, is a different story. It doesn't take up nearly as much of your time and energy, but you should be aware of a few things that are unique to study abroad applications. I also give you some helpful hints on financial aid for study abroad programs and how to coordinate your plans with multiple institutions.

Part IV: Leaving Home and Going Abroad

Your brain is in constant overdrive as you transition between your life in the U.S. and your new abroad life. It seems that in the blink of an eye (or a long plane ride), you're transported to another place where you're expected to live for an extended period of time. You don't remember all the information thrown at you during your orientation sessions — there's just too much of it! You can rely on this section to refresh your memory on what you need to pack, how to get a passport, ways to stay safe and healthy, and the best ways to blend into your new culture.

Part V: Returning Home

Time flies while you're studying abroad. Before you know it, you have to take exams, pack up, and go home. The panic of what to pack will strike — you probably have more stuff now than you did when you first arrived. What do you take and what do you leave behind? Even better, what can you legally take home and what will customs confiscate? As much as you may look forward to going home to friends, family, and a culture or place you know very well, you'll miss your abroad life. I give you some readjustment tips to help with return "homesickness" and the bizarre experience of having culture shock in the midst of your native culture! I also discuss ideas on how to work, study, or volunteer abroad after college.

Part VI: The Part of Tens

Here I've compacted helpful pieces of advice into four top ten lists for quick and easy reading. Take a look at studying in a nontraditional destination like Africa, Asia, or Latin America. Find out about study abroad programs that are just a little different from most, consider some vacation destinations you may visit while you're away, and discover the best reasons for completing your graduate degree abroad.

Icons Used in This Book

The *For Dummies* books use little pictures, or icons, throughout the text to grab your attention and point out important or special information. Here's what they mean:

This is the icon I use for "insider information." You see it when I want to point out something that I found particularly helpful when I studied abroad or to flag information that I wish I had known when I was abroad. These tidbits should save you time and frustration.

When you come across one of these icons, I'm usually cross-referencing information that appears elsewhere in the book or just reiterating a useful or practical point. If you don't remember anything else from a discussion, file away what it says next to this icon!

With this icon, I'm getting down to the nitty-gritty or highly detailed information that may or may not apply to your study abroad situation.

Don't ignore the advice that appears next to this icon or you could find yourself, at the very least, in a sticky situation, and at the worst, in jail in a foreign country.

Where to Go from Here

Abroad, of course! And use this book in the way that is most helpful for you. Feel free to use this book in conjunction with information provided by your home and abroad universities. Pack it when you go abroad, and keep it handy in your dorm room as you plan your time away. Remember, going abroad can be stressful and a lot to think about, but the fun outweighs the headaches. This book can help you problem solve and simplify!

Happy travels!

Part I
Study Abroad Basics

The 5th Wave   By Rich Tennant

"I know you want to study in a country where you'll feel comfortable and fit in easily, but never-never land doesn't actually exist as a real country."

In this part . . .

*T*his part helps you reflect on your undergraduate experience so far and figure out how studying abroad fits into your academic plans. Unfortunately, you can't just wake up tomorrow, decide to study abroad, and then be on your way. Going abroad for a semester or a year requires much preparing and planning!

Chapter 1

All Abroad! Getting the Lowdown on Studying Abroad

The best way to learn about another country's customs, languages, and people is to live in that country for an extended period of time. And what better time to do this than while you're a student. Just think, when else will you be able to earn credit for living and learning outside the U.S.? Study abroad is an amazing adventure in which you're learning all the time: both inside and outside the classroom.

With the rapid advancements in communication, transportation, and economics (to name a few), the world has become more connected and increasingly international in scope. These changes affect nearly everyone, even you! Your living space is no longer confined to your city, town, or country: You live in the world, and therefore, to achieve success on a personal, intellectual, and professional level, you have to interact with people of other cultures and think about issues on a global scale.

Studying abroad prepares you to take your place in the world by teaching you cultural awareness and respect. It also increases your self-awareness, particularly how you see yourself in relation to the rest of the world. International education not only advances learning and scholarship, but it encourages cross-cultural communication and prepares students for leadership roles in a global community.

Why Bother Going Abroad?

Once you've gotten through the first year at your home university, you probably feel like you finally know all the buildings on campus, can find your way around town, know which professors to avoid, which dining hall is busiest at lunch, and of course, have made plenty of friends. So why leave this cozy little environment you've created for yourself just to go back to being the new kid on the block? Because your experience abroad is definitely worth the few trials and tribulations of starting over!

Think of study abroad as just an extension of your studies at your home university. Your time away should be an integrated part of your four-year undergraduate academic plan. When you go abroad, you will likely take courses that, in some way, build on or add to the courses you are taking at your home university. Study abroad is also a great time to begin independent research projects. Increasing numbers of students conduct research abroad and then work with faculty members when they return to convert their projects into senior theses.

Ready, set, grow!

Studying abroad definitely challenges you on a personal level. Whether you consciously realize it or not, you develop a greater self-confidence, independence, and self-reliance. By the time you return home, you may feel like a super hero: You can do anything!

Studying abroad may be the first time you are truly away from home — all your familiar surroundings here in the U.S., as well as friends and family. While this isn't always easy, most students agree that the benefits of giving up your familiar environment for a short period of time far outweigh the reasons to stay at home. Believe it or not, if you immerse yourself in a new culture, experiment with new ways of thinking, or try a different way of living, you naturally experience some sort of personal growth. After you master your new culture and the abroad academic life, you will return home much wiser and probably slightly impressed with yourself for having had a successful time abroad.

Changing your perspective

If you go abroad with an open mind, then you're certain to return to the U.S. a more enlightened person. One of the major benefits of studying abroad is its ability to broaden your world understanding and perspective on just about anything. You gain a different view of international affairs, from politics to economics to social issues. You also return with a deeper understanding and respect for your host country, knowing how another culture approaches daily life and unusual challenges.

You may also return with a new appreciation for the U.S. Living in another culture can help you understand your own on a deeper level. You may return grateful for the way of life in the U.S., its political system, or its foreign or domestic policies. Through your interactions with your abroad professors, your new peer group, and other foreign or U.S. students on your program, you can find out what others think about the U.S. (and this is usually both positive and negative).

The top ten reasons to go abroad

For those of you who don't want to be bothered with lengthy explanations about the wonders of studying away from home, here's the abbreviated argument for studying abroad:

✔ You learn about yourself in new ways and gain self-confidence, independence, and cross-cultural skills.

✔ Studying abroad changes your perspective on the world. You're introduced to new cultures and a new way of life.

✔ Studying abroad changes your perspective on the United States. You experience an educational system different from that of the U.S. and learn how other cultures and countries view the U.S. You may even learn what it means to be an "American" and what makes life in the U.S. different from life abroad.

✔ You can earn home university course credit in many countries. You may be able to fulfill graduation requirements. Some programs may correspond nicely with your major or minor.

✔ Studying abroad gives you a unique opportunity to learn another language or improve your existing language skills, as well as meet your home university's foreign language requirements.

✔ Studying abroad is flexible! You can find programs that work with your curriculum and time schedule. You don't even need to know another language. And lots of programs are out there, so you can find one that works for you.

✔ You increase your career opportunities in the global marketplace. Most employers prefer to hire graduates with some abroad experience. If you've traveled and can show you're knowledgeable about the world, you have the competitive edge.

✔ A semester, summer, or year abroad can give you the opportunity to participate in an international internship and gain hands-on experience in a foreign country.

✔ You meet some great new friends and people you never would have encountered if you stayed in the U.S. Some of them may be lifelong friends who will invite you to visit them again. You may even find yourself "adopted" by your host family.

✔ Travel to see places you've only dreamed about! You get to experience cities and countries you've only seen in books, on TV, on postcards, or in films.

While abroad, a new academic interest or perspective on your major may emerge. Studying at an abroad university allows you to study subjects that aren't available at your home university. For example, I studied Irish History from the years 1500 to 2000 while I was studying in Ireland, a course not offered at my home university. Other U.S. students took classes in Celtic civilization or Gaelic.

You also study familiar subjects but from a different cultural perspective. For example, if you study international relations in France, it will be from a European perspective. Alternatively, studying the U.S. and American history from a different country's point of view can be fun. And, of course, all your classroom learning is enhanced by living in your abroad location and interacting with host families, housemates, roommates, or friends who are native to your abroad country.

Jump-starting your career

Studying abroad typically gives your resume a nice boost and improves your post-graduate employment prospects, particularly if you're considering a career in business, international affairs, or government service. Nowadays, employers actively seek college graduates who have spent time studying abroad because they want employees with an international knowledge base as well as foreign language skills.

The same international skills that make you more marketable for employment are also valued by graduate schools. These skills include cross-cultural communication skills, analytical skills, teamwork, flexibility, an understanding of cultural contexts, the ability to adapt to new circumstances and deal with differences, a developed view of the world outside the U.S., independence, and self-confidence.

Experiencing a different education system

Institutions of higher education outside the U.S. function differently than what you're accustomed to. Even if your program is directed by a U.S.-based school, your experience can still differ because U.S.-based programs often employ local professors.

In the U.S., most students pay to go to college. It's kind of a pay-for-service model in which students pay for the education and in return expect their professors to conduct lectures, foster class discussion, hold office hours, and so on. This isn't usually the case in other parts of the world. If students don't pay for school or if the government (maybe through taxes) subsidizes tuition, then students don't feel as entitled. The tables are turned. Students have the privilege of going to school and therefore, it is up to them to take responsibility for their own learning.

A couple of reasons why NOT to go abroad

You should not approach studying abroad as a stress-free vacation from school. While the academics may be easier for you while you're abroad, you're actively learning during most of your waking hours. You'll have stressful moments, such as speaking a foreign language in the grocery store, adapting to your new home, or finding the bus stop.

You should not approach study abroad as an escape route from problems at home or at your home university. Most likely, the same problems will still exist when you return to the U.S.

Abroad universities are much less focused on grades. They care more about learning to increase understanding and knowledge. Therefore, you can expect much more of a lecture format to your classes and not much (if any) class discussion or participation. You can also expect to have less one-on-one interaction with your professors. (Professors at your abroad university may not even be required to hold weekly office hours.) However, the flexibility of curriculums abroad often gives students at abroad universities more freedom to explore their own interests within a course than would be allowed or even feasible in the U.S.

The difference in set ups between your home university and your host university doesn't mean you should assume that academics are easier abroad.

All these differences don't mean that the education you receive while you're abroad is better or worse than the education you get at your home university — it's just bound to be different. If you don't like your abroad classroom or learning style, chalk it up to a learning experience. Accept the challenge to learn in a different way, in a different cultural setting.

Before you take the plunge, think about your own personal reasons for wanting to go abroad because when you return from studying abroad, you'll assess whether you achieved your goals or hopes for studying abroad. Whatever your reasons for studying abroad, make sure that they are not only attainable, but also positive. For example, learning a second language, studying about another culture, diversifying your studies, preparing for graduate school, or traveling to meet new people are all good reasons to study abroad.

Studying Abroad: An Overview

Studying abroad can be the best part of your college experience, provided you avoid planning your semester or year away the night before you leave. Your study abroad journey is bound to be full of plans, decisions, challenges, and maybe even a mistake or two. (Mistakes are okay, as long as you learn something from them.) Keep in mind that studying abroad is enough of a project that the *For Dummies* people asked me to write an entire book about it.

Your study abroad sojourn begins the minute you walk past the study abroad office and take a look inside, or when you meet an upperclassman who just returned from a semester in Europe, or when a professor tells you your Italian would greatly benefit from a semester in Italy, or maybe when you see the beautiful beaches of Australia on the big screen. Once the study abroad seed has been planted in your head, all you need to do is consult this book to find out how to turn that "hey, I'd like to study abroad" thought into a reality.

So pull up a chair and get started with this quick overview of what it takes to get yourself abroad. Your study abroad adventure is only a few pages away.

In the beginning

First things first. You're going to have to postpone your dreams of cruising along the Riviera sipping iced tea for a moment while you check out your home university's study abroad policies. When should you go? (See Chapter 2.) How can the study abroad office help you? What if your university doesn't have a study abroad office? What are important dates to remember for studying abroad? (See Chapter 3.) What about foreign languages — how well do you really need to speak Chinese before leaving? How will you finish your major? (See Chapter 4.)

Another huge part of going abroad is deciding where to go. This can be fun, but also stressful. Your home university may offer its own study abroad programs that perfectly suit your needs. However, you may need to go searching for a program. And believe me, there are plenty of programs to sort through. The Internet has endless information on programs, so you're much better starting with small, familiar resources like your study abroad office or recent study abroad alums at your home university (see Chapter 5). You also need to consider what to study while you're abroad. Typically science majors or premed-track students have more difficulty with finding an appropriate abroad program (see Chapter 7). Studying in a country outside Europe can also be dramatically different from anything you've ever experienced before (see Chapter 24). Going abroad to the United Kingdom is also an option with many quirks (see Chapter 8).

You may get so wrapped up in the excitement going abroad that you forget all about having to study. So pay attention to Chapter 6 to ensure that your abroad experience doesn't cost you any credits or delay your graduation date.

The study abroad process is full of the typical headaches that come with applying to any school, namely filling out applications and making plans on how to finance your adventure. These two tasks are much simpler than what you went through when you applied to undergraduate schools though. Applications tend to be less involved and financing should be easy if you're used to dealing with the financial aid offices. For more information on all these issues, check out the chapters in Part III.

Diving in

After you're into a program and ready to get on a plane, you still have loads of details to take care of, including figuring out where to live (if your program does not include housing), which courses to take, getting a passport, applying for a visa, and booking your flights (see Chapters 11 and 12). And then there's the guaranteed to be overwhelming task of packing! You get two suitcases that can weigh somewhere from 40 to 70 pounds each (depending on your airline), and that is all you can take for your semester or year abroad. How does one decide what to pack? I help you out with that in Chapter 13.

Chapters 16, 17, and 18 contain a lot of practical information that you may want to peruse before you get to your abroad country. Chapter 16 discusses everything you need to know about money, including credit cards, budgets, and best places to exchange currency. Health and safety are two other areas you need to pay attention to if you're going abroad. The best rule I can give you about safety is to use your common sense, but you can also find some other tips in Chapter 17 that may not be so familiar to you. The chapter about staying healthy abroad (Chapter 18) is not intended to turn you into a hypochondriac. Just be aware that you may run into some illnesses when you travel outside the United States. Staying safe and healthy keeps your abroad experience a pleasurable one.

Chapter 14 gets you through those first weeks or months in your abroad country. I give you some tips on settling into your new home quickly, especially if you only have a day or two before classes begin. If you're living with a host family or have roommates from your abroad country, Chapter 15 on crossing cultures should help you deal with adjusting to people, places, and situations that seem very foreign to you (at least initially).

Resuming life at home

Time flies when you're having fun, and your time abroad is guaranteed to be over before you know it. Sometimes coming home is much more difficult than going abroad. You need to, once again, pack a large amount of stuff into two suitcases. And you probably have more stuff this time around, because you'll have purchased fun things, like souvenirs, and collected notes, books, and papers that need to return to the U.S. with you. You also need to make sure you're not bringing anything home that could be illegal! (See Chapter 19.) Once you settle back in to your familiar routine at your home university, you may experience a bout of reverse culture shock. It seems hard to believe, but adjusting back to your native culture can be difficult! Don't worry, in Chapter 20, I give you some strategies for dealing with this. And, for those of you who want to go abroad again, check out Chapter 21 and start brainstorming.

Just for fun

Finally, in the last few pages of the book, I take a break from all the technical details and things to remember to give you some creative and fun ideas about places to visit and nontraditional places to study and a heads up about some unique opportunities out there (see the chapters in Part VI). I also throw in a few reasons to consider pursuing your graduate education outside of the U.S. (see Chapter 25).

Chapter 2

Timing Is Everything: Knowing When to Go

*T*raditionally, most students study abroad during their junior year because by that time, they've fulfilled most of their core requirements, chosen their major, and completed some coursework in that chosen major. For instance, at my undergraduate school about 33 percent of the junior class spends either a semester or the full year abroad. But just because this is the general rule doesn't mean that you have to follow it. With careful planning, you can study abroad during your freshman, sophomore, or senior year — it may even work better for you!

Some universities give you the option of deciding when you want to go abroad; others require you to go during a particular year or semester. Many factors influence when *you* want to go abroad, including your specific plans for a major, whether you want to write a thesis, whether you play a sport, whether you're active in various campus organizations, and whether your friends plan to go abroad. As you contemplate studying abroad, make sure your decision is the one you're most comfortable with, the one that's best for you (and not someone else).

Choosing When to Study Off-Campus

Your home university's study abroad regulations are the primary determinant of when you can and can't go abroad. The other big factor that influences your decision is how you've constructed your four-year academic program. The following sections give you some general guidelines.

Shipping out your sophomore year

Your sophomore year is probably your first opportunity to study abroad and may be a good choice for a couple reasons. Typically, juniors and seniors are accorded more privileges and opportunities, such as early registration for classes and greater access to professors. Also, you may want to pursue campus leadership or internship positions that are typically reserved for upperclassmen. With all the privileges seniority brings, why would you want to hold off and wait until your junior or senior year to go abroad?

Or maybe your sophomore year seems too soon to leave a campus you just recently got familiar and comfortable with. Perhaps you're still exploring what you want to major in, and you still need to get to know some departments better at your home university. Or maybe you're working away on completing your core requirements or taking extensive language courses during this year — better go another year.

Statistically, sophomores who choose to study abroad usually choose the second semester or the summer between sophomore and junior year because by this time their academic plan is more clearly defined than it was in first semester.

Finding yourself somewhere else in the first semester

By the time the first semester of sophomore year rolls around, most sophomores have not completed enough core requirements or work in their major to enable them to study abroad. However, if you're one of the super-organized few who has all of your coursework in order at such an early stage, by all means, go! Also, if you discover that you're unhappy at your home university and are considering a transfer, sometimes studying abroad during the first semester of sophomore year can help you decide whether another school perhaps is better for you (if that option is even available). Going abroad at this time of uncertainty allows you to get some perspective — to see the "big picture" — so that you can get some distance from your troubling home institution and see whether you really want to make a change.

Slipping away during second semester

Most sophomores who study abroad do so during the second semester. At this point, you more than likely have carefully thought out your plans to study abroad by completing core requirements and starting coursework toward your major, and thus going away is more feasible. Spending time abroad during your sophomore year may suit you for any of the following reasons:

✔ You want to complete a considerable amount of advanced coursework in your major, which requires you to stay at your home university during your junior and senior years.

✔ You want to take advantage of opportunities when you become a junior that are available to upperclassmen, such as independent research, internships, and leadership positions in campus organizations.

✔ You want to quickly improve your foreign language skills.

✔ You want to go away during the off-season semester because you're an athlete who competes and trains during only one semester. In fact, you may even want to go away during two off-seasons semesters (in other words fall sophomore year and fall junior year if you're a baseball or softball player).

✔ You want to go away to two different places each for a semester thus spreading your studies abroad over two academic years.

Cascading across continents as a junior

Junior year is the most popular year to go abroad. Some universities allow their students to go away only during the junior year for a variety of reasons.

✔ You've finished four consecutive semesters of language study, making you proficient through the intermediate level, and now you're ready for total immersion into the language to increase your fluency.

✔ You plan to write a thesis during your senior year, so you certainly cannot go away then. Furthermore, if you've determined your thesis topic and decided a semester away in a country that's relevant to your topic will benefit your research, you need to go before senior year.

✔ Your home university requires you to spend the final two semesters at home, which makes study abroad during your junior year an obvious choice.

✔ Many overseas universities and study abroad programs require study abroad students to be juniors.

Some reasons why you, personally, may find junior year a great year to study away from home could include:

- After two years at your home university, you've matured enough to venture out on your own, away from family, friends, and everything familiar.

- Many of your friends also are studying away at the same time, which means that you will have plenty of people to visit and free floors to sleep on!

- You're well established at your home university. You have professors and advisers who know you. Your social group is set, you know all the ins and outs of college life, and you won't be returning to any unexpected situations as a senior.

- You must apply to graduate school or for postgraduation jobs during your senior year.

Savoring a senior-year sojourn

Most universities require you to spend your final undergraduate semester at your home university because you'll likely need to finish one or two requirements at that time. Therefore, your last chance to spend one of your undergraduate semesters abroad is probably during the first semester of your senior year.

Most students who go abroad this late in the game usually do so because they realize that they'd be passing up an amazing opportunity by not studying abroad during their undergraduate years. Or in some cases, students decide not to write a thesis, finish satisfying their core and major requirements, and then find some time and flexibility in their schedules that they didn't originally think they'd have. Perhaps courses that you desperately wanted to take were offered during your junior year, and after having taken them, you created space in your schedule to go abroad.

If you're writing a senior thesis, you can't go away. If you have too many credits to complete, you can't go away. If you want to apply for graduate schools and fellowships or participate in on-campus job fairs, being away is a handicap.

Studying abroad during summer

When you plan out your entire undergraduate academic program and realize spending a semester abroad just isn't possible, a summer program may be just the thing for you. Studying abroad often becomes difficult whenever you're majoring in two subjects, delaying declaring a major, needing to take a particular sequence of courses before taking an exam (like the Medical College Admissions Test — for more information on this test, see Chapter 7), or applying to graduate school.

At many universities, course scheduling for majors such as science and engineering can be so tight that a semester abroad is simply not possible. For these students, summer study abroad can provide the opportunity to experience another culture, if only for a few weeks, without delaying graduation or missing important classes.

Or maybe you just have too much to accomplish, too many interesting courses are offered at home, or you're too afraid of missing out on all that your home university has to offer. If you can't bear to spend a semester away from school but still want to see a different part of the world and experience a different culture, a summer study abroad program is your best bet.

Many programs offer summer study options; however, you need to realize a few things before deciding to pursue study abroad plans during summer months:

- ✔ You lose your chance to have a summer job. If you usually depend on summer income to make money for school, this option may not work. And chances are you won't be allowed to work in a foreign country.

- ✔ Financial aid and scholarships for summer study may be limited or unavailable altogether.

- ✔ Some summer study abroad programs are watered down and glorified tours, so not much actual studying is going on. Be careful which programs you choose. If you want to receive academic credit at your home university for summer courses, you need to investigate which summer programs your school recommends.

- ✔ Most summer programs offer a small selection of courses, and most of these courses are in the humanities, fine arts, or even pop culture. You may have a hard time finding science, engineering, or social science courses in a summer program.

- ✔ You may need to petition your school for academic credit for summer courses because they may not be as structured as courses are during the regular academic year. Home universities may even impose a limit on the number of credits you can transfer from summer courses.

- ✔ Some universities abroad completely shut down or may not even offer undergraduate study during summer months. Often, the only students at school in summer are postgraduates conducting research and international students (mostly Americans) attending summer study abroad programs.

- ✔ In many countries, the majority of native students are away from university during summer months, which limits the number of courses available and the amount of contact you have with the country's culture. You can wind up on a mostly American program with few opportunities to meet and mingle with natives.

- ✔ Some summer programs offer research and internship opportunities, which may be valuable. However, your home university may not grant you credit for them.

✔ Consider the climate and weather. If you plan on studying close to the equator, be aware that some places can be very hot and without air conditioning. And if you want to study in the Southern Hemisphere, remember that our summer is their winter.

✔ When you're planning to study away from your home university during the summer between your junior and senior years, consider your post-college plans. If you're are planning to apply to graduate school and end up away from home that summer, you may miss an important opportunity to study for graduate school exams or start filing applications.

✔ When you study during the summer, you may not be giving yourself enough of a break from school and can return to your home university in the fall more burned out than when you left.

Weighing One Semester or Two?

With the notable exception of universities that do not follow a semester schedule, most study abroad programs offer you a choice of studying away during the fall or spring semesters or a full *academic year*.

The most obvious difference between studying away for one semester or two is the length of time involved. Studying abroad for two semesters offers more options and more flexibility than studying away for only one semester, but that doesn't mean that studying abroad for a year is inherently better than for only a semester. Doing so merely gives you more time.

Going abroad for a full year also has its drawbacks, including being away from the comforts of home and the familiarity of your home university. You may also return and discover that you need to scurry to finish up coursework in your remaining time on campus. Or perhaps you were the only one in your friend group to go away for a full year and have returned to find you just don't seem to fit with the friends you had before you left.

Maybe for you, going away for one semester is enough time abroad. On the other hand, you may want to spend as much time as possible away and therefore a year for you is ideal. In addition, some universities, particularly the more traditional ones in the United Kingdom and Ireland, operate on a trimester system. So if you study abroad at one of these universities in the fall, your fall "semester" abroad could be as short as nine weeks.

Deciding whether to go abroad for one semester or two is a personal choice, and you need to make that decision based on your academic plans. Studying away from home for one and two semesters each has its pros and cons. Weigh them carefully and make the decision that's best for you. To help you choose, I give you the lowdown on both options — going for a single semester or going for two — in the following sections.

Swinging singles: One semester

Reasons for studying away for one semester include any of the following:

- The number of core requirements you must fulfill or the amount of coursework required for your major allows you to go abroad only for one semester.

- You're a double major, and you find it more difficult to go away for a full year and still satisfy requirements for two majors.

- You declared your major late and have a significant amount of coursework left to complete.

- Financially, you can only afford one semester abroad.

- You get homesick easily.

- You play a sport or want to run for student government and, therefore, need to be at your home university campus during a particular semester.

Never fear! If you choose to study abroad for one semester, you still can

- Benefit from studying abroad

- Improve your language skills

- Learn about a new culture

- Find time to travel

You need to realize, however, that in one semester your time abroad is limited. Take advantage of any and all opportunities presented to you. Try new foods and force yourself to speak the language of your host country. You need to make an extra effort to be outgoing and make friends with natives as soon as possible. Join clubs and attend social events as much as possible; you don't have time to sit at home and watch the television.

If you only have one semester to study abroad, carefully research your country and region and make a list of things that you want to accomplish, places you want to visit, or experiences you want to have during your semester before you even arrive at your abroad destination. This small amount of planning keeps you from wasting a single second of your time abroad.

Double your pleasure: Two semesters

If studying abroad has been part of your college plan for awhile, you may be able to go abroad for two semesters, which means that you fulfilled, or know exactly how you plan to fulfill, all your academic responsibilities for graduation.

Spending more time in your host country usually ensures that you'll

- Make friends with native students, get to know your classmates (especially if you're in courses that last a full year), join sports teams, clubs, societies, and so on. Although you may feel like an outsider at first, after a few weeks, you'll be just like everyone else.

- Become fluent, or nearly fluent, in a foreign language. Practice makes perfect and a year gives you plenty of practice functioning in another language.

- Have plenty of time and opportunity to travel. Most likely, your host university will break between semesters for a week or more. Being away for a year guarantees you at least two extended breaks for travel. You won't have to squeeze long travel itineraries into long weekends or skip classes to travel.

- Become an expert on your host university's town or city. Knowing your way around the city will become second nature. You'll develop favorite spots for a cup of coffee, buying books, meeting up with friends for a pint — just like you have at home.

- Experience a year's worth of culture. Two semesters means you're abroad for nine or ten months. Thus, you'll get to see holiday celebrations and traditions that occur throughout the year.

- Adopt culture. More time away equals more time for developing the habits, speech patterns, or customs of your host country. You'll get used to things like having a siesta (nap) every afternoon, drinking tea instead of coffee, not going to the library on the weekends, or calling soccer "football." The longer you're in a country, the more you can incorporate the culture into your everyday life, without even realizing it in some cases. You may never be able to get through an afternoon without a cup of tea or a nap again!

An added bonus to studying abroad for two semesters is that you can often spend two semesters in two different places, if that's what you'd like. Of course, doing so means filing two sets of study abroad paperwork (including applications), packing up, moving, and then reestablishing yourself in a new city. But if you want to go two places, improve your language skills in multiple languages, and you're up for yet another adventure, this option may work for you.

Checking Out Some Alternatives to International Study

Yes, the title of this book is *Study Abroad For Dummies*, but after careful consideration and flipping through some of the chapters, you may simply decide that studying abroad is not for you. And yet, you nevertheless may still want to spend a semester or year away from your home university. It can be done without packing up and going overseas!

Lauding my year away from campus

I never questioned that I'd spend my entire junior year abroad. I wanted to be away for a year. Everyone who went abroad for only a semester regretted not going for a full year. Additionally, my first-choice university abroad wasn't on a semester schedule, so if I wanted to go to Trinity College in Dublin, which was on that kind of schedule (and I most certainly did), then I'd have to spend a full year there.

Initially, I found packing up and moving away for an entire year unsettling. You wonder things like, "What if I don't fit in?" or "What if I decide I don't like it there?" Well, as long as you at least complete one semester, you and your home university can usually find a way for you to come home early if you're unhappy.

Adjusting to a new city took me a while — an entire semester, in fact. By the time I went home at Christmas, Dublin had just started to feel like home. I had just made Irish friends, found my way around Trinity, and knew the bus routes. So, if I had to pack up and leave at that point, I'd have felt cheated.

During Christmas break, I missed Dublin and eagerly boarded the plane in January to return to my life abroad. Armed with all my newfound knowledge, gained through trial and error during my first semester, I was ready to go back and really enjoy everything. The extra semester away gave me a chance to adopt the Irish culture and attitudes (I am five minutes late for everything now), make fantastic friends, and ultimately make Dublin my second home.

You can choose to stay in your home country (most likely the U.S. for readers of this book) and go away to attend another college or university here. This alternative is actually a great idea. You still get to experience something new and different but without some of the hassle involved with going abroad. Two benefits that immediately come to mind are:

✔ You won't have to function in a language that isn't your own.

✔ You probably will have an easy time finding courses equivalent to the ones you're taking at your home university to fulfill core and major requirements.

Okay, so you still need to do your homework and investigate whether your college has exchange programs with other colleges in the U.S., but if your school already has established exchanges with other schools, usually the application/acceptance process and credit transfer is fairly smooth.

When your school hasn't set up exchanges with any U.S. schools, you need to visit your dean or adviser to determine whether they recommend studying at particular schools. Your college may enable you to choose any college/university you like and submit your plans for approval the semester before going away.

Whenever you choose to study at another school in your home country, many of the same rules and processes discussed in this book apply to you, too! Your host university requires you to submit an application, and your home university requires you to submit paperwork and plan out your course of study while away. You also need to worry about transferring course credit.

Chapter 3

Ready, Set, Plan!

In This Chapter

▶ Visiting the study abroad office

▶ Knowing what to do if your university doesn't have a study abroad office

▶ Timing your study abroad preparations

So, you're thinking about going abroad. You may not be 100 percent sure yet that study abroad is for you, but you are certainly interested in investigating what study abroad opportunities are out there. But I'm sure you're wondering where you can go to find out what you want (and need) to know. Fortunately, finding information about studying abroad is much easier than finding a needle in a haystack. A good place to start your search is at your home university's study abroad office (sometimes is referred to as the international study office).

In this chapter, I give you an overview of the study abroad office, what it is, who and what you can find there, and why it's so important. For those of you who don't have the luxury of having a study abroad office at your home university, I include a whole section on how to manage without one. And, finally, I've created two timelines for study abroad planning, one for those of you going away for a full year or fall semester and another one for those planning a spring semester abroad.

Visiting the Study Abroad Office

If a large number of students at your home university study abroad during their college experiences, chances are your school has a study abroad office and a study abroad director. So I encourage you to find out where they are and go pay them a visit! The study abroad office and its director are probably the best resources you can have when planning to study abroad. Not only is the office familiar with any existing study abroad programs, but it also is familiar with your home university's academic expectations and regulations.

Words of wisdom from a former study abroad office employee

My on-campus job during my senior year of college was as a peer adviser in Wellesley's study abroad office. I happen to think it was the best on-campus job out there because I got paid to talk about my year abroad and to act as a pseudo-travel agent, helping other students plan their abroad adventures. Besides answering general questions on Wellesley's study abroad policies, I also answered questions such as, "Should I buy a Eurail pass? What's the best way to travel from London to Paris? Do you know anyone who studied in Beijing?"

Now, while the study abroad director is usually quite knowledgeable and helpful regarding administrative and regulation questions, I recommend seeking out peer advisers for general student-related travel questions — they're the ones who have been abroad most recently and managed on a student budget. Also, peer advisers tend to be the ones who have their finger on the pulse of study abroad at your home university. They know what the re-entry process is like, how it feels to be an international student, which classmates of theirs have studied where, and who would be the most helpful for you to talk to — about Beijing, for example. So, seek them out!

Looking at the study abroad office's role

The study abroad office typically is responsible for and provides assistance to the following students:

- Students from the home university who are:
  - Planning to participate in the university's study abroad program
  - Participating in the program currently
  - Returning home from their studies abroad
- International students who come to your home university to study

If you fit into any of these categories, the study abroad office is the place for you. It helps you prepare to take your studies abroad and adjust to the idea that you'll soon become an international student!

Your host university probably has its own international student office that can help out visiting students. This office looks out for you and helps you adjust to your new home. If your host university doesn't offer such an office, feel free to get in touch with the study abroad office at your home university.

Be sure to attend all mandatory pre-study abroad orientations or meetings offered by your home university's study abroad office. Even though your host university and study abroad program probably also have orientations, only your home university study abroad office can confirm details such as credit policies and course pre-approvals.

Knowing what you can find in the study abroad office

Introduce yourself to the staff when you visit the study abroad office for the first time. Talk to whomever is there. It may be the director, assistant director, or a peer adviser (a student who has already gone abroad), but be sure to let that person know you're interested in going abroad. The person you talk to can probably give you a brief overview of what you can find in the office, put you on an e-mail distribution list for students who want to go abroad, and direct you toward any relevant handouts and promotional literature.

Most study abroad offices have some sort of library with study abroad program brochures and catalogs for programs that your home university approves. You may have to review these materials at the study abroad office, so be sure to plan enough time to sit and explore. Feel free to request brochures and catalogs by directly contacting programs in which you're interested.

Check whether the study abroad office has these three valuable collections of information available:

- ✔ **Program evaluations:** Universities with extensive study abroad programs often ask or even require students returning from study abroad to complete an evaluation of their respective programs. The study abroad office often keeps these evaluations on file and makes them available to students. Read these evaluations carefully because students who have been on the programs often provide the best and most expert information.

- ✔ **List of approved programs:** The study abroad office likely keeps an updated list of all the programs in which your home university allows its students to participate.

- ✔ **Courseload equivalents at approved universities abroad:** In addition to a list of approved programs, the office may also be able to provide you with the number of credits you're required to take at an abroad university.

In addition to the preceding resources, your study abroad office may also offer the following:

- A collection of books that provide overviews of life and customs in specific countries or regions as well as reference books about studying abroad with information about financial aid and scholarships for studying abroad.

- A computer available for student use. If such a computer is available, hop on the Internet and find out whether the office has bookmarked particularly useful Web sites. Chances are the study abroad office at your home university has a Web site of its own, too!

Meeting with a study abroad adviser

You can usually meet with a study abroad adviser during drop-in office hours or by scheduling an appointment. You don't have to arrive at your scheduled meeting with your bags packed, ready to hop on the next plane out of the country, but you do need to take some time to research and think about some of the following questions.

- Why do I want to go abroad?

- How long do I want to be away?

- When do I want to leave?

- What languages do I speak?

- What is my major?

- What countries do I want to study in?

- Have I seen or heard of any programs that interest me?

- Am I going to need financial aid or scholarships to make this experience possible?

- Do I have any concerns or fears about leaving my home university for a semester or a year?

- Will my major or academic program influence when and where I study abroad?

If you can answer most or all these questions, your study abroad director will be better able to do his or her job, giving you suggestions, presenting you with options, answering your questions, and generally pointing you in the right direction so you can begin planning a successful experience abroad.

Don't make an appointment with a study abroad adviser if you haven't done any research about studying abroad. You don't want to waste everyone's time. Directing an entire international student office is a demanding job, and appointments with the director may be hard to come by, so make sure you've planned what you want to accomplish in your meeting before you go.

Discovering some other helpful study abroad office hints

If you're waiting and waiting and waiting to hear from a study abroad program about whether you've been accepted, the study abroad office may be able to help you get an answer in a more timely fashion. Its staff is familiar with programs and often has good relationships with schools and programs where their students study abroad. Staff members often can tell you whether a lengthy wait is normal; they may even offer to contact the program on your behalf.

Here's a final tip that, although it's simple common sense, bears repeating: Be nice to members of the study abroad office staff, even if you get news you don't want. If the study abroad office notifies you that you cannot study on a certain program or that you need to take more classes to transfer a full load of credit, don't get frustrated with them. Remember, the study abroad director may not be the one to blame. Often decisions and policies coming from the study abroad office are usually made in consultation with other administration officials (like class deans).

You, and only you, ultimately are responsible for planning your study abroad experience. The study abroad office guides you but cannot do everything for you.

Coping When Your School Doesn't Have a Study Abroad Office!

If your home university doesn't have a study abroad office, don't panic. Not every school is lucky enough to have one. If students at your school study abroad (and surely some students do), information and resources must be close by for you. Someone on your campus probably knows what's going on as far as studying abroad is concerned, and you have only to do a little detective work to find out who that someone is.

If you're without the luxury of a study abroad office, you need to try to find a *study abroad mentor*. That's someone who can direct you as you make plans to study abroad and be there whenever you need to e-mail him or her with questions while you're away. The following people are potential candidates:

- Class deans
- Your major adviser
- Your favorite professor

No matter who you choose, be sure to get some kind of official approval for your study abroad experience before you leave the country. You don't want to spend time abroad and then find out that your credits don't transfer. See Chapter 6 for information on the hazards of transferring credits.

I cannot stress enough the importance of having a study abroad mentor who can clue you in to the ins and outs of going abroad, procedures your school requires, and other important details. This person also can serve as a sounding board for some of your ideas whenever you're uncertain about where to go.

Class deans and faculty members are particularly good as study abroad mentors because of their familiarity with your school's graduation requirements and study abroad programs. These people also are likely to have placed their stamps of approval on your study abroad plans before you leave campus. Additionally, if your major is art history, for example, your major adviser usually can point you in the direction of art history programs abroad that meet with the department's approval or programs that students have enjoyed in the past.

Without a study abroad office, you have to be a little bit more independent in making your plans, so contact international student offices at schools where you'd like to study to get accurate and updated information. Whenever you're considering a program that is offered by an institution in the U.S., you can often pick up the phone and call the program coordinator if you do not want to rely on e-mail or you need a quick response to a question.

And of course, another helpful tool when you don't have access to study abroad office is this book!

Sticking to the Calendar When Planning Your Studies

I've designed two study abroad calendars to help you get on track and stay on the right path when planning a study abroad adventure. There's lots to pay attention to, and some events are time sensitive. You don't want to let time slip away from you and miss your chance to go abroad! Nor should you save everything until the last minute because that is just too overwhelming. And remember that it's important to adhere to your study abroad office's deadlines for paperwork.

Calendar 1: Fall semester/full-year abroad

During the fall semester a year before you plan to depart on your studies abroad, start following the month-by-month task instructions for planning, applying for, and being accepted into a study abroad program that I provide in the following section. This first calendar works for both fall semester study abroad candidates and those of you going for a full year, because in most cases, both groups (fall semester and full year) are leaving at the same time for their abroad experience: September!

September and October

The following is a list of things to do soon after you arrive at school in the fall:

- ✔ Visit the study abroad office.

- ✔ Research program options using the study abroad library, college library, or Internet.

- ✔ Construct a list of potential programs.

- ✔ Attend any study abroad fairs or informational meetings your home university offers on studying abroad.

November

When November rolls around, be sure to do the following:

- ✔ Talk to other students who've studied abroad, especially those who've studied in the country or program in which you want to study.

- ✔ Narrow down your study abroad program choices.

- ✔ Request applications, specifying when you intend to study abroad.

- ✔ Discuss study abroad plans with an academic adviser.

December

Finish up your semester with a few more preparations:

- ✔ Begin collecting and completing any paperwork your home university requires of students planning to go abroad. Your host university will also require paperwork such as transcripts and letters of recommendation.

- ✔ When planning coursework at your home university for spring semester, take into account your potential study abroad plans.

January and February

After a relaxing winter break, it's time to hop back on the task of planning your study abroad program for next year. The following list describes things you need to do before the spring semester gets too far underway:

- ✔ Complete applications, send them in along with any required paperwork, and await decisions.

- ✔ Provide your school and advisers with a tentative idea of when you'll be departing (at the end of this semester or beginning of next school year) for an experience abroad. You may have to file paperwork that you've been collecting from your home university right away to officially declare that you may be attending school abroad next semester.

March and April

The following events/tasks pop up during the middle of the spring semester:

- ✔ Receive notice of admission from study abroad programs.

- ✔ Accept or decline abroad offers of admission.

- ✔ Promptly complete and return any housing, course preference, or other forms the study abroad program sends to you.

May

Before you leave school for the summer, be sure to take care of the following:

- ✔ Confirm with your home university that you'll be away for the next semester/year.

- ✔ File all required paperwork, including paperwork for your study abroad program or host university and leave-of-absence forms at your home university.

- ✔ Choose courses and make plans for housing for the semester you'll return to your home university, if possible.

- ✔ Attend any pre-departure meetings your home university offers for students studying abroad.

Calendar 11: Spring Semester Abroad

When planning to study abroad during the spring semester, you often apply for such a program during the fall semester right before the semester you plan to study abroad. Similarly, you're not likely to be able to apply a full year in advance for a spring-semester study abroad program.

After arriving back on campus after summer break, you immediately have to begin making plans for spring. One good thing about studying abroad during the spring is that you have the luxury of using the summer beforehand to work on your study abroad plans, rather than trying to do so during a busy semester.

During the spring semester, a year in advance of when you plan to depart on your studies abroad, start following the month-by-month task instructions for planning, applying for, and being accepted into a study abroad program that I've provided in the following sections.

January through April

- ✔ Visit the study abroad office.

- ✔ Research program options using the study abroad library, college library, or Internet.

✔ Construct a list of potential programs.

✔ Attend any study abroad fairs or informational meetings your home university may offer on studying abroad.

✔ In planning courses at your home university for next semester, take into account your potential study abroad plans.

✔ Talk to other students who've studied abroad, especially those who've studied in the country or in the program in which you want to study.

✔ Discuss study abroad plans with an adviser.

May through August

Use the summer months to do the following:

✔ Narrow down study abroad program choices.

✔ Continue research via the Internet or library.

September

As the semester before you leave to study abroad begins, make sure your plans are on the right track by setting those wheels in motion once you're back on campus and have unpacked your bags:

✔ Request applications and specify when you intend to study abroad.

✔ Meet with advisers.

✔ Collect and complete any paperwork your home university requires of students planning to go abroad.

✔ Request recommendation letters as soon as possible! Professors are busy!

October

As your fall semester progresses, you need to make your study abroad plans a priority because your departure date is closer than you think! Fall semester tends to fly because of holiday and parents' weekends.

✔ Complete applications, along with required paperwork, send them in, and await decisions.

✔ Tentatively inform your school and advisers that you'll be departing at the end of the current semester for a study abroad experience; you may now have to file paperwork that you've been collecting from your home university to officially notify the school that you may be studying abroad next semester.

December

As the excitement mounts about your impending spring semester abroad, you need to be tying up loose ends like:

- ✔ Receive notice of admission from abroad programs.

- ✔ Accept or decline abroad offers of admission.

- ✔ Promptly complete and return any housing, course preference, or other forms the study abroad program has sent to you.

- ✔ Confirm with your home university that you'll be away for the next semester.

- ✔ Fill out all required paperwork, including paperwork for your study abroad program or host university and leave of absence forms at your home university.

- ✔ Choose courses and make plans for housing for the semester you return to your home university, if possible.

- ✔ Attend any pre-departure meetings your home university offers for students studying abroad.

Remembering time sensitive calendar events

Although most of the tasks you have to complete for studying abroad depend on when you're departing, certain events are time-specific. Study abroad fairs and financial aid deadlines come and go at specific times — regardless of your departure date. Keep an eye out for them!

Fall semesters

U.S. universities tend to play host to study abroad fairs at the start of their academic years. Study abroad program representatives visit campuses to talk with prospective applicants and provide information about their programs. I strongly recommend attending a study abroad fair, whenever possible, because program representatives can offer you current information, brochures, catalogs, and other information about potential programs. Check with your study abroad office or with other local area universities to see whether a study abroad fair is planned near you.

January/February

Financial aid and scholarship deadlines tend to crop up during these two months. When you're planning to going away the following September for the full year or just the fall semester, or if you're planning to going away the following spring a year from this time, you need to apply for financial aid and scholarships now. Although it may seem a bit confusing, basically what it boils down to is that you need to apply for financial aid in the January/February time frame of the year before the academic year during which you plan to leave for your studies abroad.

Chapter 4

Thinking Ahead: Prerequisites for Studying Abroad

. . . .

In This Chapter

▶ Finishing your core and major requirements

▶ Getting your target language down pat

▶ Tuning in to international travel advisories

▶ Finding U.S. government information on foreign countries

. . . .

*1*n an ideal world, you formulate your study abroad plans the moment you arrive on campus your first year. However, you're probably too wrapped up with settling in at college to consider leaving your new school to study in another country for a semester or even a year. Although at some point along the way you decide that going abroad can enhance your college experience, you cannot treat going abroad like an exam that you can stay up all night to cram for or a paper that can be written four hours before it's due.

Going abroad takes careful thought and planning — as well it should because you're packing up and moving to another country for a semester or even a year! Most colleges and universities want you to fulfill certain academic requirements before going overseas. They do so because when you're going abroad, you need to have an idea of how you'll complete your major when you return. Having those courses already under your belt gives you a better perspective.

Additionally, if you want to study in a country where English isn't the native language, you need to spend some time sharpening your skills in the native tongue of your destination.

Before departing, you must set yourself up for a successful academic experience abroad. Believe me, returning home from abroad is stressful enough without having to scramble to finish core or major requirements, including the nightmare of reworking your entire schedule during the add/drop period or having to take extra courses to finish requirements. I promise that thoroughly thinking through your entire undergraduate course of study before you go abroad will save time and energy later on. In this chapter, I tell you what you need to know so that your home university will peacefully release you to your abroad program without worrying that you'll have to go on the six year plan to graduate from your four year college.

Planning Your Home University Courses

This may seem backwards, but after you decide that you may want to spend time studying abroad, you need to decide how to plan your coursework at your home university before you proceed with planning to go abroad. From your home university's perspective, they don't want you going abroad if you're underprepared (for example, if going abroad will delay your intended graduation date). That means you need to draft an overall battle plan, and you need:

- Pencils and paper for notes and checklists
- The most recent copy of your transcript so you remember what courses you've taken
- A current class schedule so you can include in your plan what courses you're currently taking
- Your home university's course catalog where you can find requirements for graduation and for completing your major.
- One or two hours of free time to draft your plan

The easiest way to make your plan is to take a piece of paper, fold it in half, and list requirements on one side and on the other side, list courses you've taken (or are currently taking) to satisfy those requirements. Then see which courses you still need to take to graduate on time.

Whether you're planning to be away from your home university for a semester or an entire year, this kind of planning is vital because, to be permitted to go abroad, you probably need to be in *diploma standing,* which is determined by your achieving a certain grade-point average (GPA). You can expect your class dean, study abroad office, major adviser, or registrar to check whether you're of diploma standing before your plans are approved.

Fulfilling core requirements

When you arrive at college, you're bombarded with information about what you need to accomplish to graduate *on time* (typically in four years). When you receive this information, you may completely digest it or choose to ignore it. At any rate, when you're considering a study abroad program, you need to recall this information from your memory bank or crack open that course catalog to refresh your memory.

Core requirements, which some schools refer to as general education or distribution requirements, are the courses your college wants you to take outside of your major so that you're a well-educated and well-rounded graduate, versed in English, math, and biology. Typically, universities require you to complete all or the majority of the core requirements before going abroad.

If you've completed all your core requirements, congratulations! That's one less detail you need to worry about. If you won't finish the core requirements by the time you go abroad, you need to be prepared to present a plan to your adviser showing how you plan to complete those requirements when you return.

When you have only one or two requirements outstanding, you can resolve the situation fairly quickly. Simply go back to your course catalog; assume that you're going to fulfill the requirements at your home university; figure out which classes you want to take to fulfill the requirements; and determine whether to take them before, during, or after going abroad.

When you have three or more requirements outstanding, chances are good that you'll have to complete all but one or two before going abroad. Using your course catalog, strategize how and when you can finish the courses you need so that you can go away without too much hanging over your head. For the moment, assume that you can fulfill your core requirements at your home university and don't plan for any of the courses that you take abroad to count toward your core requirements. In other words, plan on taking the one or two remaining core courses after returning from your studies abroad.

With the appropriate approval, courses taken abroad sometimes can count toward the completion of the core requirements. (If you have questions about transferring credits from abroad, see Chapter 6.)

Follow these easy steps to figure out what requirements you still need to fulfill — to help you draft your plan:

1. Create a list of the core requirements, using your course catalog.

2. Consult your most recent transcript, checking off the requirements you've already fulfilled.

3. Look at the current semester schedule and cross off any requirements you're in the process of completing.

4. Determine the requirements that you will need to finish either before you go abroad or when your return.

You don't need to panic about core requirements unless you're a second-semester sophomore who hopes to go away for your entire junior year but still needs to complete three or more core requirements. This situation can make going abroad for a full year more difficult because you inevitably need to finish major requirements during your senior year. When you find yourself in this situation, sit down with a class dean or your major adviser to get some help hammering out a plan that works. In this case, you may need to ensure that certain classes you take abroad will, in fact, count toward core or major requirements so that you graduate on time.

Colleges generally don't design core requirements so they're exceedingly difficult or impossible to fulfill; actually, it should be quite the opposite. When you think through how you'll complete the core requirements before planning your semester or year abroad, they should not become an obstacle.

Finishing your major

As a general rule, colleges won't allow you to go abroad until you've decided on and completed a certain number of courses in your major (usually 50 percent). Ideally, when you plan to study abroad during your junior year, you already have laid the groundwork for your major.

You, of course, need to consult your course catalog to determine what courses your major requires and to figure out a strategy to fulfill those requirements. You can use the steps mentioned for fulfilling core requirements in the previous section.

Some universities or departments may require that all major courses be taken at the home university and may deny credit for any major course taken while studying abroad. On the flip side, some universities require students to take at least one or two major courses while studying abroad. Get to know your university's policies well in advance!

The person who advises you on your major is a valuable resource when designing study abroad plans and can help you to create an abroad plan that works in conjunction with your major. When you're at a loss over which study abroad program to choose or which classes to take, your adviser is a great person from whom to seek advice.

Professors often are familiar with study abroad programs that are particularly good in their respective subject areas. Additionally, your adviser can probably look at an overseas university course catalog and determine whether an overseas course is either equivalent or similar to a home university course (and thus counts toward the major). Having tentative approval that classes you take overseas will count toward the completion of your major at home is in your best interest. You don't want to scramble to complete your major when you return from studies abroad.

Bear in mind that you want your studies abroad to add value to some of the work you plan to do in your major field during your senior year, including researching a thesis or an independent study project or enhancing the courses you've taken within a specialty field in your major.

This is a good time to consult with your study abroad director to find out what regulations, if any, your home university has regarding pre-approval for classes taken abroad. Some universities are very bureaucratic about having all overseas courses pre-approved and set in stone before you even get on a plane, while other universities are very flexible. In either case, make sure you know your university's rules well in advance. Regulations on course approval for credit earned abroad also varies from department to department, so be sure to check with your major department on their pre-approval policies as well.

You may want to spend a semester studying in a program that's unrelated to your major because the subject appeals to you and gives you an opportunity to explore another area of your academic interests. College is all about exploration, so if you have your heart set on a program unrelated to your major, go for it. Just be aware that doing so requires careful planning to ensure that you complete your major. In any event, you'll probably be able to spend only one semester in a program that's unrelated to your major, if, that is, you want to graduate on time. As always, check with your study abroad director or academic adviser to make sure this does not violate your home university's study abroad policies.

Language Requirements: Friend, Not Foe

Generally, studying abroad in a country where you don't speak the native language isn't a good idea. Of course, some exceptions to this rule exist, mainly if you're studying in an English-speaking program or if your program kicks off with an extensive language boot camp.

Finding out what's required

Studying abroad in any country that communicates in a language that isn't your own takes significant planning because, under normal circumstances, you need to complete four units of college-level coursework in a foreign language (usually through the intermediate level) before you can study in a location where it is spoken. Therefore, you almost need to arrive at college knowing that you want to study in Germany, for example, so you can begin completing the language classes you need to be able to go to Germany during your junior year. If, however, you complete part of this language requirement prior to attending college, you usually can avoid having to take four units of college-level language courses; however, you need to take at least one intermediate-level language course before going abroad.

Letting keen advice be a lesson to you!

Every year while I was working on my undergraduate degree, some seniors did not receive their diplomas in June with the rest of the graduating class because they'd forgotten to fulfill a requirement. A good friend of mine went abroad for her entire junior year only to return her senior year and be swept away by the craziness of a senior thesis. She forgot to pay attention to a minor graduation requirement and discovered that a somewhat ridiculous, outdated but compulsory physical education class deans had strongly recommended she fulfill before going abroad was preventing her from graduating. By not heeding this advice and not believing she'd be denied her hard-earned diploma for not taking enough gym classes, she walked through graduation exercises with our class but didn't receive her diploma until she'd successfully completed sailing lessons the following summer. Her diploma was mailed to her in September. Better planning could have prevented her graduation woes.

Consulting a foreign language professor is a good idea when you have doubts or questions about your language proficiency. The professor usually can evaluate your proficiency quickly by conversing with you in the language or by administering a short diagnostic test. You're not expected to be fluent in the language before going abroad, but you need to have a solid command of writing, speaking, reading, and comprehending the language so you can function while using the language on a daily basis.

For language majors, going abroad is almost an imperative when you want to become fluent in a language. When abroad, use as little English as possible even with your English-speaking friends.

If you're not a language major but will be studying in a language other than your own, you must stick to the language requirements of the program you choose. Remember, these requirements exist for your benefit. You don't want to find yourself in a situation where you understand very little and constantly struggle to communicate or keep up with your coursework.

Using the lingo to get your foot in the door

Because most students don't arrive at college knowing where or even if they want to study abroad, they may fail to incorporate a foreign language into their study program. Additionally, college-level language courses are time consuming and schedules don't always allow time for them. Don't distress; there are ways to go to countries where you don't speak the language.

Finding those ways may take slightly more research on your part, but a lot of programs are designed for students with no previous language training. Such programs usually require language coursework as part of your study abroad courseload. The program may start out with two or three weeks of intensive language instruction, so you're able to navigate your way through day-to-day life in your new foreign home. Additionally, the course instruction in these programs typically is given in English. All-in-all, choosing an English-speaking program to study in a country in which you have no knowledge of the native language is an excellent solution whenever you have your heart set on going to a particular country. One drawback to taking this route is that without having a good command of a language, making friends with the natives can be difficult.

If you're participating in a program designed for students with no previous language training and going abroad for only a semester, check with your home university to see what type of credit you receive for taking only one introductory semester of a foreign language. Some colleges require you to take both 101 and 102 sections of a language to receive full credit for both courses.

Investigating International Travel Advisories

Being aware of international travel advisories is an extremely important prerequisite for studying abroad. Before you even begin considering certain programs or countries for your experience abroad, you need to determine which countries the U.S. government considers unsafe and either make a note of them or promptly remove them from your list of possible places to study. The U.S. government issues warnings with the safety of its citizens in mind. Given recent world events, take these warnings seriously.

The following government agencies provide Web sites that offer up-to-date information about travel safety issues:

- ✔ **U.S. Department of State:** Travel warnings, public announcements, and Consular Sheets issued by the U.S. government are all available at www.travel.state.gov/travel_warnings.html.

- ✔ **Overseas Security Council:** You can search for security information by country at www.ds-osac.org. This site also has a daily news feature that includes news items directly related to security in foreign countries.

Some helpful nongovernment Web sites include:

✔ **Fielding's Danger Finder:** This site includes sections entitled "What Danger Awaits the Weary Traveler," and a list of places and things the Web site's authors consider dangerous for tourists. Check it out at `www.comebackalive.com/df/index.htm`.

✔ **Pinkerton Global Intelligence Services:** This site is a pay-for-service global intelligence service. Go to `pgis.pinkertons.com` if you want to take a look, but you may not want to pay for this when the free U.S. government information is more than adequate.

Make a note of these Web sites and take it with you when you go abroad. You need to consult them on a regular basis whenever you spend weekends or vacations traveling overseas. You can also check out whether your destination's government provides similar information or Web sites.

You can also obtain travel advisory information from official passport agencies, U.S. embassies, airlines, and travel agents, or ask your study abroad program or host university if it automatically sends State Department travel advisories to participants.

Heeding travel warnings

The State Department issues travel warnings based on all relevant information, such as levels of perceived safety. A travel warning is a recommendation that Americans avoid traveling to or within a certain country. Consular information sheets (see the section on "Reviewing consular information sheets," later in this chapter) also are issued for countries for which travel warnings are issued. Be sure to check out the State Department's advisories at `www.travel.state.gov/travel_warnings.html`.

Tuning in to public announcements

A public announcement is the lowest level of warning issued by the State Department. These announcements are intended to alert American citizens to specific safety issues in a particular country. These warnings are usually short-term and contain an expiration date. A public announcement does not necessarily mean that you should not study in a country, but it does mean that you should be aware of certain situations or risks there.

Worldwide cautions contain information about terrorist threats and other trans-national conditions that pose significant risks to the security of American citizens. The State Department issues a worldwide caution any time there is a perceived threat to Americans or other groups.

Reviewing consular information sheets

The State Department develops and makes consular information sheets available for every country around the world. These sheets are packed with information about locations of the U.S. Embassies or Consulates in each respective country, unusual immigration practices, health conditions, minor political disturbances, uncommon currency and entry regulations, crime and security information, and drug penalties.

If any unstable conditions that are not severe enough to warrant a travel warning exist within a country, descriptions of those conditions may be included on consular information sheets under an optional section entitled "Safety/Security."

Consular information sheets generally do not include advice. Instead, they present information in a factual manner so the traveler can make his or her own decisions concerning travel to a particular country.

Using the State Department Web site at travel.state.gov/travel, look up the consular information sheet for each country you may be visiting during your study abroad program.

Checking out other reliable information

The U.S. State Department Web page contains a wealth of regularly updated information. If you are thinking about going abroad, spending 30 minutes or more just exploring the Web site to find out what information is available regarding your potential abroad destinations is worth the effort. Check it out at www.state.gov/travel/.

The State Department publishes *Background Notes* on countries around the world. These brief, factual pamphlets provide information about each country's people and its culture, geography, history, government, economy, and political conditions. The collection covers about 170 countries worldwide for which a reading list, travel notes, and maps also are included. *Background Notes* are available through the State Department's home page on the Internet.

The State Department also publishes a *Tips for Travelers* series. These pamphlets on travel to specific regions of the world include tips on Sub-Saharan Africa, the Caribbean, Canada, Central and South America, China, Mexico, the Middle East and North Africa, Russia, and South Asia. These brochures discuss topics such as currency and customs regulations, import and export controls, dual nationality, and photography restrictions. *Tips for Travelers* are available through the State Department's Web site.

Through the Department of State Web page, you can also access the Web site of the U.S. Embassy in your potential host country.

Likewise, you can check out the Overseas Security Advisory Council (OSAC) for reliable information about foreign countries, particularly regarding safety. A link to OSAC is provided on the State Department's Web site, or you can go to www.ds-osac.org.

OSAC promotes the exchange of security-related information between the U.S. government and the American private sector operating abroad. OSAC provides timely information to help the American private sector, colleges and universities included, in making informed decisions about how to protect their investments, facilities, personnel, and intellectual property abroad.

The OSAC Daily News (available on the OSAC Web site) presents current information about foreign events and documents, especially when the news relates to regional security, security-related incidents, and threats overseas. OSAC posts news items reported in global on-line sources by 8:30 a.m. eastern time and updates the items throughout each day. Other information accessible through OSAC Daily News includes reports on terrorist group profiles, general crime information for cities and countries, State Department Travel Advisories, locations of and contacts at U.S. posts overseas, and updates on new or unusual situations.

The OSAC also maintains a helpful "Calendar Events" section that lists anniversary dates of significant events that may potentially affect travel and safety abroad.

The Library of Congress Country Studies Web site at memory.loc.gov/frd /cs/cshome.html primarily focuses on lesser known areas of the world or regions in which U.S. forces may be deployed. It currently provides information on 101 countries and regions. Notable omissions include Canada, France, the United Kingdom, and other Western nations, as well as a number of African nations.

The Country Studies Series describes and analyzes the historical setting and social, economic, political, and national security systems and institutions of countries throughout the world. Its aim is to objectively examine the interrelationships of those systems and the ways they are shaped by cultural factors.

Part II

Finding a Program That Is Right for You

The 5th Wave   By Rich Tennant

"We were looking for a college that offered an extensive night school curriculum."

In this part . . .

*T*his part helps you figure out the answers to these three questions: Where do you want to go? What do you want to study? And how do you want to study it? I give you advice on how to research programs, consider special areas of study, and think about functioning in a different language. And for those of you who want to study in the ever-popular study abroad destination of the British Isles, I give you the ins and outs of how their university system works.

Chapter 5

Hitting the Library: Researching Program Options

- -

In This Chapter

▶ Discovering various types of programs

▶ Conducting a thorough search for the program that's right for you

▶ Evaluating different programs

▶ Participating in a nonapproved program

▶ Exploring additional references for excellent study abroad programs

- -

uite an extensive variety of study abroad options are out there. Hundreds of programs offer myriad choices of location, length, program of study, language, fees, and cultural integration, to name only a few. These programs are waiting for you to explore them. When you decide to go abroad, you need to start searching for the right program for you. If you take the time to research your options, finding out as much as possible about each program you consider, then you're much more likely to succeed with your study abroad experience than is the student who only halfheartedly does the research and goes on the most convenient program.

Before Starting Your Search . . .

If your home university has a study abroad office, start your search there. Use study abroad advisers as a resource because they are familiar with many programs and know exactly what types of programs your university approves. They also can suggest alternative study abroad ideas and make sure the program you choose coincides with your academic aspirations. See Chapter 3 for more about working with a study abroad office.

If, however, your university doesn't have a study abroad adviser or office, visit your class dean's office, the office of the dean of the college you're attending, or your major adviser. While these offices may not have the extensive library a study abroad office would have, they should be able to, at the very least, provide you with your home university's study abroad regulations, including a list of programs approved by your home university and a few general reference books on studying abroad.

Taking stock of your needs

You also need to do a little bit of a self-assessment so you can determine what type of study abroad experience works best for you. The following list of questions can help you know thyself (and lead you to a suitable study abroad program):

- ✔ What do you want to study? The most likely answer to this question is your major subject. Or maybe you'd like to satisfy some general education requirements while you're away.

- ✔ Where do you want to study and why? Which continent? Which region? Which country? Try to narrow it down a little here.

- ✔ Do you need to earn credit for studying abroad? (The answer to this is probably yes.) What is the minimum amount of credit you need to earn while you're away? What is the maximum amount of credit you can earn? This will get you thinking about credit transfer issues. See Chapter 6 for an in-depth discussion of credit transfer.

- ✔ How proficient are you in a foreign language? Are you fluent (and comfortable) enough to take classes in another language, or would you be better off taking your classes in English? If you only speak English, consider a country where English is the national language. Or you could look for an English-language program in a non-English speaking country. Assess whether you know another language well enough to function in it on a day-to-day basis.

- ✔ As far as academics are concerned, how much time can you reasonably afford to spend away from your home university? Your options run the gamut — a full year, a semester, or few weeks in the summer.

- ✔ Would you feel better on a highly structured program or would you be happier on a program that enables you to be a little more independent? Decide how much freedom you want. Would you rather go off exploring on your own or be shepherded around with other international or American students on a weekend trip?

- ✔ Where do you want to live while you're abroad? With whom do you want to live? Do you want to live in a dorm, with a host family, or in your own apartment? Do you want to live with other Americans, other international students, or with native students? You'll probably get some choice in deciding where you want to live, so start thinking about your preferences now.

✔ What is all this going to cost? Add up the tuition and fees, room and board, transportation, visa fees, additional study abroad program fees, and everyday living costs, which may be much higher in some countries than what you're used to at home. Figure out what you can afford before looking at programs.

✔ Are you currently receiving financial aid? Will you be able to take your home university financial aid with you, or will you have to search for other funding sources?

Although answering the above listed questions is important for you in determining your study abroad plans, you also need to remember that maximizing your study abroad program largely depends on your attitude when you board that plane and head for lands unknown. Be honest with yourself when considering programs. Be aware that some programs require more independence and sense of adventure than others. Regardless of which program you choose, you must maintain an open mind from the start to finish.

Gaining a sense of what's available

Roughly two-thirds of U.S. undergrads who study abroad choose programs specifically organized for U.S. students. The program sponsor can be the student's home university, another U.S. university with which the home university has an agreement, or a consortium to which the home university belongs. Other possible sponsors include domestic or foreign organizations that organize international student exchanges, or even a university located abroad.

Your home university, in general, dictates which program options are available to you, based largely upon their academic standards and credit transfer policies from other universities, domestic or foreign.

In the sections that follow, I cover and explain different programs that may be available to you.

U.S. university-affiliated programs for American students

Some of the more popular study abroad programs are sponsored by U.S. universities. The attraction of studying with a U.S.-based program is that you're able to study in a foreign place, but your credits are transferred through a U.S. university, which sometimes is easier than transferring credits through universities abroad. Even when you take most or all of your courses at an abroad university, academic credit, transcripts, and most or all of the required paperwork are managed through the U.S. sponsor. Other benefits of U.S.-based programs are special language courses, prearranged housing, weekend trips, and group travel discounts.

Although students derive this wide range of benefits from these programs, U.S. universities, for the most part, offer three basic types of study abroad programs, *island programs, semi-integrated programs,* and *integrated programs.* In an island program, sponsoring U.S. institutions plan all courses for the group of U.S. students who participate, and you usually don't have contact with host country students in the classroom — you only study with the other American students in the program. In a semi-integrated program, you take classes offered by your sponsoring U.S. university *and* you also get to enroll in courses at a foreign university or institution. In an integrated program, you enroll directly in a university abroad with the help of a U.S. university, and you probably live in the host university's dorms or student apartments, rather than with other Americans.

U.S. university-sponsored island programs

In an island program, courses are taught by home-university faculty members or by foreign faculty hired by the U.S. sponsor. Courses may be taught in English, in the language of the host country, or both. The costs of these programs typically are equal to the costs of studying at your home university. Financial aid that you receive from your home university and from the government usually transfers to your program of study abroad.

Most summer study abroad programs are island programs because universities in many countries do not offer regular courses during the summer.

An island program is a great idea when you want to live in a certain country but don't speak the local language or you're not fluent enough to take courses in any language other than English. Likewise, the program staff of your U.S. sponsor more than likely will be easily accessible and probably will arrange different cultural trips, some meals, and weekend excursions to keep you busy. If you're hesitant about going abroad and want a program that can give you services and support similar to what you're used to having at your home university, then consider this option.

An island program probably is a terrible option when you:

- ✔ Are independent and confident in your ability to navigate a new and unknown place.
- ✔ Don't want to be tied down by group activities with a bunch of Americans.
- ✔ Want to become fluent in the language and spend plenty of time interacting with the locals.
- ✔ Need the credits to count toward your academic goals — some home universities are reluctant to grant credit for participation in these types of programs.

If you go abroad with a group of Americans, chances are you're less likely to venture outside of that group, particularly when your local language skills need some work.

U.S. university-sponsored semi-integrated programs

When you're an independent student, want a more authentic experience in your host country, and have some knowledge of the host country's language, a semi-integrated program may be a good choice for you. You can take courses at a foreign institution and also complete courses designed by your U.S. sponsor (which means a few of your courses will be with Americans also studying on the same U.S.-sponsored program). A semi-integrated program enables you to improve your language skills so you can make new friends and maybe even join some of the university clubs and societies.

Semi-integrated programs in non-English-speaking countries, in particular, will arrange a few courses for program participants only. So, like island programs, you'll probably have an attentive program staff looking after you and planning various group outings.

Avoid enrolling in more than one or two classes that were specially designed for U.S. or international students. These classes tend to have less demanding requirements, particularly where language is concerned. Even though you're on a semi-integrated program, aim to maximize your integration at the abroad university. If you're looking for full immersion in another university, opt for an integrated program or take the leap into direct enrollment.

U.S.-sponsored integrated programs

Some U.S. universities offer fully integrated study abroad programs where you can enroll in a host university and take classes with native students, taught by faculty from the host institution. In some cases, you live in the university dorms or student apartments with native and other international students, not just Americans. In non-English-speaking countries, these programs require a high level of language proficiency. If the program has strict language requirements or if you're studying in a country where college students traditionally live at home, you may live with a host family.

This kind of setup usually solves the credit transfer problem because the grades for your coursework abroad are translated to an American university transcript. These programs also handle most or all applications and other paperwork, can process financial aid, and usually offer support services abroad. Your experience abroad is supported not only by program staff at the abroad location, but also by the international student offices of each university, abroad and at home. The U.S. program staff makes your transition as smooth as possible by giving an orientation when you arrive, arranging housing, and planning occasional trips and meals. For these reasons, most students find that participating in an integrated program is more convenient than directly enrolling in a foreign university.

Arcadia University's Center for Study Abroad (www.beaver.edu/cea) and Butler University's Institute for Study Abroad (www.ifsa-butler.org) have numerous offerings for integrated programs. Students without extensive study abroad options at their home university often choose to study with Arcadia or Butler because they take care of your application process, run an orientation for you when you arrive in your host country, and set up housing. Program staff, located in your host country, check in with you on a regular basis and are always available for emergencies or just to answer questions. But don't go this route if you're trying to save money. Using a U.S. university as a middle man can and often does increase the costs. Also, the programs don't always offer integrated housing, which is a disappointment if you want to live in dorms with the natives.

Exchange programs, arranged through your home university, are another type of integrated program. Most exchange programs are direct exchanges, in which a student at your host university takes your place at your home university. These are good for students who are independent and fluent in another language, but not for those who need support while abroad.

Non-U.S. university-sponsored programs

Some programs are sponsored by organizations that aren't universities. Several not-for-profit (NFP) and for-profit organizations in the U.S. and abroad sponsor study abroad programs. In general, any NFP that is sponsoring a study abroad program is doing so to promote understanding between people of different cultures or nations.

Two examples of this type of program include CIEE (Council on International Educational Exchange) and SIT (School for International Training). CIEE offers opportunities to work, study, teach, or volunteer abroad. SIT offers experiential, field-based learning programs for undergraduate students, graduate students, professionals, and even high school students.

Whenever you choose a program sponsored by an organization other than a U.S. university and that program doesn't have any sort of standing agreement with your home university, you must arrange for and verify the credit transfer between the sponsoring organization and your home university. So, be sure to thoroughly investigate your school's credit transfer policies and your study abroad program's policy. Otherwise, your home university may refuse to transfer your study abroad credits.

International student programs abroad

Some universities abroad design programs exclusively for international students. (Don't forget; you'll be an international student once you leave your home country.) These international student programs often feature courses in the host language, literature, culture, and history.

In the 1990s, an increase in European academic exchange prompted the development of several English-language programs designed for students from other countries. Some of these programs now are available to U.S. students as well.

This type of program may be a perfect fit for you when you want to interact and learn with students from other countries. Courses are offered in English and in the host country's language. Even if the overseas university arranges to transfer credit through an accredited U.S. university, make sure that you find out from the appropriate authorities at your home university before you enter the program whether those credits will actually transfer.

Keep in mind that international student programs generally are created to meet the needs of English-speaking students, so your chances of meeting other students from far off places may decrease. You may not meet many natives in such a program, either. If you find out that credit doesn't transfer automatically from the overseas university or that it doesn't transfer at all, then look for another program.

Direct enrollment in a university abroad

Direct enrollment is a system where universities abroad actually accept students from other countries for a semester or a year and classify them as special, visiting, or international students. You take classes taught by your host university faculty with students from your host country, perhaps even in another language. This experience can be the kind that often provides the best opportunity for you to assimilate the culture and language of your new country and university.

Direct enrollment is a good option when you're looking for an exciting and challenging adventure. You need to be especially enterprising and resourceful because every detail is in your hands, from submitting applications to arranging housing to signing up for courses and transferring credit to your home university. You won't receive much support beyond what's provided by your host university's international student office and your home university's study abroad office.

One disadvantage to direct enrollment is that you have to be a full-time student and earn good grades for the courses you take before you can begin to consider transferring those credits back home. Some U.S. university registrars have rules against transferring credit from a foreign transcript. If the design of the program you want to attend is similar to taking U.S. classes as a nonadmitted, auditing, or part-time student, credit may not be transferable. Your financial aid is another thing that may not transfer if you directly enroll in a school abroad.

Thinking outside the box: Other paths to a study abroad experience

If going abroad on a program for one or two semesters isn't for you, and you want to try something different or more independent, the following sections present a couple of ideas.

Working independently

With the approval of your major adviser, design an independent project that you complete while abroad. Perhaps you want to travel through Ireland to study the iconography of the Celtic crosses for an art history paper or maybe you want to interview Indian women living in London for a sociology project. Most U.S. universities offer an independent study option to qualified students who want to conduct preapproved research or in-depth study projects in a specific field or on a certain topic. Remember that you must complete the research and write up the results on your own while you're abroad, and your final paper or project usually is evaluated by a faculty member (or members) when you return home.

If you're working independently, you won't be affiliated with an abroad institution unless your university or adviser has a friendly relationship with a foreign university and can obtain visiting student privileges to libraries for you before you depart.

Doing something for nothing

You don't always have to go abroad in search of undergraduate credit. In fact, relatively little hassle is involved in pursuing coursework, learning a language, conducting research, or undertaking an unpaid internship abroad after graduation or during the summer. If you're not receiving credit for what you're doing, consider it a learning opportunity by which you can advance your knowledge and career exploration.

Matching the Right Option to Your Needs

After you think through which type of program is right for you and find out what you're looking for, you're ready to start researching options that best meet your academic requirements, schedule, budget, and interests.

One of the easier avenues to explore are programs sponsored by your home university. In fact, they're often listed on your university's Web site, which you can access from the comfort of your dorm room! Likewise, you can simply visit the study abroad office or the department that oversees your school's study abroad programs.

At some universities, students who want to study abroad are required to participate only in programs sponsored by or affiliated with their respective schools. Whenever that is the case, those universities usually create a number of academic and economic obstacles that prevent their students from going on outside programs of any kind. Other universities maintain lists of approved programs (which means credit will transfer); however, just because a program is approved doesn't mean that you can take your financial aid with you. And still other universities enable their students to choose from hundreds of available programs for which they qualify.

If your home university neither sponsors study abroad programs nor offers a program that suits your needs, you must start looking outside of your home university for program options.

Looking in the library

The university library is always a good place to go when you're doing research, and study abroad research is no different! Many U.S. universities maintain a study abroad library or, at the very least, devote a section of the university library to studies abroad. The study abroad library contains an array of information from reference books that list thousands of study abroad programs to catalogs and brochures from other U.S. university programs to course catalogs (sometimes called programs of studies) for universities located abroad.

Asking an adviser or librarian whether they keep any multimedia information about programs often yields videos, slides, CD-ROMs, photos of programs and program sites, and other types of information. Many study abroad libraries and offices also maintain files containing written evaluations about various programs. Home universities often require students returning from abroad to submit evaluations for prospective study abroad students to use. You may find evaluations of places and programs you're considering incredibly valuable.

Going global: Exploring the Internet

Using your personal computer and campus network, you can find endless numbers of Web pages that give you information on hundreds of programs, financial aid, scholarships, fellowships, and grants specifically geared to studying abroad. You can also find information about internships and volunteer opportunities, international travel, particular countries, specific fields, and international currency exchange rates and banking.

Although the Web is a great research tool, remember to be critical of information you find out there. Just because it's on the Web doesn't mean it's true or reliable! Gather, study, and analyze what you find and what you're thinking about for your study abroad experience, and then share your thoughts with your advisers and friends.

A few good Web sites to start with include:

- ✔ **GoAbroad.com** (`www.goabroad.com`): GoAbroad.com has an international education database. The site is frequently updated, contains fairly accurate information, and maintains user-friendly travel information.

- ✔ **IIEPassport** (`www.IIEpassport.org`): IIE Passport, the Web site for Institute of International Education, includes databases with information about spending an academic year abroad and scholarships.

✔ **SECUSSA** (www.nafsa.org/secussa): SECUSSA is a Web site maintained by NAFSA (National Association of Foreign Student Advisers): Association of International Educators. It provides links to other education-abroad Web sites and to information for students and advisers about studying, working, and traveling abroad. It also has an excellent bibliography.

✔ **StudyAbroad.com** (www.studyabroad.com): The site offers a flexible search feature that enables you to look for programs using a variety of fields, including how long you plan to study abroad, language, subject, and country.

Reference books and catalogs typically have very general information about programs while brochures may focus on making the program or school look inviting by showing more about social life and benefits of living in a particular city. Brochures may fall short when it comes to information on academics. Once you know you're interested in a program, check out its Web site and get in touch with the sponsor for more information and application forms. Many U.S.-based programs have toll free telephone numbers you can call to request information, which sometimes is quicker than e-mail. If your parents have questions or concerns, they should feel free to call the same numbers and ask to speak with a program adviser, too.

Getting a fresh perspective from returning students

Talking to students at your home university who already have studied abroad is one of the most valuable tools in choosing and planning your own program. This strategy helped me choose a program and enabled me to work as a peer adviser in the study abroad office at my home university when I returned from my studies in Ireland. I got to spend most of my time telling other students about my experiences and why they, too, should pack up and go away. I even tried to convince a few to go to Dublin. If your home university uses students returning from study abroad programs as peer advisers, seek them out — they're a valuable resource, too!

Don't be afraid to contact students who've studied abroad! You probably won't be bothering them at all, and they'll more than likely welcome the opportunity to share their study abroad story with you. In fact, you may have a hard time getting them to stop talking about it!

Whenever you're interested in a particular program, find students who recently went on that program. Call them up or e-mail them, asking whether they're willing to meet you for lunch to discuss their time abroad. If your study abroad office sets up a question-and-answer session with students returning from abroad, attend these events! Returning students give you the best picture of what the experience was like. If several students who went on the same program are on campus, talk to a few of them, because no two experiences are the same and you can find out something valuable from each student you talk to. Ask questions like the ones that follow to help you discover whether a particular program meets your study abroad goals:

- How challenging were the courses?
- Was there enough time for traveling and socializing?
- What were the best and worst things about the program?
- How "American" did the program feel?
- Are optional program trips worth the time and money?
- Was the international student office/program staff as helpful as possible?
- What one place should you not miss on your visit?
- What was the housing like?

If you can't find any students who've been on a program you're considering or to a country where you want to study, talk to any students who have been abroad. Their perspectives on what living and studying is like in a foreign country, what they wished they'd packed, why they're glad they went away, what most surprised them about being abroad, and how it felt coming home, still provide you with insight.

When you want to study abroad with a program that is not sponsored by your home university, contact the representative of that program and ask them for telephone numbers or e-mail addresses of students who have participated in the program.

If a program refuses to let you contact former participants, start looking for another more reputable program.

Meeting with program representatives

Talking with program representatives is a great way of getting the kind of personal attention you need to get answers for all your questions. They usually are the experts on the programs their universities or organizations offer. Program representatives often visit campuses of U.S. universities to promote their programs and meet with interested students. Some universities invite a number of program representatives to campus every year for a day or evening Study Abroad Fair. The program representatives set up booths with plenty of brochures, course catalogs, and applications. They also talk with and recruit interested students. As an added bonus, program representatives may bring a student who has studied with their particular program to the fair. You can use these opportunities to collect up-to-date information, resolve questions, and discover more about programs from the people who know them best.

Evaluating a Program

Once you've selected a variety of potential study abroad programs, you need to take a careful look at each program. Maybe you're wondering why you placed a particular program on your list of possibilities. Was it simply because the brochure looked cool? Be honest with yourself. Studying abroad is an important educational and financial investment that you're making in yourself!

The following sections cover the major considerations for evaluating study abroad programs. In addition to these, remember that cost, safety, and health are other important considerations. See Chapters 10, 17, and 18 for more information on these topics.

Location, location, location!

A program's location definitely has an impact on your decision. Deciding to study abroad is impossible without considering where in the world you want to go for a semester or year. And the options literally extend around the globe.

Western Europe is the most popular study abroad destination for U.S. students. In fact, two-thirds of all U.S. study abroad students go there, primarily because Europe has many extensive and well-developed study abroad programs. And yet its popularity doesn't mean Western Europe is the best place for you to study. Where you need to study depends upon personal, academic, and home-university considerations. Each town, city, country, region, and continent has something to offer. Although no one place is likely to suit all your desires, some will come close.

These days students are diversifying, visiting regions other than Western Europe because of attractive academic, language, cultural, internship, and traveling opportunities. Consider programs in Africa, Asia, the Caribbean, Eastern Europe, Latin America, the Middle East, South America, the islands of the South Pacific, and the former Soviet Union. You can study rain forests in South America, politics in Eastern Europe, Hinduism in India, or the roots of African music in Nigeria.

Challenge yourself to explore a culture that may be radically different than your own — it's not only an invaluable learning experience, but you also gain a better perspective of your own beliefs and traditions through different and unfamiliar cultural lenses.

Seventy-five percent of the world's population lives in developing nations. How does that affect world politics and history? You probably don't know that U.S. trade with developing countries currently approaches 40 percent of all U.S. imports and exports. How are U.S. politics affecting these developing nations? You'd probably be surprised. Because today's world is global in nature, and almost without boundaries because of the Internet, being able to focus your knowledge of a developing nation or simply any nation other than your own may become a major career asset. What has colonialism done to the developing nation you visit? What languages are the citizens learning in the country where you're studying? What primary language is used in higher education institutions where you spent a semester or two?

Tracing your roots

Although some students go abroad to discover more about a culture that is not their own, some do the exact opposite. For example, students from Arabic-speaking families often study in the Middle East, and Hispanic students may select any of the countries where Spanish is spoken. Likewise, Jewish students may choose to go to Israel, African American students may seek out a program located in Africa, and Asian American students may look to programs in Asia. Students search for information about their own culture, ancestors, national heritage, or ethnic and religious identities. Seeking your own identity is another excellent reason for pursuing studies abroad, and your experience will be just as rewarding as students who study abroad to find out about others. The hope is that you find what you're searching for, deepen your understanding of yourself, and come home more connected with your background.

Initially, students in search of their backgrounds always are perceived and treated as Americans, regardless of their efforts to blend in, properly speak the native language, or even look like the local people. So, be wary; your assimilation efforts may not always work the first few times around.

Mousing between city or country digs

Do you prefer studying in the city, the country, or in the suburbs somewhere in between? All three locations have something to offer. A large city often is a mecca of cultural experiences and social opportunities. On the flip side, cities tend to be more expensive, impersonal, trendy, and busy. Sometimes cities fail to have much of a national identity and you need to venture out to the country to experience it. On the other hand, although a suburb or rural area is often more traditional and offers plenty of contact with local residents, you may go stir crazy, feeling confined in such a small place. Think about what type of residential area your university is in now and ask yourself whether you want to live somewhere similar or different? Sometimes a city mouse can use a break from the city life.

Double-dipping: Visiting two countries

Despite the benefits of being in one place for awhile, you may prefer traveling to several places during the time you spend abroad. Perhaps glimpses of many cultures, countries, or regions can help you reach a different goal, perhaps discovering common themes or issues in a number of places or exploring different forms of government, education, or healthcare.

Although finding and being approved for a study abroad program is going to be easier when it's based in one specific location with occasional visits to other nearby cities, programs that involve a high amount of travel do exist. Such programs frequently use travel as a way of comparing and contrasting differences in various locales. Semester at Sea, for example, enables students to compare and contrast the oceanography of different places along the Atlantic coast of the U.S.

Measuring compatibility with your home school

Some study abroad programs dovetail nicely with your home university's schedule and academics better than others. You want to attend a foreign university where the academic calendar is compatible with your home university's academic calendar, particularly if you are only going for one semester. You want to be able to return to your home university at a convenient time, like at the start of a fall or spring semester.

If your abroad university schedule is such that you have a month or two or three of downtime before being able to go back to your home university, make sure you have a way of keeping yourself busy. For example, if your abroad semester goes from July through November, what are you going to do until classes start up again? Travel? You could return home and try and make some extra money at a part-time job.

Choose an institution abroad that is as academically rigorous as your home university. You'll need to check out whether your abroad university offers your major and what level courses you can to take in that field. If the abroad university is going to limit you to entry level or intermediate level major courses, you may end up bored. If it's important that you do some advanced work in your major while you're abroad, make sure you're allowed to enroll in advanced courses.

Persevering with a nonapproved program

Picture this scenario. You're at your computer, surfing the Net for potential study abroad programs, and you discover a program in Timbuktu (otherwise known as Tombouctou, a real town in Mali in West Africa). It is perfect! Exactly what you've been looking for. The price is right, it has your major, and you can study there for just one semester. You jump up and run to the study abroad office to check their list of approved study abroad programs. And, you find a problem. The Timbuktu program is not approved. Crestfallen, you think of heading back to your computer to look for another program.

Ah, but wait! Not so fast. Although your home university doesn't currently approve a program abroad, that doesn't mean you can't persuade your school to approve the program you want to go on. Maybe no one until now has wanted to go to Timbuktu, so the university didn't need to offer a Timbuktu program option.

Typically, whenever you'd like to receive credit for a study abroad program that isn't currently included on your home university's list of approved programs, you can petition the study abroad office, dean's office, or if your home university has one, an International Study Committee, for program and credit approval.

Be aware that petitioning for approval of any study abroad program is a tedious and detail-oriented process. Every university has its own procedures for what you need to do to be granted program approval. Pay close attention to them, follow directions, and provide as much information as you can.

You usually need to include the following in your petition:

✔ A brief statement saying why you want to attend this particular program. Explain how the program can benefit your education and why you've chosen this specific program over other similar programs that may already be approved.

✔ As much program material as you can get your hands on. School officials considering your petition primarily are concerned with the academic merit of the program, so providing a course catalog or syllabi from courses you want to take is a nice touch.

✔ A list of other universities that approve the program. Call the program for this, or if it's on their Web site, print it out.

✔ A letter supporting the program from one of your professors — if possible. A professor who examines the program, thinks it has merit, and writes a letter supporting the program is definitely a feather in your cap. If you can get the chairman of the department in which you're majoring to back your request, that's even better.

✔ Any forms that need to be filled out and submitted with the petition.

✔ Several copies of the entire petition package. Check with your study abroad office or dean to find out how many people will review the petition so you can provide copies for each of them. (You probably won't need to submit several copies of a course catalog. Instead, you can photocopy the relevant pages, like the ones from your major department.)

As with all study abroad–related matters, meet the deadline when the petition is due! Submit it well in advance of when it's to be reviewed. If you fail to submit your materials on time, the committee reviewing your petition can refuse to accept or review it.

Hitting the Books to Find Out More

Thanks to the Internet, students are often able to research and write papers from the comfort of their dorm room without having to set foot in the library. However, you may be selling yourself short if you keep your study abroad search confined to the Internet. Many comprehensive guides to studying abroad have been written that you can't find on the Web.

Your nearest study abroad office, library, or bookstore offers an opportunity to check out the valuable information in these study abroad guides:

- *Academic Year Abroad 2003* by the Institute of International Education (www.iiebooks.org). This publication provides listings for almost 3,000 semester and academic-year programs offered by U.S. and foreign universities and private organizations and key information about application procedures and requirements, academic credit, contact addresses, e-mail, phone, fax, costs, fields of study, language of instruction, housing, travel and orientation. You can look up programs by location, course of study, and so on.

- *Vacation Study Abroad: The Complete Guide to Summer and Short Term Study* by Sara Steen. International Institute of Education (September 1999). Describes more than 2,000 programs sponsored by U.S. and foreign universities, language schools, and a wide variety of other organizations.

  Considered the best study abroad reference guides, the first two publications in this list are U.S. higher education's standard information resources on international study. They're used by students and academic advisers nationwide. U.S. undergraduates find information about programs that combine travel and study in Eastern and Western Europe, Asia, Africa, Oceania, the Middle East and the Americas — more than 70 countries worldwide.

- *China Bound: A Guide to Academic Life and Work in the PRC* by Anne F. Thurston, Karen Turner-Gottschange, and Linda A. Reed, National Academy Press; Revised edition (January 1994). This guide provides information about living and working in China as an international student or scholar.

- *International Handbook of Universities* by the International Association of Universities, Grove's Dictionaries, Inc.; 16th edition (June 2001). An up-to-date guide to more than 7,300 higher education institutions in more than 175 countries, this handbook features more than 1,000 new entries added since the previous edition.

- *The Jewish Travel Guide* by Michael Zaidner, Vallentine Mitchell (February 2003). This study abroad guide covers Great Britain, Israel, the U.S., and other African, European, and Latin American countries. It lists community centers, synagogues, kosher restaurants, and so on.

✔ ***Smart Vacations: The Traveler's Guide to Learning Adventures Abroad*** by the Council of International Educational Exchange. St. Martin's Press, March 1993. Featured in this travel guide are 200 learning vacations of one to six weeks duration that are available throughout the world, including study tours, outdoor adventures, voluntary service, field research, archaeological digs, and others. It gives you practical details about programs and tips about how to select a program and prepare for traveling abroad.

✔ ***Students Abroad: Strangers at Home — Education for a Global Society*** by Norman L. Kauffmann, Judith N. Martin, Henry D. Weaver, and Judy Weaver, Intercultural Press (February 1992). This book discusses studying abroad from the students' viewpoint.

✔ ***Transitions Abroad.*** Your campus library may also carry this magazine, which features articles about study, work, and travel abroad. It's written by students who've recently returned from studies abroad. The magazine's Web site, www.transitionsabroad.com, also is a good study abroad resource.

Chapter 6

Beware: Hazards in Transferring Credit

....

In This Chapter

▶ Determining your courseload

▶ Weeding through technical aspects of transferring credit

▶ Averting common mistakes

▶ Reviewing differences in the U.K.

▶ Covering a few final notes on transferring credit

....

Studying abroad is not a vacation . . . at least as far as your home university is concerned. You need to assume that your home university expects you to take as many courses and study just as hard in taking them as you would if you were staying home for the year. And because you want to blend in with the students at your university abroad, you need to expect to take the same amount of classes and do the same work that is required of native students.

Now that you know you'll be working hard in your classes, I can let you in on an important secret. Transferring credit has the potential of becoming one of the trickiest parts of studying abroad. If you don't pay attention to your home university's rules regarding the transfer of credits from other schools, you can end up making mistakes when choosing courses while studying abroad. Some of those mistakes can prevent you from returning to your home university with a full semester or year's worth of credits. Preplanning and keeping someone at your home university apprised of your studies abroad are the best ways of guaranteeing that you'll return home with all your credits intact.

You can consult your study abroad adviser, major adviser, class dean, or registrar at your home university to determine whether the classes you plan to take while studying abroad actually meet credit transfer requirements.

I spend most of this chapter warning you about all the things that can go wrong when transferring credit, but I must remind you that at most universities, students go abroad on a regular basis and credit from universities abroad is, more often than not, routinely and easily approved. You may be lucky enough to find that transferring credit turns out to be one of the easier parts of going abroad because your home university approved your study abroad program and you shouldn't be studying abroad on an unsatisfactory program.

Determining Your Courseload

Universal standards for credits and credit-weighting systems do not exist. Just among U.S. colleges, some students need to earn 32 credits to graduate while others need 132 credits to graduate. Considerable variation in credit structures also occurs among schools abroad. A few programs may use the same credit-weighting system as your home university, so that credit weights are identical. This situation likely happens with study abroad programs that are directed by your home university, which makes transfers of credit very simple. When that's the case, you probably don't need to read any further.

Most American universities use the semester credit system, and by now you know how many credits you need to earn per semester at your home university to carry a full courseload and graduate on time. When you study abroad on a program that also uses the semester credit system, determining how many credits you need to take while you're away probably won't be too difficult. However, you need to realize that many Australian and European universities have credit systems that vary significantly from what you're used to. At some schools, credit weights may vary even from department to department.

Ultimately, how the credits that you earn abroad actually translate to home-university credits is at the discretion of your home university. Before going abroad you need to understand how your home university defines a full courseload and how many courses you're expected to take while you're away to be considered carrying a full courseload. Similarly, you shouldn't leave campus without first knowing how your university defines a full courseload for students on your particular study abroad program.

Don't confuse full courseload with the minimum full-time courseload required for financial aid purposes. Often the minimum full-time courseload doesn't equal the number of courses per semester required to receive your undergraduate degree in four years at U.S colleges.

When your study abroad program doesn't have the same credit weight or semester system as your home university, determining how many courses you need to take while studying abroad can be as simple as visiting the study abroad office. Many offices keep lists of approved programs with full courseload requirements clearly defined. As such, you need to look up your program in the study abroad office files to find out how many credits you need to take during the semester or year you're away to meet the full-semester or year's worth of requirements at your home institution.

Taking a full program of study

My college's general rule for courseloads was as follows: It transferred credit on a full-load basis, which means I was required to take the same number of courses that students at the university abroad were required to take, regardless of whether that meant three or eight courses. This system didn't pose too much of a problem for me because I ended up taking four full-year courses. However, other students on my program from different universities were subject to similar rules, but they found themselves juggling six, seven, or eight courses per semester, because one course at the abroad university was equal to only half a course at their home universities. So be aware of what you're getting yourself into!

If your study abroad office doesn't have this type of list, you must consult other resources, such as a dean, major adviser, or registrar to agree on what a full-time courseload is at your university abroad. Whenever you've had to negotiate your courseload, make sure that your home university puts these expectations in writing and keeps them on file before you leave campus.

When you choose your study abroad courses before leaving your home university, make sure that you sign up for a full-time courseload and submit your planned courses to the study abroad office, dean, major adviser, or registrar for approval.

When you choose your study abroad courses or change one while you are away, make sure that you send an e-mail with your course information to the study abroad office, dean, major adviser, or registrar, confirming your course plan, or any changes, and asking for approval.

Getting home-university approval for your study abroad courses is a necessity. Approval typically is granted either before you go away or right at the start of the semester you begin your studies abroad. Home universities sometimes refuse to transfer credit to your permanent transcript for unapproved courses and won't retroactively approve courses taken abroad after you return to campus. Therefore, communicating your study abroad course plans with your home university is important.

If, for some reason, you must leave a study abroad program early, you probably will jeopardize most or all your program credits.

Transferring Credit

The grade transcript from your study abroad program is the most important piece of paper you have to guarantee that your credits transfer. It proves that you completed study abroad classes and provides the grades that you received. Be sure to request that the official transcript from your studies abroad be sent from your university abroad to your home university. Provide your university abroad with the name of the appropriate contact person and address for sending the transcript to your home university. You won't usually be allowed to deliver these official documents to your home university, because in most cases the university abroad must send them. However, you also need to receive a grade report or unofficial transcript from the university abroad at the end of your program.

If you're participating in a U.S.-based study abroad program, your transcript probably will come from the program or from the U.S. university it's affiliated with. Most colleges will treat these transcripts as transfer credits from a U.S. university.

Sending a course description, or even a syllabus, helps your home university determine whether or not to accept your transferred credits. Try to anticipate course-approval problems at the beginning of the semester, which enables you to use the add/drop period to enroll in an extra course or two while waiting for an answer from home.

Use the tips in the following list to ensure your credits transfer smoothly:

- ✔ **Save e-mails.** Saving e-mails about course credit that you send to and receive from your home university is a good idea. Whenever a question comes up about course credit when you return home, you'll be better prepared to deal with it when you saved your messages.

- ✔ **Save course materials.** Bring syllabuses, reading lists, papers, portfolios, exams, and so on home with you because having them may make getting courses approved for credit much easier. Yes, having to pack all these materials to bring them home is a pain, but doing so often is the only way your home university can assess the work that you did abroad and grant you credit for it.

- ✔ **Go to class.** Be aware that instructors of courses abroad may take attendance, and showing up for class can influence your final grade. You may even be granted only partial credit for a class when you don't attend on a regular basis.

Receiving credit toward graduation

Regardless of whether you receive credit toward general education or major requirements, you'll likely receive credit toward graduation for every course that you take while studying abroad. For example, if you earn four credits while away for a semester, the credits count toward the number of credits (say 32, for instance) that you need to graduate.

Most universities stipulate, however, that you must receive a certain grade in a course, in other words a C or better, to receive credit toward graduation at your home university. For that reason, as a general rule, you don't want to take any courses pass/fail while studying abroad. When a course is offered only on a pass/fail basis, you may have to prove that the grade you would have received was a C or better.

When your university has a study abroad office, making sure that you receive credit toward graduation while studying abroad usually is its responsibility, but when you want to seek credit toward core requirements or your major for courses you've taken abroad, you must consult the appropriate people — in other words a dean or major adviser.

Making the grade

Universities usually handle grades earned abroad in one of two ways:

- ✔ Home universities may take the grades from your study abroad transcript and transfer them directly onto your home university transcript. Using this method means that grades earned abroad will be counted toward your overall grade-point average (GPA).

- ✔ Home universities may not transfer your grades directly from abroad university transcripts onto your home university transcript. Using this method means your home university will note the courses that you took and that you received credit for them while studying abroad, but it will neither report the grades on your home university transcript nor count them toward your overall GPA.

If your home university doesn't transfer your grades from abroad onto your permanent transcript, you need a way to access your study abroad transcript in the future for employment or graduate school purposes. For example, two years from now, you may need to request a transcript from your study abroad program. If a U.S. institution operates your program, obtaining a transcript usually is easy. However, some foreign universities will neither provide additional transcripts nor have them available when you request them. When that's the case, your home university needs to have your transcript from the university abroad on file and be able to make a copy of it for you.

Receiving credit toward core requirements

Your home university typically requires you to complete the majority of your core requirements (also known as general education or distribution requirements) before ever going abroad. When you want a course from abroad to count toward your core requirements, you must first receive school approval. As a general rule, if a similar or equivalent course is available at your home university, gaining approval is relatively easy. However, having a course from abroad count toward general education requirements is more difficult when an equivalent course isn't listed in your home university's program of studies. If you plan for a course that you're taking abroad to count toward your core requirements, you need to seek out your home university's approval before ever going abroad. Some universities simply won't provide retroactive approval for such measures.

Some liberal arts colleges require you to take a certain number of courses outside of any one department to graduate. When you spend a year abroad at a U.K. or Irish university, meeting those requirements may become difficult to accomplish because those universities allow you to take courses in only one or two departments while enrolled as a visiting student. Be aware of this potential problem when planning your coursework abroad.

Receiving credit toward your major

When you want to receive credit toward your major for courses taken abroad, you must discuss this issue with someone from your major department or your major adviser. The study abroad office, dean, and registrar usually cannot grant credit toward your major for courses taken abroad.

Each academic department may make its own rules regarding how to provide credit for work done abroad. Be aware of these rules. Discuss receiving credit toward your major with your major adviser before you go abroad. When you meet with your major adviser to discuss course plans for study abroad, bring along a copy of the study abroad course catalog so your adviser can refer to course descriptions and determine equivalencies with home university courses.

You may be required to submit paperwork (sometimes called a petition) to your major department for the credit from your studies abroad to count toward your major. These forms need to be signed by your major adviser. The major department will likely grant credit toward your major upon your return when you present your major adviser or the department with the syllabuses, papers, and exams from courses you want to count toward your major.

Maintain communication with your major adviser via e-mail while studying abroad. Keep your adviser updated on the courses that you want to count toward your major. Doing so helps eliminate problems when you return home. Save the e-mails you exchange just in case your major adviser has a change of heart after you return home and decides not to grant credit for a course that the two of you previously had agreed would count toward your major.

If you're accelerating

If you're planning to complete a four-year degree in less than four years (accelerating) you may find that studying abroad can make fulfilling those plans difficult. Some colleges require you to spend two of your last four semesters at your home university. Thus, if you go abroad during your junior year, you may not be able to graduate in December of your senior year. Consider a short-term or summer program instead.

Confirming credit transfer

When you return to your home university, confirm that your credits from abroad actually transfer. Don't wait until two weeks before graduation to find out that there was a problem with your transfer of credit from abroad. Remember, you ultimately are responsible for meeting your home university's credit requirements.

Check with the registrar or dean's office to make sure each received your transcript from abroad. If you need to file specific forms for credit to count toward core requirements or your major, submit the forms with appropriate signatures. Clear up any credit transfer discrepancies as soon as you return home.

Avoiding Some Common Mistakes

Although I cannot speak for all universities, I can say that making any of the following course choices while studying abroad can lead to problems.

Taking only one semester of a foreign language

You've probably heard the rule, "You cannot have an A without a B." Well, that rule often rings true when receiving credit for foreign language courses: You cannot receive credit for 101 if you don't take 102. Credit may not be granted for an introductory or intermediate first semester of a foreign language unless you also take a second semester of the language. You can take this second semester while you're abroad or when you return home, but you must take it at some point before graduating or you won't receive credit for the one semester you completed abroad. An exception to this rule is when you attend a one-semester program that requires you to take a language that your home university doesn't offer. Your home university should, in that case, grant you credit for one semester of the language when it can't offer you a second semester.

Recognizing that liberals and nonliberals don't always mix well

Most liberal arts colleges won't grant credit for courses that are not considered liberal arts. If you study abroad at a big university, you may have the option of taking courses that don't qualify as liberal arts. Bear in mind that if you cannot find an equivalent course in your home-university course catalog, chances are good that the course is not liberal-arts related, and if you take it, you may not receive credit. Check with someone at your home university whenever you have any doubts about how your school defines liberal arts courses. Accounting, business, public speaking, and cooking courses typically are not considered liberal arts.

Taking short courses before your program begins

Some study abroad programs require you to take short two- to six-week courses prior to the official start of your program. You often must attend these preliminary sessions, but you won't receive any credit for them. However, these courses sometimes lead to semester or yearlong courses for which you will receive credit. For example, you may be required to take four weeks of intensive French before beginning your semester of study at a French-speaking university. As part of your study abroad program, you continue your language study in French 201 and receive credit for this course (provided, in some cases, that you take French 202).

Doing independent study, internships, and research projects

Most liberal arts colleges won't grant credit for independent study, internships, or research projects that you complete while studying abroad. The reason: Your home college simply wants to supervise your undertaking of these projects to make sure that you're doing enough work to receive credit.

Determining whether your work is of the same caliber and difficulty that you'd be doing at home is difficult for liberal arts colleges in these situations. Some colleges make exceptions or have special requirements when you want to complete an independent study, internship, or research project abroad. For example, if your study abroad program requires an internship or research project component, your home college should give you credit for it. However, as a general rule, when given a choice between taking a course and doing an internship or independent study, choosing the course is usually better.

Duplicating courses

While studying abroad, you definitely don't want to take a course that duplicates or repeats course material for which you've already received credit at your home university — you probably won't receive credit for it. Whenever you take a course that's similar in name but different in content when compared to one you've already taken at home, then you must bring all course materials (syllabus, notes, exams) home with you and be prepared to explain the differences between the two courses when you return to your home university. A faculty member or adviser probably has to vouch for the fact that you did not repeat any course material while studying abroad. For example, if you took abnormal psychology at your home university and advanced abnormal psychology while abroad, you need to describe the differences between the two courses when you return home. If, at the beginning of the semester, you question whether an abroad course duplicates one that you've already taken at home, contact someone at your home university or choose another course.

Receiving less than a C

Your home university may have rules about minimum grades that you must receive while studying abroad to be able to receive credit toward graduation. Remember, your home university isn't sending you on an academic vacation. Some schools require a C or better to receive credit, which means that if you receive a C–, you won't receive credit for the course. Make sure you know whether your home university requires you to receive a minimum grade to ensure that your credit for courses taken abroad will transfer.

Enrolling in upper-level courses

You typically must complete most of your advanced coursework (particularly in your major) at your home university. Again, your home university wants to ensure that your advanced coursework meets its expectations. Home university officials don't want to grant credit for advanced coursework abroad that, in reality, may equal only intermediate-level coursework at home. The only way to ensure that you meet your school's expectations is to require you to complete your advanced coursework at home. Thus, this requirement means one of two things to students studying abroad. You can either rejoice that you don't have to kill yourself by taking advanced courses while abroad, or you can take advanced courses while abroad and petition for advanced course credit approval when you return. Be aware, however, that just because you petition for advanced credit, that doesn't mean your petition will be granted. Although you may, however, still receive credit toward graduation for the course, it won't count toward the number of advanced courses you need to take to graduate.

Understanding the woes of a transfer student

If you attended another school for any amount of time before transferring to your current university, the way your credits transferred from the original school can affect your study abroad plans. Most universities allow only a certain number of transfer credits to contribute toward your degree. You need to check with your dean or registrar if this situation applies to you. Policies vary and universities sometimes make exceptions or compromises if you present a strong case explaining why you need to study abroad (for example, you're a foreign language major and need to improve your language skills) even though you've nearly met the maximum allowable transfer credit threshold.

Taking Exams and Receiving Credit in the U.K.

Be aware that when you're planning on studying abroad at a university in England, Ireland, North Ireland, Scotland, or Wales, you need to know that universities in those countries have dramatically different credit-weight systems and semester schedules than what you may be used to. I discuss other unique characteristics of the British university system in Chapter 8.

Matching courseloads to U.K. standards

Even though I mention this earlier in this chapter, it bears repeating here: Courseload requirements may vary from department to department at schools in the U.K. Although 30 credits may constitute a full courseload in the physics department, you may need 45 credits for a full courseload in the English department. Remember that determining and then carrying exactly what constitutes a full courseload for a native student at your university abroad is your sole responsibility. Your home university can help you with this issue.

When you study in only one department while attending a U.K. university, you need to worry only about carrying a full courseload for that department. However, if you study in two departments while abroad, you must calculate how many credits constitute a full courseload in your particular situation. When taking 50 percent of your courses in each department, you can expect to take half of a full-time courseload in each department. If you're not splitting your time that evenly, you need to work with your home university to determine the number of credits you need. Your school probably has experience with other students who've studied abroad at the same university and can tell you how many credits you need to take within each of your departments to for your courseload to be considered a full one.

When studying at Oxford and Cambridge, a full courseload may entail two or three Tutorials per term. No written work is attached to lectures at Oxford and Cambridge, and as such, lectures may not count as part of your official home-university courseload. Lectures may, however, complement your courseload. For a detailed discussion of lectures and tutorials, see Chapter 8.

Defining semesters in the U.K.

Many British universities are on a trimester system, which makes them better suited to a full year of study. These universities often have yearlong courses and award credits based on a full year of study. Trimesters usually mean teaching periods of different lengths, which can complicate the number of credits available to students who want to study abroad for only a semester. If you're more interested in a full semester of study abroad, ask your study abroad program or study abroad adviser about U.K. universities that have moved to the semester system.

A semester courseload at U.K. universities needs to be somewhere in the range of 60 units; however, those 60 units can include as few as two or as many as six courses. At some schools within the National University of Ireland, students may take as many as eight courses, each of which is worth about half the course credit at your home university.

Examining U.K. exams

Your home university likely requires you to take all exams in all courses in which they're offered when you're studying in the U.K. Some U.K. universities provide visiting students with the option of whether to sit for exams; nevertheless, you need to plan on taking exams when you want to receive credit for your courses.

Besides, in some courses, your final exam counts for 100 percent of your final grade. That may well explain why taking the exams is so important, don't you think? A final grade must be recorded on the transcript from your university abroad if you want to receive credit for a course at home. Additionally, courses for which the final accounts for 100 percent of your final grade may periodically require you to submit written work that won't be graded. Although you may not understand the point of handing in work that isn't graded, departments often require all written assignments to be turned in if you expect to receive a grade for the course.

Other departments give cumulative exams. For instance, their exams may cover material from two semesters. So if you studied at the school for only one semester, your home university won't expect you to take exams on material that you didn't cover in your course. At your abroad university, however, some instructors will forget or won't even care that you attended only half of a course. Study abroad students should not assume that an instructor will be willing to administer half of an exam. Although you shouldn't need to ask instructors to make up special exams for you, some students have to do exactly that. Discuss this situation with your professor, study abroad program, and home university.

When exams are held for degree-granting purposes, you may, however, find that university policies won't allow you to take exams. When that happens, you need to follow the policy of the university abroad but notify your home university.

As a visiting student, you never want to become a nuisance to your department by asking for special exceptions to be made to accommodate your exam needs.

Whenever a department offers a dissertation option, in lieu of an exam, to all its students, British and international alike, your home university will likely allow you to choose. However, make sure that you check in with your home university about this issue before you choose.

If you earn a certain grade in the course, some departments may exempt you from taking an exam.

Chapter 7

Doctor, Lawyer, Indian Chief: Considering Special Areas of Study

Some subjects are easier to study while abroad than others. For example, planning to study French language and literature in France is a straightforward task. By the same token, traveling to any English-speaking country to study the social sciences or humanities is also relatively simple. You shouldn't have to jump through many hoops to get these study abroad plans to work. Hopefully, you know some French before you arrive in France or are participating in an intensive language program when you get there. If you're studying in an English-speaking country, you don't have a language barrier to contend with and just have to make sure that your credits transfer to your home university.

But study abroad plans sometimes get tricky for students studying science, engineering, math, or economics. Some U.S. universities consider studying these subjects in another country so tricky that they discourage students in these disciplines from studying abroad at all. But if you truly want to study abroad, you can make it happen, regardless of your major or future career plans. In this chapter I discuss those subjects that sometimes make studying abroad quite a challenge.

The Troubled Invasion of the Mad Scientists

Research shows that U.S. science and engineering students are an underrepresented group of study abroad students. For the most part, the low number of science and engineering students studying abroad has to do with the policy of the home department or university, not with a lack of desire to go abroad on students' parts.

One of the top reasons science and engineering departments discourage their students from studying abroad is that the courses required to graduate with a degree in science or engineering have been carefully mapped out and sequenced. Going away for a semester may mean that you fall off this carefully constructed path and are unable to catch up in order to graduate on time.

Furthermore, finding exact equivalents to U.S. science and engineering courses may be difficult, if not impossible. Abroad universities may teach organic chemistry over the course of several semesters or modules instead of during one intensive semester, like in the United States.

Another problem that crops up for students who want to study abroad for only one semester is that many abroad universities offer science courses on an annual basis. This means that exams usually fall at the end of the entire school year as opposed to the end of the semester or term, making it difficult for the U.S. university to accept grades (if the student didn't take the entire course) or translate grades into matching equivalents.

Other reasons U.S. science and engineering students are discouraged from studying abroad include the following:

- **Inadequate math skills:** American undergraduate math skills tend to fall behind those of European undergraduates. The entrance requirements to European universities often include math skills that exceed math-skill expectations for first-year undergraduates in the U.S.

- **Limited faculty support at home:** Often, U.S. science and engineering students are hard pressed to find an adviser to assist them in finding an appropriate study abroad program because finding an adequate abroad program is a labor-intensive process that requires time and effort.

- **Lack of sufficient funding:** Finally, because of the way science and engineering curriculums have been designed, many science and engineering students who want to study abroad must add a fifth year or extra semester to their studies. This, of course, costs extra money! And if the student opts to study abroad in the summer instead, not only is finding funding difficult, but the possibility of summer employment is often eliminated.

So, given all these reasons not to go abroad, why should you bother? (If you're really wondering, see Chapter 1.) If you come up against a department with a firm "no credit will be granted for study abroad" policy, you may have to accept this and find another time to go abroad. If your department permits you to study abroad, but isn't exactly encouraging you to buy your plane ticket, you may hesitate to carry out your plans. Don't change your mind! You should still go!

To maximize your chances to study abroad, do lots of research to find a country and university where your major is taught similarly to the way your home university teaches it. For example, many Australian universities' engineering programs are similar to those in the U.S., whereas the trimester system and other factors make the British system unsuitable for many students. Discuss your options with your home university study abroad office or your study abroad program.

Most science students can only study abroad for a semester and so you can usually control any "damage" study abroad does to your plans to complete your major. Before or after you return, you can double up on lab courses. Being away for only one semester also allows you to not stray too far off the path for completing all the required classes for your major on time.

While there are numerous challenges to studying science or engineering abroad, you shouldn't give up! The sections that follow provide arguments that should help strengthen your resolve to study abroad.

Science, science everywhere

Although you may find it hard to believe at times because of the prevalence of science and technology stories in the media, the U.S. is not the end-all or be-all as far as science is concerned. Every country throughout the world, to some extent, has a well-educated scientific community that is responsible not only for teaching science, but also for discovering new things.

Remember that part of what keeps science and technology continuously advancing is the exchange of ideas between scientists all over the world. The ability to collaborate with members of the global scientific community is a useful skill, particularly for those students planning to continue studying science at the master's and PhD levels. Therefore, developing a global perspective by studying abroad is important for science students. Scientists and engineers benefit from foreign language and intercultural skills.

If science or engineering is your strong suit, and you want to study abroad, with a thorough enough search and some help from your study abroad office or major adviser, you should be able to find courses that meet your degree needs at any abroad university with a relatively large science curriculum. (For help conducting a study abroad search, check out Chapter 5.)

Thinking globally, locally, and scientifically

You can't find a better way to understand different environmental conditions, agriculture, and health than with an on-site study experience. What better way to study the rain forest than by spending a semester in the Amazon? Why not study potato growth in the west of Ireland? Studying on location not only places your studies in a social and cultural context, but it also gives you a much richer perspective on global problems and solutions. In your abroad environment, you can observe how natives approach science and find ways of linking your academic knowledge with what you learn on-site.

Frequently, developing countries can benefit from the knowledge study abroad undergraduates have to offer. You may have a chance to participate in significant research projects, as developing countries can't always afford senior researchers.

How Do You Say "I'm Sick?": Premed Students Abroad

Most universities tell their premed students that if they're interested in studying abroad, then by all means, they should go. Medical schools like to see that students have had a variety of college experiences. However, studying abroad for premed students is a sticky situation because of the Medical College Admissions Testing (MCAT), the medical school application process, and the amount of course work involved with finishing premed *and* major requirements.

Some schools allow you to take premed courses while abroad and others strictly advise against it. So you need to check with your home university's premed committee about completing premed requirements while abroad. Also keep in mind that it is *always* your responsibility to know what you need to do to apply to medical school before you go abroad.

Taking the MCAT: Timing it right

Most schools advise you to complete the science courses required for medical school (introductory chemistry, organic chemistry, and introductory physics) at a U.S. school if possible. This guarantees that you not only cover all topics on the MCAT but also have taken most (or all) prerequisite courses for any advanced level science courses you want to take when you get back.

Taking the MCAT the summer before or after you go abroad allows you to take an MCAT review course during the summer months before the exam. If you need to take the MCAT while you're abroad, get in touch with the premed committee or career service center at your home university to obtain a copy of the registration packet.

Study abroad students and AMCAS

The American Medical College Application Service (AMCAS) is the service you use to apply to most American medical schools. AMCAS is a non-profit, centralized application processing service for applicants entering first-year classes at participating U.S. medical schools. Find them on the web at www.aamc.org.

Yet another reason you may want to complete your premed classes in the U.S. has to do with credit transfer and grade reporting. You want your grades for coursework completed abroad to transfer on the American scale (A, B, C, D, F) so that they can be included in your AMCAS composite grade-point average (GPA). If your abroad school uses a grading system other than the American system, then your abroad grades won't be recorded in your AMCAS GPA; these courses will only appear as pass/fail semester hours. Discuss this issue with your home university study abroad director or study abroad program.

Preparing med school applications

Typically, students apply to medical school more than one year before they plan to matriculate, usually in the summer between their junior and senior years. If you want to study abroad during your undergraduate career, you need to carefully plan your classes (from your first day at college) in order to apply to medical school at the end of your junior year.

Most students planning to go abroad during their junior year can usually complete all the premed classes before they go if they take some premed classes during the summer months. If you can achieve this, then you may even be able to take the MCAT in August before going abroad. With these requirements out of the way, you can return from studying abroad in June of your junior year and fill out the online AMCAS.

If you choose to study abroad during your sophomore year, you may need to take summer classes after you get back in order to complete all premed class requirements before the start of your senior year.

Because medical school interviews are usually scheduled from September until February, senior year study abroad for premed students is not at all practical if you've applied to medical school.

Premed study abroad options

Here's a good list of premed programs abroad to give you a sampling of what's out there. I list them here with their Web site information to help you get started on your study abroad options and give you a sampling of what is out there.

- England: University of Bristol (www.bris.ac.uk/Depts/IC/jya)

    The University of Bristol's premed program allows students to combine courses in Biomedical Studies (anatomy, biochemistry, and physiology) with courses from the Biological Sciences units (such as molecular genetics and cell biology). You can also take courses from the Department of Chemical and Physical Sciences to prepare for the MCAT, which can be taken in the U.K. You can study at Bristol for the full year, or for just a fall or spring semester.

- England: University of Lancaster (www.lancs.ac.uk)

    The University of Lancaster has both a premed program and a healthcare program. The university offers a range of science courses to study abroad students, including almost all of the core MCAT courses. All courses have laboratory and/or fieldwork available. Lancaster has made an effort to establish itself as a center for science and premedical studies in the U.K. The MCAT is given at a site in Lancashire, and a premed adviser facilitates contacts among premeds so that students can study together for the MCAT. You can study at Lancaster for the full year or for the spring semester only.

- England: University of Sussex (www.sussex.ac.uk)

    The University of Sussex offers a program specifically designed for the needs of premed students from North America. At Sussex, students have an opportunity to volunteer at places such as the Royal Sussex County Hospital, a drop-in center for people with HIV, a hospice, and in the campus rescue team. You can take the MCAT in Sussex at the same time as in the U.S., and MCAT review classes are available in the Spring Term (January–March). You can study at Sussex for the full year or for spring semester only.

- Denmark's International Studies (DIS) Medical Practice and Policy Program (www.disp.dk)

    DIS offers a study abroad program for non-Danish speaking juniors and seniors who have a serious interest in medicine. Courses offered include: Human Health and Disease, Health Care in Scandinavia, Biomedical Ethics, Brain Functioning and the Experience of Self, Developmental Psychopathology, and the Impact of Epidemic Disease upon European History. Courses offer students privileged access to the National University Hospital, the National Science and Medical Library, and the Macroanatomical Laboratory at the Medical School of the University of Copenhagen. Field trips to the World Health Organization (WHO), whose European headquarters is located in Copenhagen, and the Danish Institute for Clinical Epidemiology also coincide with some courses.

Some students wait and apply to medical school after they've finished their senior year. Applying at the end of senior year may work better for students who are away during their junior year — you will not feel as rushed. However, this also means that you'll have to take a year off between finishing your undergraduate degree and starting medical school.

Gathering recommendations

Before going abroad, speak to the professors who will write your letters of recommendation for medical school. Make sure you give them waiver forms and any other materials they will need to complete your recommendation. You may want to check in with them again while you're abroad as a helpful reminder and to see whether they need any more information from you. If you anticipate requesting recommendations from faculty members at your abroad university or program, be sure to take additional waiver forms and materials with you.

Writing a personal statement

Your adviser and other faculty members writing recommendations usually need to have your personal statement and resume in front of them when they write their letters. Most medical school application forms give you plenty of freedom to write an essay in which you can discuss your achievements that aren't reflected in other parts of your application or talk about how events have shaped your attitude, focus, and desire to attend medical school. If you do not have your personal statement completed before going abroad, work on it while abroad and e-mail a draft to your adviser and other recommenders.

An added benefit of e-mailing your personal statement while abroad: It reminds your adviser and recommenders that you're expecting a letter from them.

Supply and Demand: Studying Economics Abroad

Most of the economics majors at my undergraduate university studied abroad at the London School of Economics. I always wondered why that particular school attracted so many economics majors but have since discovered that this is because most study abroad programs have limited offerings in economics.

Keep in mind that there are many different approaches to the study of economics. Review your study abroad program or host university's course descriptions carefully to make sure your economics courses abroad match those required for your major.

Many programs offer principles of economics courses (typically microeconomics and macroeconomics), some programs offer intermediate economics courses, but few offer advanced or field-based courses. So if you're an economics major, study abroad takes a little bit of extra careful planning. The best times for you to study abroad are during your sophomore or junior years, before you need to take the advanced-level courses required for your major.

After you have found two or three programs you're interested in, bring the course descriptions and any other pertinent information to the chair of your home university's economics department. This way, the chair can review the courses and let you know which courses may count towards your major. Find out if the department grants credit for upper-level economics courses completed abroad. Such courses may count for college credit, but won't advance your standing as a major.

Keep in mind that if your home economics department requires one or two semesters of calculus, you should get this out of the way as soon as possible. Typically, after this requirement has been met, majors can begin taking intermediate economic theory courses. If you put off the calculus requirement until your sophomore year, you may run into difficulties studying abroad and completing your major.

Additionally, try to complete some intermediate course requirements before traveling abroad (usually econometrics or intermediate micro/macro economic analysis). This allows you to easily finish the rest of your requirements when you return.

As with premed students, economics students may be able to gain a little bit of flexibility by completing some of their required economics courses in summer school. Remember to get summer school courses pre-approved for credit transfer by your home university's economics department.

Taking Advantage of Summer Internships

Perhaps you're planning to spend all or part of a year abroad, but for whatever reason (academic or just to strengthen your resume), you need to acquire a internship for the summer after you've completed your study abroad experience.

If you're studying abroad during the fall semester only, you probably don't have worry about searching for an internship until you return to your home university for the spring semester. Most students successfully conduct their internship searches in the spring, with two exceptions:

✔ If your home university has an active on-campus recruiting program, you may want to check with the career office to see what opportunities may be available in the fall when employers tend to visit campus.

✔ If you are interested in journalism or government, internships in these fields generally have early deadlines (before the end of fall semester). Take time to do some research before leaving the U.S. to determine deadlines. After you're abroad, you can use the Internet or snail mail to apply for these positions.

If you're studying abroad during the spring semester, when internship searches are at their busiest, you're going to need to follow the steps I outline in the following sections to ensure a successful search from abroad.

Before you go . . .

The key to getting an internship when you return from your study abroad experience is excellent preparation before you leave the U.S. Get a jump on your internship search by taking care of the following details:

✔ Write your resume and a good sample cover letter before you go abroad. This way your home university's career office can help if you get stuck. Also, create your resume in multiple electronic formats (such as an e-mail version and on your Web site) just in case employers can't receive your resume when it is attached to an e-mail message.

✔ Choose and research industries that you're interested in. If you have no idea what you want to do, meet with a counselor from the career office.

✔ Start networking! Use alumni contacts when possible. Select companies and/or professionals which reflect your career goals. Set up phone or in-person informational interviews.

✔ If you're really interested in a particular employer or internship opportunity, take the time to contact them before you go abroad. Request an early interview, if possible.

While you're away . . .

To keep the ball rolling on your internship search and to stay motivated while you're studying abroad, work on these tasks while you're gone:

✔ You're going to be busy with your classes, activities, and friends while you're abroad and it will be very easy to avoid or ignore your internship search. Schedule some time to work on your search each week, to make phone calls, e-mail, or do research.

✔ If you have Internet access, check to see what internship opportunities have been posted at your home university (provided your home university posts opportunities on their Web site or affiliated Web sites).

- ✔ When you apply for internship positions, mention that you are currently studying abroad, but are available via telephone and e-mail.

- ✔ Follow up with any employers you spoke with before going abroad by letter, e-mail, or phone.

- ✔ Use e-mail or snail mail when possible because they are cheaper and more convenient for everyone. If the employer has a Web site, see whether you can apply for positions online. If you must use the phone, make sure to leave messages that mention convenient times (during the workday in the U.S.) you can be reached and leave your e-mail address.

- ✔ Don't be afraid to follow up! Keep track of the contacts you have made and follow up at least once with each employer. Politely inquire if your materials have been received and ask about the timeline of the internship selection process.

Chapter 8

Daring to Be Different: The British University System

University-level courses in the United Kingdom are taught in English, but few other similarities exist between British and American universities. From grading to scheduling classes to choosing a major, the Brits do things their own way. But, hey, you were the one who decided to study abroad to experience something different, right? Studying in the U.K. offers the chance to soak up another culture without having to soak up another language.

Studying in England

British students planning to attend university begin specializing in an academic subject while they still are in high school. Students choose their university majors essentially during the years that are equivalent to 11th and 12th grades in the U.S. In 11th grade, students study four or five courses and take the first round of exams, called *A levels,* before proceeding to a second year of advanced A-level study in three subjects. Students emerge from these two years of study with the equivalent of what is considered advanced placement or freshman-year credit in the U.S. Therefore, in England, most university degrees are completed after only three years of study rather than four.

Students apply directly to a university's academic departments (such as history or biology) for admission to bachelor's degree programs. The specific academic department makes admission decisions, not a centralized admissions office. For students entering an English university, majors are determined when they apply, and they're permitted to take only courses that are within their majors. As an applicant to an English university, the department in which you plan to study reviews your application and admits you. Additionally, you can expect to study in no more than two departments at most British universities. Some universities, however, have become more flexible and are allowing study abroad students to study in multiple departments at the introductory (first- or second-year) level.

Because of the preparation U.K. students go through before arriving at university, many first-year courses at British universities equal courses at a U.S. university's sophomore year level, especially where languages, science, and math are concerned. As a visiting student, the university may allow you to take only first- and second-year courses. Be aware that second-year courses match junior-year courses in the U.S. British universities often limit admission to final-year (third-year) courses to students with extensive backgrounds in their respective fields of study.

Learning the ropes

Your attendance is expected at lectures, discussion groups, and lab practical classes. You need to realize that in England, much of your academic work is left up to you. Professors often provide lengthy reading lists at the start of their courses, and you then decide how much reading you complete each week. Professors usually refrain from giving give you specific reading assignments for each class. What, when, and how much you read for the course is entirely up to you.

Lectures may be organized in such a way that the professor covers or highlights specific topics, but you, through your independent reading, are responsible for covering the topic's broader content by exploring recommended texts on the reading list. Professors assume that you're continuously reading on your own, and so can contribute to classroom discussions and pass an exam at the end of the course. In general, there is much less hand holding in British universities, on both an academic and a personal level. Students are assumed to have adult independence and responsibility.

Although the amount of reading is entirely up to you, you need to understand that a final exam may be the only means of assessing your progress in the course, and believe me, cramming a semester or year's worth of reading into two or three weeks isn't a very wise idea.

Making the grade

Although courses at American universities typically offer several chances to improve your grade — a midterm exam, final exam or final paper, quizzes, and periodic writing assignments — universities in England generally focus on just a few papers or exams that count for all or most of your grade. Although smaller essay grades may contribute to your overall grade for the course, the final exam, project, or paper usually counts most in determining your final grade.

British universities assign percentage grades to all courses and you need to consult your study abroad program, host university's international student office, or home university to find out how to translate the grading scale of your British university to the grading scale at home.

You are responsible for completing the same amount of work as a British student. This includes taking exams! Do not take courses pass/fail because your home university won't be able to factor a passing/failing grade into your overall grade-point average (GPA). Additionally, the definition of a passing grade may differ between your home and host universities.

Studying in Scotland

Scottish universities are more similar to U.S. schools than English universities. In fact, the American educational system is based on the Scottish system. Students enter university without the specialized backgrounds of their English counterparts. Scottish students take an exam called the "higher" after studying four or five subjects. Instead of spending another year studying two or three subjects and taking an advanced exam like English students, Scottish students enroll in a university after the higher.

In Scotland, students don't choose their major until the end of their second year at the university. Although they do not apply directly to specific academic departments for admission, they nevertheless apply to *faculties* such as humanities, science, social science, law, medicine, or engineering. Professional courses like law or medicine have prescribed courses that students must take each year, but humanities and science students often can choose which classes they want to take. After choosing a major, Scottish students spend two more years at the university concentrating on their majors before earning an *honours degree*. After choosing a major, students may also choose to spend only one more year at university, earning a general education degree.

Scottish universities are more flexible in nature than many English universities, especially the more traditional ones. Students are admitted to a specific faculty at Scottish universities, but are likely to be able to take courses at various levels (provided they meet course prerequisites) and in a number of subjects within your faculty. You may even receive permission to take courses in another faculty.

Learning the ropes

Scottish universities may provide you with more course information than English universities, including course objectives, a reading list, lecture syllabus for an entire semester, essay topics, and schedules of important events like exams or presentations. However, considerable variation in course expectations exists from department to department.

In Scotland, introductory courses usually are large lectures. Don't let the large lecture style of intro courses mislead you into thinking that you don't need to attend to class. On the contrary, class attendance is important in introductory courses because professors rarely follow or use textbooks. Higher level courses tend to be taught seminar style or as a mixture of lectures and seminars.

As in England, Scottish professors assume that you are continuously reading on your own so that you can contribute to classroom discussions and pass an exam at the end of the course. Attendance is usually mandatory at discussions, labs, and tutorials.

Making the grade

Traditionally, Scottish universities rely heavily on final exams to determine 100 percent of the final grade for a course. The system has shifted toward more continuous assessment models, like you're probably familiar with at your home university, but the final exam for a course still can carry a significant amount of weight. Scottish universities usually use the A through F grading scale.

Timing Your Trip: The Trimester System

Universities in the U.K. are designed differently than schools in the United States. One major difference: Many universities still operate on a trimester system, which means that you won't receive a full semester's worth of credit for fall study abroad because you'll be there for a term, not a semester. Although most trimester universities accept students for just one or two terms, studying abroad for less than a year may be easier and less confusing at British universities that have adopted semester schedules. In addition, some universities require full-year study in certain disciplines such as English, science, and engineering.

When a school has adopted a semester schedule, you need to be very careful about when to go. Remember the following caveats:

✔ If the fall semester, including exams, ends before Christmas, you can return to your home university in January.

✔ Universities that formerly followed a trimester schedule often have a second semester and a mini semester in the spring. You should plan to stay for both.

✔ Some universities that have switched to a semester schedule have a fall semester that begins in late September and ends with exams in late January, which often makes returning to your home university in time for the start of spring semester impossible.

Some universities (and this is the exception here, not the rule) have an arrangement in which international students studying in the fall semester can submit essays in place of final exams given in January (details must be worked out between professors and students) so that international students can still study in the fall, but return to their home university in time to start the spring semester in January. If you must study abroad in the fall, you may want to find out if this is possible at your potential host university.

Considering Oxford and Cambridge

The Universities of Cambridge and Oxford are among the oldest universities in the world and among the largest in the United Kingdom. Both have worldwide reputations for outstanding academics and original research.

In general, Oxford and Cambridge universities prefer to accept full-year visiting students who demonstrate exceptional motivation and enthusiasm for their major subjects. Visiting student applicants must have a solid foundation in their majors, a strong grade-point average (GPA) — 3.5 or higher — and they must already have completed two years of study at their own universities.

At most colleges, you're allowed to study in only one department (your major) during your time at Cambridge or Oxford, or no more than two. Cambridge tends to restrict students to one subject more often than Oxford. This limitation may cause difficulties for students with plans for completing more than one major at their home universities, so be careful. Oxford offers a number of combined courses, or *joint schools,* as they are often called. They allow you to choose areas that interest you from two different disciplines, sometimes across arts and sciences, such as physics and philosophy. If you are a double major in, for example, English and biology, you probably will have to choose study in just one of those subjects.

Oxford and Cambridge are on trimester schedules. The first term, which is known as *Michaelmas*, runs from the beginning of October until the first or second week of December. The second term, known as *Hilary* (at Oxford) or *Lent* (at Cambridge), runs from the beginning of January until Easter. Third term, *Trinity* (at Oxford) or *Easter* (at Cambridge), which is slightly shorter than the first two terms, runs from after Easter until mid-June. The third term is primarily for studying and exams, but because visiting students don't take degree exams, they spend the third term taking tutorials, just as they would in the previous two terms.

Understanding the university structure

The structure of the undergraduate education system at Oxford and Cambridge is different than that of undergraduate institutions in the U.S. and even other British universities. The *university* handles administrative duties such as defining academic standards and degree requirements and maintaining facilities.

The *college* is another thing entirely: Imagine that at your current university, you live, eat, study, go to class, and have access to a library all within your dorm. You don't have to leave your dorm to go to class, unless you wanted to hear a large lecture or go to a sporting event. That's what a college is at Oxford and Cambridge.

The college is the center of university life at Oxford and Cambridge. Students live, study, and socialize within their own colleges. The many small colleges, with between 200 and 700 students, make up the larger university. Oxford has 30 undergraduate colleges, and 6 private halls that were founded by different Christian denominations and still retain a religious character. Cambridge has 31 colleges, three of which are for women and two that are exclusively for graduate students. When applying to Oxford or Cambridge, students are admitted to a college and are members of the university by default.

If you're attending a women's college, you still can eat and attend social events at any other colleges. The colleges tend to be located fairly close to each other. Going to a women's college doesn't mean that you'll have a single-sex educational experience. Your experience still will be coed.

College communities include undergraduate and postgraduate students, teachers, and lecturers. Students attend tutorials within their colleges. Each college has libraries, computers, common rooms, and academic and personal support. They provide recreational activities, including entertainment, sports, music, drama, and other special events.

Delving in to your topic: Tutorials

The tutorial system at Oxford (known as the supervision system at Cambridge) is organized by each college and is a highly individualized approach to learning, where you meet weekly with a tutor (sometimes with another student) to discuss a particular subject in depth. The tutorial usually centers around an essay, which you prepare the previous week and then submit to the tutor, or, if the tutor is a very traditional one, read aloud during the tutorial. The tutorial allows you to receive focused instruction from the tutor, and you can also learn from the other student in your tutorial.

While studying at Oxford or Cambridge you attend lectures and labs offered by the university and tutorials organized by your college. Generally, lectures are not required but are available to supplement your education at your discretion. Your tutor often can advise you about which university-run lectures and practical classes are useful for your studies.

The people who lead tutorials are professors. The tutorial system is not equivalent to having a discussion or conference section led by a graduate student in the U.S.

The goal of the tutorial is to review your answers and theories and to raise new issues related to your topic. The tutor may also critique your essay's content and approach. Your tutor may even ask to take the essay at the end of the session to read it over and make comments — or not.

At the end of the session, you and your tutor decide on a topic for the following week and suggested readings. You usually are free to explore the tutor's suggested readings or to venture out and find your own readings related to what you're studying.

The tutorial system is a highly personalized form of teaching and learning designed to show students how to think critically, independently, and creatively. Tutors are more concerned with increasing your knowledge than they are with awarding grades.

Success with tutorials is really up to you, the student. You need to adequately prepare for tutorials so that you're ready to exchange ideas with your tutor and other (one or two) students during your meetings. Don't worry about arriving at Oxford with polished presentation or public speaking skills. Part of tutorials is discovering how to prepare and present your ideas and how to defend your opinions or theories.

Your tutor may arrange for you to have tutorials in another college whenever he or she doesn't cover a certain specialty. Doing so exposes you to different points of view and different ways of conducting tutorials.

In nearly all cases, Oxford colleges will not accept a study abroad student without a good idea of what the student wants to study, and it's difficult or impossible to change these tutorials once a student has arrived at college. A list of tutorial subjects is actually part of the admissions process for most Oxford colleges. At Cambridge, students don't generally finalize supervision subjects until their arrival, but they do have to submit the subject area in which they are interested at the time of application to a college.

Trying triposes at Cambridge

Degree courses at Cambridge are called *triposes*. Cambridge courses cover subjects very broadly before becoming more specialized and offering a wider range of options. Triposes are divided into blocks lasting one or two years. In some subjects, there is a two-year Part I (which may be divided into Part IA and Part IB) and a one-year Part II. In others, Part I lasts a year and is followed by a two-year Part II.

Visiting students typically study at the second-year level. After consulting your director of studies, you register for one part of a tripos relating to your major field and take the appropriate courses. Depending on which part of a tripos you take, you may or may not have to sit for an exam.

Applying to Oxford and Cambridge

Applying to Oxford and Cambridge is a rigorous process. In addition to an application form and academic transcripts, these universities typically require two recommendations from college professors and two graded writing samples.

Oxford offers a circulating application that enables you to list four colleges of choice in order of preference. Candidates are considered by their respective colleges, in turn, by the order of preference. Oxford encourages prospective visiting students to write to the tutor in charge of admissions at their first-choice colleges during the September or October of the year before admission so they can discuss possible supervisors and branches of study. The circulating application isn't available for applicants who apply through a U.S. university or program.

Cambridge, on the other hand, doesn't have a circulating application. If you're interested in studying as a visiting student at Cambridge, you need to write or e-mail your first-choice college early in the fall semester of your sophomore year, making sure that you to state your major field and request an application form.

Students applying to Cambridge need to submit SAT scores. Because you'll be reporting your scores more than a year after your high school graduation, you need to contact the College Board in Princeton, New Jersey, at 609-771-7600 to make this report request.

Admissions at Oxford and Cambridge are made on a rolling basis. Spaces can fill before the program deadline dates, so, apply to these schools as early as possible in the fall semester of your sophomore year for admission during the following fall. Plan to send an updated transcript after you finish the fall semester of your sophomore year.

Oxford and Cambridge colleges, whether through a U.S.-based program or direct enrollment, are expensive. A few U.S. universities have direct exchanges with one or two Oxford and Cambridge colleges. This can be the easiest and least expensive way of studying at Oxford or Cambridge, so ask your study abroad director if your home university has an exchange like this. If you're on a tight budget for study abroad, you can still have a great academic experience at a less expensive university in the U.K.

Admission for visiting students at Oxford or Cambridge is, at times, peculiar. Outstanding, well-rounded students have a good chance at being admitted. Factors that often affect admission include the popularity of the subject you want to study there and how many other U.S. students are applying. So don't be discouraged if you are not admitted; not only is Visiting Student admission at these colleges extremely competitive, but factors that are beyond your control also are involved.

Studying American-style

Several institutions in the United States sponsor programs at Oxford and Cambridge. The experience provided by these programs is often not the same as it is when you're admitted via direct enrollment as a *visiting student*. Visiting student status means that visiting students have all the privileges and status of regular degree-seeking students, both within their college and throughout the university. The only restriction on visiting students is the Oxford and Cambridge rule that limits degree exams to full degree students only.

If you study with an American program that grants you *associate student status*, this means that that your privileges at the University are more limited than if you were a visiting student. You also have limited or no access to libraries, university facilities, or college grounds. Furthermore, you usually do not live in an Oxford or Cambridge college but rather off-campus with other Americans. If you chose to pursue one of these programs, you won't have a very authentic experience and you'll most certainly need to get the approval of your home university.

Getting social: The "scene" at Oxford and Cambridge

Some students find that the college they attended while at Oxford and Cambridge had a bustling social life, while others think the social scene was fairly boring or they had trouble making friends because of the tutorial system.

Firstly, the tutorial system at Oxford and Cambridge don't exactly make it easy to meet other students. You probably will only meet a handful of students in your tutorials, whereas in the U.S. it is easy to meet many other students who have class with you — class size at home is much better! Additionally, realize that much of the on-campus accommodation at Oxford and Cambridge are single, as opposed to shared, bedrooms. While this may be a nice break from having to share a small dorm room, it makes it very possible for you to go through your day with a limited amount of contact with other human beings!

Students who've studied at Oxford and Cambridge report that in general, you're going to have to be extra outgoing to make friends. The best way to meet people is through events sponsored within your college or by joining societies. One student joined as many as five societies in order to meet people! However, students who studied at either school for only one term explain that that limited amount of time (eight weeks) is really too short to get into societies and other social groups.

A great kick-off to the year and way to make friends happens in the fall during "Fresher's Week," which international students are invited to attend There's plenty of orientation sessions designed to introduce you to all aspects of college and university life. During this week, there will be a fair where most of the university societies, clubs, and sports teams have booths promoting their activities where you can sign up to join. While initially this sounds appealing and as if you'll emerge from Fresher's Week with many new-found friends, realize that the primary audience for Fresher's Week is first-year students and you're probably a junior. Students report that it is difficult to find Oxford and Cambridge students who are third years; students your own age have already formed their social cliques.

Students who did not live within a college at Oxford and Cambridge, and for one reason or another, lived away from campus, highly advise against this choice if you're hoping to have a social life. Most students who live off-campus find it difficult to be part of the social life when living off campus and don't feel 100 percent a part of the community — they report going into college just for tutorials and computer access.

Another social trap to be extra careful of at Oxford is Cambridge is the tendency to hang out with other American visiting students. There are so many Americans at Oxford and Cambridge that it is easy to find them and stick with them as opposed to meeting native or other international students. And, this tendency will cheat you out of part of the experience of living in England.

Butler University's Institute for Study Abroad has a visiting student program with several colleges at both Oxford and Cambridge and you can apply through Butler to several colleges. See www.ifsa-butler.org.

Part III
Applying to Schools and Programs Abroad

The 5th Wave   By Rich Tennant

"Oh, him? He's some guy from Muncie, Indiana looking for a way to pay for his daughter's semester abroad."

In this part . . .

This part may initially give you a slight feeling of déjà vu from your senior year of high school when you were filling out college applications and financial aid forms. But applying to study abroad is, for the most part, less complicated than the college application process (partly because you've already been through a rigorous application process and also because you don't need to write as many essays or complete as much paperwork). I guide you through the process of applying to abroad programs and coordinating your abroad plans with a number of departments and institutions.

Chapter 9

Submitting Applications

· ·

In This Chapter

▶ The essentials of applying to universities abroad

▶ Making essays easy

▶ Waiting and backup plans

· ·

*1*t wasn't long ago that you endured the tiring and arduous process of applying for admission to college. Remember the SATs? Writing six different college essays? Interviews and campus visits? Running home to check the mail every day? Well, in case you're afraid that applying for admission to a study abroad program is going to cause you to relive that nightmare — it isn't.

Submitting applications to study abroad is a shorter, less involved, and therefore less painful process. No standardized tests, interviews, campus visits, or tours are required. In fact, you most likely board a plane to your destination abroad never having seen the university in person (other than in pictures) nor visited the country to which you're going. That's all part of the adventure on which you're about to embark.

This chapter presents seven simple steps for completing your study abroad application process.

Getting an Application

Although obtaining an application may seem like an obvious first step, you need to remember that, in most cases, you're dealing with a university that's overseas and therefore forced to reckon with international mail. Believe me, that can take awhile, so request an application as far in advance of any deadlines as possible.

You likewise need to be persistent in your request. When an application doesn't arrive in your mailbox within two to three weeks, don't hesitate to make another request or send a friendly e-mail asking where your application is. Universities in other countries sometimes do not act as quickly on requests as students in the U.S. may like.

If the application you need is available online, print it out, or if your home university's study abroad office has one, take advantage of this convenience by stopping by the office to collect materials.

Requesting Supporting Documents

You need to submit several documents to support your application to a university located abroad. These documents include recommendations, academic transcripts, foreign language proficiency forms, and program approval paperwork. Make sure you request these documents as soon as possible. Professors, deans, and registrar's office staff members are busy people and fulfilling your request can take awhile. As soon as you receive your application, determine what documents you need to complete it and then make all the necessary requests.

Because of confidentiality issues, the universities you are applying to may require that some, if not all, of these supporting documents are sent directly by the person who supplies the information (such as your professor, dean, or registrar). In this case, be sure that addressed and stamped envelopes accompany your request.

Recommendations

You need anywhere from two to three letters of recommendation, which are one of the most important parts of your application. Letters from professors and other mentors who know you well and are familiar with your performance, character, and goals can make a difference during the selection process, explaining gaps between grades and test scores or illuminating areas in which you excel that otherwise may be overlooked. Letters from employers also can help, but rarely do the general platitudes of an acquaintance — alumni included — make a difference.

Good people to ask include the following:

- ✔ **Your academic adviser.** An adviser in your major with whom you frequently meet or someone who has known you most of the time you've been at school are good sources.

- ✔ **A professor within your major department.** Host universities typically are department-based and having a professor who has taught you in a given subject write a recommendation is a good idea.

- ✔ **A professor with whom you've taken more than one class.** Ask only the professors of classes in which you've done well.

> ✔ **Academic deans.** Letters from academic administrators always are help-ful. If you happen to know your class dean fairly well (and not because you've been on academic or social probation), ask him or her to write you a letter of recommendation.

Do not ask a professor who doesn't even know your name to write your letter. If a professor doesn't know your name, then he could easily confuse you with another student when writing a letter of recommendation. Furthermore, if a professor never took the time to learn your name when you were in his class, do you think he'll take the time to write you a decent recommendation letter? Probably not; you could get stuck with a generic letter of recommendation or worse, no letter at all.

Whenever a professor agrees to write a recommendation for you, organize your recommendation materials for him or her. I suggest putting all your materials in a folder before giving them to the professor. You need to clearly indicate on the envelope what the recommendation is for and when the dead-line is! In the folder, include any recommendation forms that the university abroad has sent.

Don't forget to sign any forms that waive your right of access to your recom-mendation! Current federal law provides that students may review letters of reference written for them. Applicants may also choose to waive this statutory right. While admissions officers respect that it is within the applicant's legal right not to sign the waiver, some schools may take confidential letters more seriously. Faculty members may also refuse to write a recommendation letter if it is not confidential.

Giving the professors who are writing your recommendations copies of your academic transcript, current resume, or a paper you wrote and earned you a good grade in his or her class sometimes is helpful, but be sure to include a stamped, self-addressed envelope to the university abroad school for the pro-fessor's convenience. When you need to send the recommendation along with your application, ask that the professor put it in an envelope and sign across the envelope's seal before giving it back to you.

Whenever your academic record shows some inconsistencies either because you had a rough semester or suffered through an illness or other family prob-lem, you can ask whomever is writing your recommendation to explain.

Foreign language proficiency form

If your study abroad program features a language requirement, you will more than likely need to file a foreign language proficiency form. The for-eign language proficiency form asks the professor filling it out to comment on your oral fluency in the language, grammatical accuracy, pronunciation and intonation, and which level class you should be placed in while abroad. Ask the faculty member who most recently taught you the language to complete this form. He or she can best assess your current ability to speak, read, listen to, and write in a foreign language.

Academic transcripts

You also need to send an up-to-date and official copy of your academic transcripts to your host university. You can usually make this request through the registrar's office at your home university. A nominal fee sometimes is charged for processing and mailing the transcript. Be sure to provide your host university's address, pay the fee, and sign the release form that comes with your request. Your home university cannot legally release your transcripts unless it has your signature. Therefore, e-mail requests are not acceptable. It's best to personally visit the registrar's office to take care of this matter.

Be aware that sometimes an application deadline may occur before the end of a semester. When that's the case, you must plan to send:

✔ A current transcript before the deadline

✔ An updated transcript after the deadline when your most recent semester grades are posted

Program approval form

Most study abroad programs and host universities require an international studies adviser, academic dean, or registrar at your home university to complete a program-approval form before they will admit you. This form confirms that you're a student in good academic standing at your home university, that you haven't had any disciplinary action taken against you, and that your plans to study abroad at a specific university have been okayed by your home institution.

Completing the Application

The actual study abroad application (minus any essays) is fairly short and need not take you hours and hours to complete. It asks for basic information, such as your name, address, which academic department you're applying to, when you plan to study abroad, and where tuition bills should be sent. However, bear in mind that your application is a reflection of who you are. Follow instructions on filling it out completely and as neatly as possible.

Whenever possible, either type your application or fill it out online. Always use proper grammar, punctuation, and spelling. Furthermore, meeting the application deadline is critical.

Deadlines vary. In general, deadlines for fall and full-year programs occur anytime from December to mid-April. Spring program deadlines tend to fall from October to mid-November. Many programs have rolling admissions instead of a specific deadline, so submit your application as soon as you know that you intend to apply to a program!

Otherwise, check deadline dates carefully. Some universities and programs have strict policies requiring that applications received after the deadline be reviewed only if space is still available in the program after on-time applications have been reviewed.

Other important details to bear in mind include:

- Keeping a copy of everything you send in case your application package gets lost in the mail.

- Supplying your signature where necessary. The application may request it in many different places.

- Making sure you've supplied your school abroad with enough information about you so that it has a complete picture of who you are and what your academic strengths are. Doing so is the only way admissions committee at your host school will find out about you.

- Providing up-to-date contact information so that if anything is missing the host university can reach you as soon as possible.

  The application asks for your school address and home address, so be sure to indicate to which address the school abroad needs to send any correspondence, including any acceptance packet.

- Include a check, money order, or credit-card information to pay the application fee that most programs and schools charge. Never send cash! Whenever you need to pay the application fee in your host country's currency, the easiest way is to use a credit card. Otherwise, you must work with your bank's international department to be able to pay the fee.

- Sending an I.D.-sized photo whenever the host program or university requests one (usually 2 inches by 2 inches). Universities abroad often require these photos and use them to make your student I.D.

- Sending a copy of your birth certificate or passport whenever required. A copy of the identification page of your passport usually will suffice. If you don't yet have a passport or passport number, let your host school know that you're in the process of applying for one and will send that information as soon as you have it.

Writing Those Essays

If your university abroad requires you to write a personal essay or statement for your application (some don't!), doing so isn't as big a deal as those essays you wrote for admission to college — unless it must be written in a foreign language. The host school usually merely wants to find out more about you, why you want to study abroad, and whether you can intelligently think and express yourself in writing. The length requirement for these essays is typically less than two typed pages.

Whenever you need to write your essay in a foreign language, make sure to have a professor or student who's proficient in the language review it for major errors before sending it off.

Examples of short-answer/essay questions and imperatives include the following:

- Have you traveled or studied abroad before? Where?
- Describe your family.
- Tell us about your personal interests and hobbies.
- Why are you a good candidate for studying abroad?
- Why do you want to study in this country? At this institution?
- How does a semester or year of studying and living abroad fit into your overall educational goals?
- What do you want to achieve during your experience?

If your program doesn't ask a particular question but requests a study abroad statement, then address why you want to study abroad and what you want to study.

Although you need not stress too much over this essay, it nevertheless can make you or break you. Students with excellent personal statements have been admitted to programs even when they've fallen short of the program's grade-point average (GPA) requirements. Your essay can be the deciding factor, especially when you're a borderline case. Because the essay can be a good indicator of your personality, make sure that you communicate your enthusiasm for studying at the host university and let officials there know about your unique qualities.

Here's a quick list of dos (mixed with a few don'ts) for effective essay writing:

- Do stay upbeat. Admissions committees generally like positive, lively students. Don't belabor any of the three Ds: Divorce, Disease, Death.

✔ Do make sure that your essay shows your creative side, whenever possible.

✔ Do proofread! Have others proofread! Don't rely on the computer's spelling and grammar checker.

✔ Do make sure your essay has a point. Don't make it a laundry list of everything you've ever done or a chronology of your life. Make sure to say something meaningful.

A quick list of don'ts (spiced with a few crucial to dos) for effective essay writing includes:

✔ Don't focus on quantity. Quality is preferable. Say what you need to say in as few words as possible. Concise, well thought out essays are the best.

✔ Don't exceed the page or word limit.

✔ Don't overuse the thesaurus. Clear and direct writing in your own words is more impressive than writing tangled up topics with big words.

✔ Don't use trite phases. In other words: "I hope that by learning more about Africa, I can save the world someday." Unless, of course, you can back it up.

✔ Don't aim for a polished, PR statement. Make sure your essay reveals something about you.

✔ Don't brag that being a student at your home university makes you more qualified for admission. Your home university may be well known in your state or region, but the U.S. has thousands of colleges, and it's quite possible that the person reviewing your application has never heard of it.

Gimmicks don't work. When your program is particularly competitive and you're concerned about being admitted, don't resort to using gimmicks to help you stand out and get accepted. The quality of your application gets you in, not stunts or flashy paper.

Submitting Special Application Material

Some universities or university departments abroad require additional application material. The most common requests for additional material include writing samples, art portfolios, and audition tapes. If a school requires you to submit a writing sample, make sure you choose one that meets the length requirement. Sometimes a university or program asks for a graded copy of a paper, so make sure that you choose a paper on which you received a good grade! Likewise, make sure that you submit a paper that you wrote for a course in your major subject area because you're probably applying to a department representing the same or similar major at the university abroad. If you're a visual or studio art major, most universities will ask you to submit a portfolio. If you're a music major, you may need to send a portfolio or an audition tape, depending on your area of expertise.

In general, do not send additional application material unless the school specifically requests it. Some schools specifically prohibit you from sending additional information. Large packages of materials don't make you a stronger candidate. You do not want to overload an admissions committee with too much information because its members may get lost in it, not know what to read, or not have time to read everything.

Submit portfolios, audition tapes, and your application well in advance of the deadline, so the admissions committee has plenty of time to review it and to contact you if they have any problems with your materials. Remember that videotape formats differ from country to country.

Putting It in the Mail

I know, this also seems obvious, but prepare a checklist of everything that you need to send with your application. Go through this checklist after you complete your application. Make sure that you have the correct mailing address and have affixed adequate postage when mailing your application. If some not-too-expensive means of delivery confirmation, signature on delivery, or other way of tracking your envelope is available when you send in your application, it may be worth what you spend for the service. And don't forget to ask the postal worker who helps you for an estimate of when your package will reach its destination.

Without being too much of a pest, follow up with your study abroad program or university abroad to find out whether and when your application arrived safely and whether it is complete. It is not unusual that everything that you send will arrive on time, but a recommendation or transcript still ends up missing. When that is the case, you may need to give professors and staff at the registrar's offices gentle reminders to send the documents as soon as possible (if they haven't already). It doesn't hurt to tell them that because your school abroad already has received your application, it will be processed as soon as they submit the outstanding documents.

Waiting

After your application is submitted and complete, you cannot do anything but wait. Be patient! Most programs notify you of acceptance or rejection anywhere between two and eight weeks. Because of differing university calendars at home compared with those abroad, you may often be waiting on a decision from a university abroad when planning for the next semester at your home university begins. My best advice in this situation is to pretend that you won't be accepted into your study abroad program and thus will be spending the next semester or year at your home university. Go ahead and fill out registration forms for classes and apply for housing as if you're not going anywhere. Making these plans at your home university is easier when everyone else on campus is making them, besides when you find out that you're definitely going abroad, you can simply cancel them.

Assuming you'll be studying abroad isn't any fun, especially when you find out that you're not going away because your application was rejected or you didn't get enough financial aid. When that happens, you end up having to scramble to choose courses or risk not having any housing because you missed the deadlines. It is a little bit of a juggling act to have to think about being in two places at once for one semester, but a little extra work now is worth not having so many headaches later on!

The waiting is the hardest part

I can sympathize with the slowness of universities abroad. I submitted my study abroad application in December and didn't get an official response until the end of April. In the meantime, I had to pretend that I was going to be staying at my home university for the following year. What fun it is to be leading a double life! Despite many phone calls to my study abroad program and potential university, there was nothing I could do to get the process to move more quickly.

One reason it took so long is because the academic departments I was planning to study in made the admissions decisions for visiting students. Without the luxury of an admissions office, the departments were juggling normal teaching and research responsibilities with the task of reviewing applications. The other reason my application took so long to process and review is simply because of "Irish time." The Irish are always late for everything and there's never any rushing around — in other words, what you can't do today you can do tomorrow. In fact, many countries and cultures outside the U.S. don't have the same regard for time and punctuality as we do. You just have to be patient.

Chapter 10

What Will It Cost and How Will I Pay for It?

. . . .

In This Chapter

▶ Determining costs

▶ Applying for financial aid

▶ Finding additional resources for money

. . . .

*B*udgeting is a tricky business, and budgeting across currencies is trickier still. Not only do your potential expenses determine how you prepare for and finance your study abroad, they may very well determine which program you choose. Careful planning is imperative for determining what type of financial aid you seek.

Finding a way to finance your study abroad experience may take some work. The financial aid package that you currently have at your home university may or may not be completely or partially transferable to your schooling abroad. Most U.S. loan programs serve only institutions in the U.S. and Canada. Although this type of financing is changing, you may nevertheless have to research alternative ways of financing your experiences abroad, perhaps by using a combination of loans, scholarships, or grants. However, you have no need to panic, yet. This chapter gives you details about what to think about and where to look to rearrange your financial aid package to make paying for an abroad experience a nonissue.

I talk about the nitty-gritty of budgeting for laundry, food, and other day-to-day expenses in Chapter 14. In this chapter, I focus on the bigger picture of program costs and tuition.

Adding Up the Costs

Thinking about how much your experience abroad is going to cost you (and your parents) relative to what you pay per semester or per year at your home university is important. Basically, studying abroad can cost you more, less, or the same as studying at home. The bottom-line cost depends on a variety of factors that may or may not be within your control. For example, you can control how many times you eat out or cook in while abroad, but you cannot control things like your home university's tuition policies, whether your financial aid is transferable, costs of living in another country, tuition at an overseas school, or international currency exchange rates.

Looking at the major expenses

Study abroad programs package major costs in various ways. Some may include tuition, housing, meals, airfare, insurance, and other program-related expenses in one all-inclusive fee. Others may include some but not all of these items. Collecting all the information and trying to come up with complete figures so you can arrive at the bottom line of what studying abroad will cost you is entirely your responsibility. And you need these calculations so you know whether you can afford a particular study abroad program. Never be afraid to make phone calls or send e-mails asking about what something costs.

Be aware that program costs frequently change because of varying exchange rates and changes in the types of services provided for the program fee. As a result, the cost listed in last year's catalog or study abroad guide may no longer be accurate!

The following variables often affect the overall cost of your study abroad experience:

- **Location, location, location:** In general, living in a big, bustling, cosmopolitan city is probably going to cost you more than living in a quiet countryside location. When the U.S. dollar is weak in comparison to a local currency (say for example, the British pound), then the cost of living is going to be higher. Conversely, when the U.S. dollar is stronger than the local currency, the cost of living will be lower — that is for U.S. students studying abroad. Additionally, the cost of your study abroad program depends on which part of the world you choose to study in. Programs in Western Europe tend to be more expensive than those in most other parts of the world (Canada, Africa, Asia, or South America). But take note that it is not unheard of for programs to be expensive in countries with lower costs of living.

- **The length of your stay:** This factor, although obvious, is important: The longer the program, the more money you're going to pay. If you're away for a full year and fly home for vacations or holidays, that means paying for more than one airfare to and from your destination at the beginning and end of a semester. However, be aware that costs can fluctuate based on the time of year you happen to be studying abroad. For example, the per-week/per-credit cost of a summer program may be greater than the per-week/per-credit costs of a semester program.

✔ **Your class load:** You may pay tuition at your home university on what is called a *semester basis,* which means everyone pays the same tuition for the semester regardless of how many or what type of classes you take. Realize that outside of the U.S., many universities determine tuition based on a per-credit basis. Taking five classes can cost more than taking four, and taking science courses with laboratory components can cost more than taking an English class.

✔ **The program you choose:** Study abroad programs offered by private colleges or organizations (such as the Counsel for International Education Exchange — CIEE) cost more than programs sponsored by public institutions. A great way to reduce costs is to go abroad through the public university of the state in which you're a resident because paying the reduced in-state tuition may be less expensive.

Shop around. Some destination cities and countries are more popular than others; therefore, any number of universities may offer study abroad programs in a given location, which means that prices will vary.

✔ **The services offered:** The type of program in which you plan to study also determines cost. When you choose go with an island program (See Chapter 5 for an explanation) that caters to groups of U.S. students, the costs typically are more than directly enrolling at an abroad university. For more money, you're getting more services, such as program staff support in the country you're studying in, language training or orientation programs, social activities, and sight-seeing trips.

✔ **Hidden expenses:** In addition to your program fee, you may find yourself paying a number of other *hidden expenses.* A few to watch out for and put into your budget/overall cost scheme (again, see Chapter 14 for more detail) are application fees, extracurricular fees (in other words sports center access), housing deposits, room and board for vacation periods, passport fees, student I.D. fees, commuting costs, insurance (health, accident, traveler's, renter's), phone calls home, laundry, luggage, and weather appropriate clothing.

Understanding home-university tuition policies

Your home university's tuition policy is probably the single most influential factor that determines how much you pay for your study abroad experience. What your home university's policy is regarding fees to study abroad also determines whether your financial aid transfers.

When you receive financial aid to help pay for schooling and you've applied to go abroad (or you're at least considering it), you need to meet with your financial aid officer or study abroad adviser at your home university to start figuring out how you can pay for your abroad experience. Bring a proposed study abroad budget with you to this meeting. Preemptively taking this step is a good idea because you'll probably have to submit one to the financial aid office eventually anyway. (For more help with study abroad budgeting, see Chapter 16.) Be sure to ask what funds can and can't be applied to a study abroad program. Each home university has different rules and quirks about financial aid and going abroad, and although I try to cover some of these here, your financial aid office is the better authority on this situation. Financial aid representatives can advise you what your particular situation is — based on the amount of aid you're receiving and where you intend to study — and then adjust your financial aid package accordingly.

Because many foreign universities are state supported, the cost of tuition is much lower than what is charged at many U.S. schools, particularly private colleges and universities in the U.S. Conversely, some foreign universities have different levels of tuition and charge higher tuition fees to foreign students. For example, Trinity College, where I studied in Dublin, Ireland, charged its lowest tuition rate for Irish students, a middle-level tuition rate for European Union nationals, and its highest tuition rate for non-E.U. students. Yeah, they apparently believe Americans are made of money!

The following is a list of possible study abroad tuition and financial aid scenarios, from the simplest to the most complicated.

Taking advantage of your home university's program

You're going on a home-university sponsored study abroad program. Tuition is the same regardless of whether you're studying with your home university in another country or in the U.S. If you're currently receiving financial aid, then it's highly unlikely that anything needs to be done differently than in any other semesters you've been at school. You and your parents fill out an endless pile of forms, send them to the appropriate places, and your school gets the correct amount of funds. Just make sure that you budget for things you don't normally pay for when you're staying in the U.S. Airfare may be one such item; groceries are another (if you're on a meal plan at school and don't usually cook for yourself).

Traveling through a different university

You choose to go on a study abroad program sponsored by another U.S. school. Your home university requires you to pay full home-university tuition, and through a written agreement between it and your abroad U.S.-based program, you're allowed to use your financial aid. Policies on whether you're entitled to your financial aid vary, and you need to double-check this with your study abroad or financial aid office.

Getting stuck paying excess tuition

You choose a program sponsored by your home university or another U.S. university, and you're required to pay full home-university tuition even though the tuition at the school you'll be attending is much lower. The U.S. schools tend to justify this in one of the following ways:

✔ You're paying not only for school credits you earn through the home university but also study abroad advising and other administrative and support services. While studying abroad, you accumulate credit toward the degree you receive from your home university. When that's the case, it is hoped that the courses and grades appear on your transcript just as if you were at your home university for a year.

✔ While you're away, the home university cannot really fill your space, for a number of reasons, one of which is that the university budget assumes a certain number of students attend school for four years, and the budget doesn't work whenever a certain percentage of the student body is away on leave.

✔ The principle of equality of opportunity for abroad studies to be accessible to all students means that your home university needs to be able to provide financial aid. Thus, it needs to rely on certain tuition revenues, especially when it provides an extensive amount of institutional financial aid.

You may be irritated knowing that your inexpensive study abroad program is actually subsidizing other people's pricey abroad experiences. Think of it this way: Classes in humanities and social sciences, which cost less to administer and often have larger enrollments, can be thought of as subsidizing classes in fine arts and sciences, which are more expensive to run. When your school doesn't charge different fees for these different types of classes, then it can justifiably make the argument for charging the higher home-university tuition.

If your abroad program only charges you tuition and expects you to arrange your own room and board, make sure that you're billed only for home-university tuition.

Whenever you're paying home-university tuition, you are more than likely responsible for airfare and other nontuition charges. An exception would be if your abroad program offers some sort of group airfare as part of its comprehensive fee.

Taking a leave of absence

Yep, you guessed it. Taking a leave of absence can get a little bit tricky, but you may be able to take advantage of lower-cost tuition at foreign universities. Some universities will approve your study abroad plans and transfer your abroad credit if you decide to go abroad through a U.S.-sponsored program or direct enrollment at a foreign university; however, doing so requires you to take a leave of absence. Technically that means you're not a student at your home university for the duration of your abroad program, regardless of whether it lasts a semester or a year.

Unfortunately, taking a leave of absence is likely to change your financial aid and funding status. You won't be allowed to take your institutional aid with you, and you may need to seek other scholarship or grant opportunities through your U.S.-sponsored program or foreign university. When you're going with a U.S. program, you can adjust your federal and state aid accordingly, but if you're directly enrolling at a foreign university, the general rule (at this point, anyway) is that you cannot take federal or state financial aid with you. Thus you're going to have to look for other ways of funding your abroad experience. Check out the list of additional resources in the "Utilizing Other Resources for Finding Money" section at the end of this chapter to jump-start your search.

If your home university requires or recommends taking a leave of absence, you should discuss all the ramifications of this with your study abroad adviser. Not only do leaves of absence cause credit issues with your home university, but they can also cause financial problems. If you take a leave of absence because you are not officially enrolled at your home university, financial lenders may demand repayment on student loans!

Ah yes, but hope for the federal government doth spring eternal. Some recent developments in how financial aid is administered have proven beneficial for students wanting to study abroad. Stafford loans now are made available to U.S. students studying in Canada. See the section, "Looking at the legalities of funding," later in this chapter for more on using federal aid to study abroad.

For you to be able to study abroad, as many as five different groups of people or organizations can become involved in getting your financial aid straightened out. (They should award parents with special degrees in filling out more and more (and more) financial aid forms.) If you're already receiving financial aid (see the next section), you're familiar with three of them: you and your parents, your home-university financial aid office, and whatever organization/bank/educational-funding agency is loaning or giving you the money. When you throw an abroad university into the mix, the number of players climbs to four. That is a great deal of coordinating to accomplish, and ultimately, you're the one responsible for making sure that the money gets where it needs to go.

Exploring the Ins and Outs of Financial Aid

This section includes a brief overview of financial aid for undergrads. If you're currently on financial aid, have met with your financial aid officer, and your financial aid for the time you plan to spend abroad is all straightened out, then you can skip this section. I'm providing this information for those of you out there who may need to pursue some alternative financial avenues because your current financial aid plan doesn't quite work for a semester or year abroad.

Looking at the legalities of funding

Most U.S. institutions dictate that for financial aid to transfer to a study abroad program, you must carry and receive credit toward your degree for at least a half-time courseload at the abroad university. Study abroad must, in some way, be academically pertinent and not merely an enrichment experience or vacation.

Universities may also impose eligibility restrictions, particularly with institutional aid. As far as financial aid is concerned, many students are able to take their government aid (state and federal funding, including Pell Grants and Stafford and PLUS loans) abroad with them. Merit scholarships also can be used abroad, although they must be used for programs sponsored by U.S. institutions. If the school grants a student credit for a proposed study abroad program, and the student meets requirements for federal aid, then the school is not permitted to deny federal aid to the student just because he or she is going abroad.

The Higher Education Act (HEA) of 1992 mandates that a student can receive financial aid for study abroad when the student is enrolled in a program approved by the home university. Moreover, the student is eligible to receive "grants, loans, or work assistance without regard to whether the study abroad program is required as a part of the student's degree."

Understanding the types of financial aid

Education in the U.S. is expensive. In fact, few students can afford to pay for college without some sort of educational financing plan. Recent statistics show that two-thirds of undergraduate students graduate with some debt, and the average federal student loan debt is $16,888 (Stafford and Perkins loans). When you include PLUS Loans in the total, the average cumulative debt incurred is $19,785.

The reality is that grants, scholarships, work-study, and other forms of *gift aid* (aid that doesn't need to be repaid) just cannot completely cover the full cost of a college education. Education loans come in three major categories: student loans, parent loans, and private loans. The federal education loan program is most attractive because of lower interest rates and flexible repayment plans.

The FinAid Web site (www.FinAid.org) provides numerous calculators that can help you understand your loan options. The calculators offer:

- ✔ Estimates of monthly loan payments and the amount of debt you can afford to repay

- ✔ Analysis of the cost of capitalizing the interest

- ✔ Tools for comparing loan costs

Here's a breakdown of the types of aid out there:

- ✔ **Federal government aid:** The federal government offers a variety of loan programs. Unfortunately, the federal work-study program won't be of any use to you during your semester or year abroad. You can only use this program to make money via employment while at your home university. Among the types of federal aid you may be able to use to study abroad are:

  - • **Loans:** The Federal Stafford Loan and the Federal Parent Loan for Undergraduate Education (also known as the PLUS Loan) are good options for those families who are looking for loans with low interest rates to help pay for college. See the sidebar in this section for more about these loans.

  - • **Grants:** The government also offers Pell Grants and Federal Supplemental Educational Opportunity Grants (FSEOG). Some universities are allocated funds by the government and administer these funds via the financial aid office in the form of Perkins Loans and SEOGs.

- ✔ **State government aid:** Many states maintain funding for higher education. You need to contact your state's department of education or student financial assistance program to determine what amount of aid your state offers and how you apply for it. Be aware that state aid may be limited to only state residents.

- ✔ **Institutional aid:** Most universities award their own institutional grants and scholarships to students based on financial need or merit.

- ✔ **Private funding:** Private organizations such as local clubs (Lions and Kiwanis clubs and Elks lodges) and religious groups may be another resource to tap for scholarships. You can also try tapping professional associations for scholarships available for higher education.

- ✔ **Alternative loans:** Alternative loans that are available through Sallie Mae or major banks are based on good credit and enable you to borrow up to the full cost of education less any financial aid received.

Getting the scoop on Stafford and PLUS loans

Federal Stafford Loans don't require a cosigner or prior credit history. The interest rate on a Stafford Loan is a variable percentage and changes annually, based on the 91-day Treasury Bill rate plus either 1.7 percent while you're in school or during grace and deferment periods or 2.3 percent while you're repaying it. The interest rate can never exceed an 8.25 percent interest rate cap. Your university's financial aid office determines whether you're eligible for either a Subsidized Stafford Loan on the basis of financial need or an Unsubsidized Stafford Loan (which is not need based). A subsidized loan means that the interest of the loan is paid by the federal government until you start repaying the loan six months after you graduate or leave college. In the case of an Unsubsidized Stafford Loan, you must pay the interest on the loan from the time funds are dispersed, although these loans carry an option to defer payment of principal and interest until six months after you leave school. The maximum repayment term for Stafford Loans usually is usually ten years, again, starting six months after you graduate or leave school. To obtain a Stafford Loan, you must complete a Free

Application for Federal Student Aid (FAFSA), which you can obtain from your college's financial aid office. You can also complete the FAFSA form online at www.fafsa.ed.gov.

With a PLUS Loan, parents (or legal guardians) may borrow up to the full cost of attendance for education, minus any financial aid received. PLUS Loan eligibility is not based on financial need, and any family may apply. A FAFSA is not required to obtain a PLUS Loan, but a credit application is, and a bad credit history can cause you to be denied a PLUS Loan. The borrower and the student must be U.S. citizens or eligible permanent residents, and both must have valid Social Security numbers. The interest rate on PLUS Loans is variable and changes annually on July 1. It's based on the 91-day Treasury Bill rate plus 3.1 percent. The interest rate for PLUS Loans can never exceed a 9.0 percent interest rate cap. Repayment of a PLUS Loan usually begins within 60 days after funds are disbursed. The maximum repayment term is 10 years, and the minimum required monthly payment is $50.

Paperwork, paperwork, and more paperwork

If you thought the paperwork for applying to college or a study abroad program was overwhelming, then obviously you have yet to encounter financial aid applications! The federal government and financial aid offices across the country have admissions offices beat where paperwork is concerned.

The most commonly used financial aid forms include the following:

- ✔ The FAFSA is a federal form that colleges and universities that accept federal funding require, and is available on January 1 of each year.

- ✔ CSS/Financial Aid PROFILE is a second application that some private colleges and universities require. The PROFILE asks more in-depth information for the purpose of awarding institutional aid. The PROFILE registration form is available through the College Board at `www.collegeboard.org/profile`.

- ✔ Some universities may also require their own application form. Call the financial aid office to find out whether your home university has its own institutional aid application.

On these forms, you need to report your yearly family income and assets. Keep in mind the following tips when filling out financial aid forms:

- ✔ Keep copies of any and all financial aid forms you fill out and send in (including tax forms). If they get lost in the mail or in a financial aid office pile, you don't want to have to start from scratch and fill them all out again.

- ✔ Estimate income figures if necessary to meet your deadlines. You can correct or verify information later. Be as accurate as possible because your figures impact the award you receive.

- ✔ Ask questions if you need help. Contact your university's financial aid office for assistance in completing your forms.

Determining your financial need

The information you supply on the financial aid forms is plugged into a formula to determine your *expected family contribution (EFC)*.

The EFC is an estimate of your family's ability to contribute toward your educational expenses. Although it estimates how much you and your family can contribute relative to other families, it does not assume how you will finance that contribution. Your home university then compares your EFC to its total cost of attendance, which includes tuition, fees, room and board, books, supplies, transportation, and living expenses.

To determine your eligibility for financial aid, your home university subtracts your EFC from its cost of attendance. If your EFC isn't sufficient to pay the full cost of attendance, you have *financial need* and therefore become eligible for financial aid.

In determining how much your family is expected to contribute toward your education, a number of factors are considered, including dependency status, income, assets, family size, and number of family members in college. You can estimate your EFC by visiting www.finaid.org. Most U.S. universities use this federal methodology in determining your EFC.

Your financial need may be met with a combination of grants, loans, and work-study depending upon your eligibility and funds availability. Families are not always awarded enough aid to meet their full financial need.

Because funds often are limited, applying for financial aid on time is important for priority consideration. Note: Finding out which applications you must complete is also very important.

Digging Under the Mattress: Other Funding Sources

Okay, so we can all use some more money; however, this section is designed as a place to start when you need to look for more loans, scholarships, or grants to defray the cost of your time abroad. By no means is this list exhaustive. Plenty of money for education is out there! You just need to look around for it! Use the Web, reference books, your study abroad office, your home-university financial aid office, and your abroad university's international student office. If you or your parents are involved with any community organizations, religious groups, or special interest organizations, ask about the possibility of scholarship money for your study abroad experience.

Useful Web sites

When it comes to looking for money, often the Internet is the easiest place to start. The following list includes some of the most comprehensive and reliable sites on educational funding out there:

- **Department of Education (www.ed.gov):** The Department of Education provides financial aid information and the FAFSA online. You can determine your eligibility for federal aid, fill out, renew, or check the status of your FAFSA online.

- **Students.gov (www.students.gov):** Students.gov provides easy access to information and services you can use for planning and paying for a semester or year abroad. This site is a cooperative effort between federal agencies, students, and other parts of the higher education community, under the leadership of the U.S. Department of Education.

✔ **FinAid.org** (www.finaid.org): FinAid's homepage features a "SmartStudent Guide to Financial Aid," information about scholarships and loans, and calculators that help you come up with your EFC, loan repayment plans, and loan comparison information.

✔ **FASTWEB** (www.fastweb.com): FASTWEB offers online scholarship and college search services that compare your background with a database of awards. Only those awards that fit your profile are identified as matches. This free service is part of the largest, most accurate, and most frequently updated scholarship database.

✔ **The College Board Homepage** (www.collegeboard.com): The College Board Homepage provides PROFILE form registrations, an online PROFILE application process, and articles about paying for college.

✔ **International Education Financial Aid** (www.iefa.org): International Education Financial Aid is a scholarship search tool for students who want to study abroad. It also features grant listings and links to international student loan programs.

✔ **International Education Finance Corporation** (www.iefc.com): International Education Finance Corporation provides international student loans to students who want to study in foreign countries.

✔ **International Student.com** (www.internationalstudent.com/scholarships): This Web site offers a Study Abroad Scholarship Search tool for international students. On it you can find college scholarship programs by country, field of study, or university name. Lists of programs are available for undergraduate students anywhere in the world.

✔ **Sallie Mae** (www.salliemae.com): Sallie Mae provides numerous consumer credit loans for education.

Scholarship and grant information

Scholarships and grants qualify as gift aid, which means they're *free money,* or money that you won't have to repay. Grants are based on financial need, and some can be used to pay any education-related expense. On the other hand, most scholarships are restricted to paying all or part of tuition expenses, but some also cover room and board. Scholarships tend to be restricted to students in specific courses of study, from particular ethnic or geographic backgrounds, or with academic, athletic, or artistic talents — your intention to study abroad qualifies you as special, too. Most U.S.-based study abroad programs offer some kind of scholarship or grant program to participants, ranging from several hundred dollars to fully paid tuition. Ask your study abroad program or university about award amounts, applications, and criteria.

Scholarship search services charge fees to compare your profile against a database of scholarship programs. Few students who use a scholarship search service actually win a scholarship. I include only free scholarship databases in this chapter.

Competition for gift aid can be tough (who wouldn't want free money?), so be sure to give yourself plenty of time to complete scholarship or grant applications and adhere to deadlines.

An abbreviated sampling of the type of study abroad scholarships and grants that are available follows:

- **AIFS International Scholarships:** Each year the American Institute for Foreign Study (AIFS) offers 100 semester-long scholarships of $1,000 each (50 for the fall semester and 50 for the spring semester) and 10 summer scholarships of $500 each. AIFS also offers one full minority scholarship and five $1,000 grants to minority students each semester. For more information call 800-727-2437 or visit its Web site at www.aifs.com.

- **Council for International Educational Exchange (CIEE):** CIEE has an extensive offering of need- and merit-based scholarships for its own sponsored programs. Check out the Web site at www.ciee.org.

- **Institute for International Education:** Institute for International Education (IIE) administers many worldwide programs for students to share ideas and work for common goals, including international exchange programs, scholarships, and grants. For more information visit www.iie.org. Two programs administered through IIE include:

  - **Freeman-Asia Program Awards for Study in Asia:** The Freeman-ASIA Program awards scholarships for study in Asia. Its aim is to increase the number of American undergraduates who study in East and Southeast Asia. Awardees are expected to share their experiences with their home universities to encourage study abroad by others and to spread understanding of Asia in their home communities. For more information, call 212-984-5542, or check out the Web site at www.iie.org/programs/freeman-asia/default.htm.

  - **Gilman International Scholarship Program:** Gilman offers awards for study abroad for U.S. students who are also receiving federal Pell Grants at a two-year or four-year colleges and universities. The Gillman program is sponsored by the Bureau of Educational and Cultural Affairs of the U.S. Department of State. Check it out at www.iie.org/gilman.

- **International and Research Exchange Board (IREX):** IREX promotes academic exchanges between the United States and Eastern European and other nations that were part of the former Soviet Union. Check out its Web site (www.irex.org) for information on exchange programs, scholarships, and grants, particularly the USIA Regional Scholar Exchange Program (RSEP).

✔ **National Security Education Program (NSEP):** The NSEP administers the David L. Boren Scholarship, which funds undergraduates studying abroad in areas outside of Western Europe, Canada, New Zealand, and Australia. NSEP sponsors study in areas of the world critical to U.S. national security, where most U.S. students do not study — such as Africa, Asia, Eastern and Central Europe, Latin America, the Caribbean, and the Middle East. NSEP particularly encourages and seeks applications in fields of study critical to U.S. national security, such as engineering, applied sciences, business and economics, international affairs, political policy and social sciences, health, and law. Call 800-618-6737 for more information or visit www.iie.org/nsep.

✔ **The Rotary Foundation:** The Rotary Foundation, a part of Rotary International, offers grants to undergraduate and graduate students to serve as goodwill ambassadors around the world. Rotary's Ambassadorial Scholarship program strives to further international understanding and friendly relations among people of different countries. While abroad, students are expected serve as ambassadors to the people of the host country and give presentations about their homelands to Rotary clubs and other groups. Upon returning home, students are expected to make several presentations to local Rotarians and others about their experiences in their host countries.

This foundation boasts the world's largest privately sponsored international scholarship program. These scholarships are awarded on an extremely competitive basis. Rotary Foundation scholarships provide money for travel and living expenses, in addition to tuition and academic fees. Contact your local Rotary Club for application information or visit www.rotary.org.

Books

I realize that with the widespread use of the Web, books may seem a rather outdated mode for conducting research. But I don't think you should eliminate them entirely from your research radar screen. One of the best, of course, is Wiley's *Free $ For College For Dummies* by David Rosen and Caryn Mladen. You'll probably discover many scholarship and grant opportunities that are not listed or found on the Web, which means that there are probably fewer students applying for them.

Check out some of these for more information:

✔ *The College Board Cost & Financial Aid 2003*. NJ: College Board, August 2002.

✔ *The College Board Scholarship Handbook,* 6th edition. NJ: College Board, August 2002.

✔ *Fellowships, Scholarships, and Related Opportunities.* University of Tennessee-Knoxville: Center for International Education. Phone: 423-974-3177.

✔ *Financial Aid for Research and Creative Activities Abroad 2002–2004.* By Gail Ann Schlachter and R. David Weber. San Carlos, CA: Reference Service Press, July 2002.

✔ *Financial Resources for International Study: A Guide for U.S. Students and Professionals (1996).* By Sara J. Steen (Editor) and Marie O'Sullivan (Editor). Inst of Intl Education; October 1996.

✔ *Financial Resources for International Study.* Princeton, NJ: Peterson's Guide. Phone: 800-338-3282.

✔ *Free Money for Foreign Study: A Guide to More Than 1,000 Grants and Scholarships for Study Abroad.* By Laurie Blum. New York: Facts on File, March 1992.

✔ *Foundation Grants to Individuals.* New York: The Foundation Center. Phone: 212-620-4230.

✔ *The International Scholarship Book,* 2nd edition. New York: Prentice-Hall. Phone: 212-373-8500.

✔ *International Scholarship Directory: The Complete Guide to Financial Aid for Study Anywhere in the World.* By Daniel J. Cassidy. Career Press; 3rd edition, September 1993.

✔ *Financial Resources for International Study: A Guide for US Nationals.* . Lists more than 650 awards offered by governments, foundations, universities, and so on. The cost is $39.95 plus $4 shipping. For more information, call 800-445-0443 or 301-617-7804, fax 301-953-2838, or send e-mail to iiebooks@iie.org. IIE also publishes *Academic Abroad* and *Short Term Study Abroad,* which offer information on scholarships or work-study assistance.

✔ *The Scholarship Book 2003: The Complete Guide to Private-Sector Scholarships, Fellowships, Grants and Loans for the Undergraduate.* By National Scholarship Research Service. NJ: Prentice-Hall, June 2002.

✔ *Winning Grants: Step by Step,* 2nd edition. By Mimi Carlson and the Alliance for Nonprofit Management. NY: Jossey-Bass, June 2002.

Chapter 11

I've Been Accepted! Now What?

*B*y the time you read this chapter, acceptance letters from programs of study abroad are probably flooding your mailbox! Hooray! After basking in the glow of being accepted for a few days, you must decide where you're going to spend your next semester or year and then start thinking about the details of leaving your home university. Completing all predeparture responsibilities at your universities at home and abroad makes leaving home and going abroad and then leaving abroad and going home transitions much easier. Considering the courses and housing options you'll choose at your schools at home and abroad before going away can save you time and energy later on. Now that you know where you're studying abroad, you can take time to research your destination and make sure you're well educated about the country you currently live in!

Making It Official: Enrolling in Your New University

The list of things to do and people to contact to ensure a smooth study abroad experience is long. Of paramount importance is enrolling at your new university and letting your home university know your study abroad intentions. Another detail to consider is the courses you'll take while abroad and what you're going to take the semester you return to the U.S. (for more information on transferring credits, see Chapter 6). Paying attention to these details will make arriving abroad and returning home as easy as possible.

Notifying schools

Before making a final decision about where you're going to spend your time abroad, make sure that you've considered all your options, weighed the pros and cons of each program, and figured out a way to fund your adventure. (Check out Chapter 10 for information about financial aid.) Don't forget you can use your study abroad director as a sounding board while making your decision. He or she can provide useful hints on how each program will affect transfer credits and financial aid. Once you've made your decision, notify all the schools to which you applied, regardless of which one you've chosen.

While feeling excited about your upcoming trip and studies abroad is natural, if you feel indifferent toward it, that's probably a good indication that you prefer one of the other programs to which you were accepted or that maybe you'd simply rather stay at your home university.

Notifying your home university

Your registrar's office, bursar's office, dean's office, and major department and adviser need to know about where you've decided to study, so you need to tell them. And you need to fill out all the necessary paperwork. Your home university requires you to fill out papers detailing your plans for studying abroad, provide an address where you can be reached while abroad (your program can provide you with this information, or you can use your U.S. home address until you know where you'll be living), commit to the specific number of semesters you'll be away, and provide information about when you expect to return. Your home university also may technically need to place you on a leave of absence while you study abroad with an institution other than your own.

Notifying your abroad university

You also must accept one study abroad offer (or possibly two if you plan to visit two different places for a semester each) and decline the rest. Accepting and declining offers to study abroad is fairly easy and quick when done via e-mail; however, as a courtesy, I also suggest that you send a letter via mail to formally decline offers from particular programs or schools.

In addition to notification, the school or program that you've chosen more than likely will want you to fill out a few forms (one of which is an official acceptance of the offer) and send a deposit to guarantee your place in the program. You may even be asked to send a deposit in the currency of your destination country. When you need to exchange U.S. currency for that of the country where you'll be staying, a bank with an international branch should be able to help you sort out this dilemma quickly. Don't forget to find out what your deposit pays for and whether it will eventually be returned to you or applied toward your program costs. Likewise, make sure you get a written acknowledgement of your deposit. You wouldn't do it any differently if you were dealing with a program in the U.S., would you?

You'll probably have a small window of time to decide about a study abroad program once you're accepted. Having to give the study abroad program your answer (yes or no) within 10 days is typical. If, however, you need more time to decide, don't hesitate to call and ask for more time. Be mindful, however, that the sooner you decline an offer, the sooner you open up a place for someone else out there who may be on a waiting list.

Choosing and registering for courses

The first caveat to choosing courses when you're studying abroad is understanding that in some foreign countries, a secondary-school education is more advanced and specialized than in U.S. high schools. In many cases, foreign students enter universities at the same level as an American sophomore in college. Additionally, some foreign students graduate from secondary school later than in the U.S., and then may take some time off before heading to universities.

Foreign universities may therefore allow you to take courses only at the first- or second-year level while studying there.

Initially, first- or second-year courses may not sound all that appealing when you're a junior looking to complete advanced coursework in your major subject. However, at some schools, third-and fourth-year courses are equivalent to *graduate-level* work in the U.S. The host university probably established this rule based on experiences with other U.S. students, knowing that you don't want to get in over your head. If you're determined to try a higher-level course, you need to consult with the chairman of the abroad department in which you're studying to find out whether you can. Then make sure that you shop around for different courses and levels before deciding what is best for you.

If you're only taking first- and second-year courses at your abroad university, make sure that doing so is acceptable to your home university.

Registering for abroad courses can happen in a number of ways. Depending upon the school and program, you may need to choose courses at one of the following three times:

- ✔ When you send in your place-holding deposit
- ✔ About a month before departure
- ✔ When you arrive at your abroad destination

If you're registering from the U.S. before entering your program, you need to do so in the most expedient way possible. Just like at U.S. universities, students register for courses at abroad universities for the most part on a first-come basis. Even more convenient, you can make use of online or telephone registration systems at abroad universities that offer such services, but make sure that you follow up these options with a paper copy of the courses for which you registered. When you receive a confirmation number after you register, make note of it and keep it in a safe place. When you register by mail, fill out forms as soon as you can after receiving them and mail them back to your school immediately.

If you don't have to register for courses until you arrive on campus, rest assured that you're also likely to have a fairly substantial class-shopping period. In fact, most abroad universities, like in the U.S., reserve a specified time frame for adding or dropping courses at the beginning of each semester.

If you absolutely must take a particular course to graduate from your home university on time while you're abroad, make your request known as soon as possible — either in your application package or when you send the acceptance notice with your deposit. Making this kind of request in writing is important, so remember to save any correspondence between you and academic officials at your abroad university regarding the course. Typically, an abroad program cannot guarantee that a course will be offered or that you'll even be accepted to take the course, so be sure to have a backup plan — just in case. If you're attending a school abroad via a U.S. university, let the program office know about your request, so it can do whatever it can to help you get the course you need. In terms of requesting special courses, the international office at your abroad school also may have some clout with academic departments.

If your host university allows it, consider registering for more classes than you actually plan to take in case one or more courses are unavailable. You can then drop the least interesting courses after you arrive. This also will give you one or two backup courses in case another choice isn't available to you for some reason.

Schools abroad offer more full-year courses than you may be used to here in the U.S. As a result, you need to be careful steering clear of full-year courses when you're going to study abroad for only one semester. Being in a full-year course for only one semester can be disastrous because the final exam typically is cumulative (and you'll have been there for only half the course!) and at the end of the year. You may end up departing at the end of the semester without taking the exam, which makes getting credit for the course impossible.

Finding a Place to Live

By the time you're ready to study abroad, you've realized that your living situation affects your college experience. Where and with whom you live can make college more fun or turn life into a total nightmare. The same is true for your study abroad experience: Where you live significantly impacts your experience while abroad, so when given a choice of where to live, choose carefully!

As part of your research, you probably discovered whether the programs you're interested in actually arrange housing or whether finding a place to live is your responsibility. When you need to find your own housing, ask representatives of your program, the international student office, or student housing office at your abroad university to assist you. Ask around to find out what is considered reasonable and fair rent for the city you're living in.

Student housing is at a premium in most countries! Whenever your study abroad program does not provide housing for you, give yourself plenty of time to arrange it.

If you're going on a short-term program or one that requires frequent travel, you may stay in hotels, pensions, or student hostels. If you're lucky, your program offers you a choice of where to live. However, choices probably are limited, and your first choice is not guaranteed because student housing is difficult to find almost everywhere. Space within on-campus dorms usually is the most limited, and many abroad universities reserve only a certain number of rooms for international students.

One way to make sure that you have a pleasant living situation is to inform your program or housing office about any special needs you may have before you're assigned accommodation. Fill out any housing forms honestly. Smoking is far more common and acceptable abroad than in the U.S., so if a nonsmoking environment is important to you, request a nonsmoking home-stay or nonsmoking roommates in dorms and apartments.

Confirm all housing arrangements before you depart. Get the address and directions to your new home. Let the landlord or housing office know approximately what time you will be arriving at so you can arrange to pick up the keys to your place. (The "landlord" in many cases may be your program office or university accommodation office. You will not have to deal with the person who owns the property unless you have to find your own housing.) Also, upon arrival, ask about housing rules and if you're paying rent on a monthly/weekly basis, and find out the most convenient way to get the rent to your landlord.

Living in dorms or apartments

Most study abroad students live in dorms or apartments with roommates from the host country, other foreign countries, or from the United States. You can expect to share your accommodations, regardless of whether it's a dorm room or an apartment, with other students. However, dorms at abroad universities commonly provide students with their own rooms that share an adjoining common room and kitchen with three to seven other students.

Most dorms and apartments abroad are *self-catering*, which means you prepare your own meals. Meal plans and dining halls in most study abroad situations are very limited when compared with the offerings of U.S. schools.

If you'll be living in an apartment in the middle of a major metropolitan area, you may want to consider investing in renter's insurance to protect your personal belongings. Renter's insurance is relatively inexpensive, considering it covers repair or replacement of damaged, destroyed or stolen personal property in case of fire, theft, vandalism, or water-related damage. Where you live, your deductible, what your building is made of, and a variety of other factors determine the cost of your policy. Renter's insurance also comes in handy in covering your personal belongings while traveling. Consult your insurance agent for more information.

Home-stays: Living with a host family

When you choose or are placed in a home-stay situation, you'll live with a local family. Major benefits of a home-stay are that you:

✔ Have the greatest opportunity for immersion in the host language and culture.

✔ Learn how the local population really lives on a day-to-day basis.

✔ Live with a family that treats you like a family member (in the most optimal home-stay situation), takes the time to get to know you, and includes you in all their family activities. You eventually feel as if you have a second home with them!

In some cases, however, home-stays are less than perfect. Your host family may consider their relationship with you as strictly landlord/tenant: They have an extra room to rent out, and you have little social interaction with them. Realize that although the program should screen these families to ensure suitability, not-so-great host families do slip through the cracks! When that happens, these families consider you just an extra source of income. Because you're paying for the experience, however, if your living situation becomes unpleasant or unbearable, contact your program immediately to find out what can be done to fix the situation.

Your home-stay hosts will, more than likely, provide most of your meals. If you're a vegetarian or have other dietary needs, check to see whether your host family can accommodate them. Bear in mind that vegetarian menus are not as readily available as they are in the U.S. Your host family may perceive your refusing meals they serve as rudeness. So, at least temporarily, you may need to compromise your food choices or spend your own money to make special meals for yourself.

After you've settled in with your host family, make sure to clarify what's expected of you. Do you have weekly or daily chores? What can you do to help around the house? Should you call when you'll be staying late at school or missing dinner? Or should you let someone know before leaving for the day what your evening plans are? Be polite and courteous to your host family and respect their cultural or family traditions, and you shouldn't have any problems getting along with them.

Always on the go: Living in hotels, hostels, and pensions

Some study abroad programs allow you to study and travel to multiple places during your semester or year abroad. Because you'll be moving around so much, it's possible you won't have a permanent place to call home while you're away. Programs may choose to house you in hotels, hostels and pensions for a week or two at a time while you're studying in a particular city or town. Depending on where you stay, you'll probably be sharing a room with at least one other person, or as many as 6 or 8 if you're living in a hostel for the week.

If you don't have a permanent "home away from home," you'll be traveling from place to place with all your personal belongings, constantly living out of a suitcase. Remember to pack light and don't pack anything too valuable in case of theft.

Deciding to room with U.S. or foreign students

If you select a U.S.-based program, you may get to choose whether you live with foreign students or U.S. students. If you apply directly to an abroad university, you won't usually get a choice about the nationality of the students with whom you live.

You may feel more comfortable living with other U.S. students, because just about everything else about your new home is going to be so new and different to you. At times, living with people who are experiencing similar culture shock, homesickness, or adjustment issues can be very reassuring. Realize, however, that unless you make a conscious effort to avoid it, living with students from the same culture as you can also be isolating. When cultural immersion or an authentic experience of your host culture is important to you, you may want to choose to live with students from the host country.

If you're attending a major university or living in a major city, you'll always be able to find Americans whenever you need a reminder of home, someone to celebrate Thanksgiving with, or a sympathetic ear to listen to the trials of being an American abroad.

When you feel strongly that your living situation is a quintessential part of your study abroad experience, then opt for living with students from your host country. If your program provides you with housing in university dorms, be aware that in some places, host-country students live in dorms only during their first year of school and then move to off-campus apartments. In other countries, it may be traditional for students to continue living at home while attending the nearest university, which means that few native students will live in university dorms. Likewise, you need to realize that some universities house all foreign students (and remember, that includes you!) in special dorms for international students. While living in an international dorm, you won't encounter host-country students, but you will have the benefit of knowing many other students who share the experiences of being new to the school and country.

If you've rented an apartment and need to find a roommate, usually the best place to start is at your host university's accommodations office. Sometimes an accommodations office dedicates space within their office (such as a bulletin board or binder) for students to post if they're looking for a roommate. Otherwise, the accommodation office can usually advise you whether it's best to post in a local newspaper or on the Internet — and can suggest which newspapers and sites seem to get the most traffic.

When interviewing potential roommates, make sure you ask about their daily schedules to assess compatibility.

Asking the right questions

When it comes to housing, no amount of knowledge is too much. You want to gather as much information as possible about your potential housing situation before you go abroad so you know what to expect. In addition to helping you decide whether a program is right for you, knowing as much as you can about your housing can also prevent total shock when you see your new home for the first time.

Student housing abroad is almost never as luxurious as it is at American universities. Try to maintain realistic and unprejudiced expectations about your housing. Student apartments in the United Kingdom and Ireland are likely to be old, drafty, and damp, and your London dorm won't look like Buckingham Palace. In big cities, housing may be located on dingy, noisy streets. Give your housing a chance before becoming too critical, and remember that part of the purpose of study abroad is to live and study like students from your host country.

Regardless of where you may be living, you need to find out whether your dorm, apartment, or home-stay is located in a safe part of town. Although you may be able to save a little on rent by living in less desirable digs, the potential risk to your safety is never worth the money. Determining what areas are safe to live in is as easy as consulting your program representatives, asking students who've studied abroad before you, or checking with your abroad university's international student or housing offices. If you want to be extra cautious, you can even go to a police station and find out whether local law enforcement can provide you with some guidance or even a crime report for the neighborhood you're considering. Don't assume that your housing is in a bad neighborhood just because it's home to immigrants, minorities, or working-class families.

Ask the following questions to make an informed decision about whatever housing option you choose:

- ✔ Is the dorm or apartment fully furnished? Partially furnished?

- ✔ What kinds of appliances and utensils are available in the kitchen?

- ✔ Will I have a workspace that includes a desk or table?

- ✔ Do I need to supply my own linens (sheets, blankets, pillows, and so on)? If so, is there a service available to rent linens?

- ✔ Are there laundry facilities (a washer and dryer) in the building? How much does it cost to use them?

- ✔ What kind of telecommunication facilities are available? Will I have access to a phone or high-speed Internet?

- ✔ Who pays the utility bills? If I pay them, how much per month do they typically cost?

If you'll be studying and living in a developing country, make sure you also ask if there is suitable drinking water available, hot water for showers, and electricity.

Learning About Foreign Cultures — and Your Own

It should go almost without saying that you need to try to find out as much as you can about your host country before beginning your studies abroad. Uncovering the details about your new home and its language, culture, history, political structure, economic conditions, education systems, popular religions, and social structures gives you a good jumping-off point for when you arrive in your host country. You'll be able to observe your surroundings, quickly assimilate information, incorporate yourself into the culture, and more important, ask intelligent questions. Similarly, as a student studying abroad, you're likewise viewed as a source of knowledge for all things American, so brushing up on your knowledge of U.S. history, government, and culture is also important.

Getting the facts about your host country

You can pursue many avenues to discover more about your new home. Here are a few suggested (and easy) strategies:

✔ During the semester before you go abroad, take a course that focuses on the history, politics, or economics of the country or region you'll be visiting.

✔ Check out books and magazines about your country at the study abroad office, library, or bookstore. Aim for an overall picture of the country you're going to, but don't worry too much about detailed information. Student travel guides such as *Lonely Planet* or *Let's Go* give basic and easily digestible background information about countries. Read internationally oriented papers like *The New York Times*. Try *The Economist* for political and economic information about your country.

✔ Surf the Web — cautiously, of course. You can't believe everything that is published on the Internet, but you may find some useful information.

✔ Get personal perspectives by talking with people from your host country or people who have spent time there. This is a good time to explore ethnic student unions — a great place to find people who may have spent time in the country or region you're traveling to.

Besides consulting study abroad returnees, find out whether any faculty members hail from, have spent time in, or are experts on the area of the world you're planning to visit. Be sure to seek out any international students from that locale who happen to be attending your home university. They, too, are invaluable resources. Your home university's study abroad/international student office is often the on-campus expert about who on campus has spent time in the country you're going to.

When you're enrolling in a foreign university, arriving in your host country with an understanding of its educational system is important, because you'll be a part of it for the next semester or year. A university-level education varies from one corner of the globe to another, and it varies from what you're probably used to as a U.S. student. Remember that just because a foreign university may do things a little differently doesn't make it better or worse than what you're used to — it's just different. That said, finding out how classes generally are organized at your abroad school is a necessity. Be sure to ask:

✔ Are classes lecture or discussion based?

✔ How large will my classes be?

✔ Is learning classroom based? Computer based? Or is there a hands-on approach?

✔ What is the class attendance policy?

✔ How will my learning be evaluated (through papers, tests, practical exams)?

✔ Does the school have a letter-based or number-based grading system?

Assessing your current knowledge

I've composed the following list of questions for you to use as a guide to what you need to know about your host country. By answering some of these questions, you may be able to determine what types of information you need to share with your host country friends about differences between your cultures. It may also become clear what information you want to tone down because your culture may be drastically opposed to or the opposite of theirs. In any case, first see how many answers you already know before heading to the library. You may surprise yourself.

✔ What are the important and traditional holidays? When do they fall during the calendar year?

✔ What are favorite or popular leisure activities? Is there a national sport?

✔ What is the national cuisine? Is there an authentic dish or two that you must try while you're abroad?

✔ What is the current pop culture? TV shows? Music? Movies?

✔ What other languages are spoken besides the dominant one? Does using one language rather than another have social and cultural implications?

✔ What is the predominant religion? What important religious ceremonies and occasions are observed? How do members of the predominant religion feel about other religions?

✔ What is the general attitude toward divorce? (Is divorce even legal?) Multiple marriages? Illegitimate children?

✔ How does the culture celebrate births and weddings? How do its people mourn deaths?

✔ Is there a cultural attitude toward drinking? What about drugs?

✔ When shopping, are you expected to pay a fixed price for items, or is bargaining more typical? What are the best ways to bargain?

✔ What is a typical daily schedule like in your new home? When do people eat? When do they visit friends? Is there a daytime rest period or lunch hour during which no one is available?

✔ How do people greet each other? In other words, do they shake hands, hug, or kiss? How do people say goodbye?

✔ What topics, issues, or items are considered taboo?

✔ How do men and women dress on a regular basis? What is casual dress, and what is formal dress? For women, is wearing shorts or trousers appropriate?

✔ When is it okay to receive (or give) gifts from people in that country? What types of gifts are appropriate?

✔ What types of public transportation are available? Who has the right of way: drivers, cyclists, or pedestrians?

✔ Is military service mandatory?

✔ How does the local newspaper and government view the U.S.?

✔ What is the structure of their health-care system?

✔ Is all education free? How much do university students pay to go to school? Is education through a certain grade level mandatory? Are schools public, private, or parochial?

✔ Is receiving a university level education considered important? Do many students go abroad to study? Why? Where?

✔ Who are considered minority groups in your host country? Will you be a minority? Where do women and minorities fit into the social hierarchy?

✔ What roles do men and women have (currently and historically), and how do the sexes relate to one another?

✔ Which famous people hail from your host country, and what did they contribute to the culture? (Think politicians, athletes, artists, and so on.)

Being a smart American

On the other side of the coin, as you discover more about your host country, you probably want to make sure that you have a good understanding of the goings on of the country you're from. Be forewarned that, like it or not, in a foreign country you are occasionally put in the position of being a representative of the United States and American culture.

What I learned not to say

I'm thankful that before sending us off to our respective universities at the start of the school year, my study abroad program gave participating students some hints about what types of information they should and should not share with their new foreign friends. In Ireland, education is pretty much free, and the privilege of driving a car comes at a very high cost in terms of many taxes for owning a car and using the roads. Not everyone gets a driver's license at age 16, and not every family owns two cars. Thus, telling my Irish friends about the $100,000 price tag on my college education was not advisable, because I'd be perceived as a rich, spoiled American. It was better to say, "The cost of education in America is higher than in Ireland." I had to use a similar tack when explaining that I'd been driving for years: "Well, I live a considerable distance outside the city, and there's no public transportation so walking anywhere is out of the question, because everything is just too spread out! Besides, chauffeuring me around would be an inconvenience to my parents if I didn't have my license and access to a car."

Most foreigners expect you to have an extensive knowledge about the country you hail from, the same way you expect your host country friends to be experts on where you're studying. You may encounter some foreign students who want to play 20 or 40 questions with you about America. Be patient with their curiosity; it's harmless, and they're just anxious to find out about America, particularly when it's a place they hope to visit someday. You'll probably encounter a wide variety of questions, so try to know a little bit about everything from music and movies to politics and policy. Keep up on current events. Know how to discuss issues intelligently and without offending your audience. (Check out the nearby sidebar about "What I learned not to say.")

News stories from the U.S. or information about U.S. foreign policies that travels throughout the world usually prompts questions from your non-American friends. So you want to make sure that you know enough about your own country to discuss these issues intelligently. Returned study abroad students often remark about how they sometimes had a difficult time explaining U.S. history, politics, and culture when asked about particular topics by friends.

Watch out — because you may also find professors asking you questions if you're the token American in the class. Professors have a tendency to turn American students into spokespeople for the U.S.

Review your American history and consider what your cultural values are before going abroad. What are the American values? Will you be able to adequately describe the characteristics of the U.S. to someone else? Be prepared with some answers!

How they saw me

Shortly after I arrived in Dublin, I became tuned in to how I was perceived as an American. The Irish generally are friendly and welcoming. So it was not surprising that I felt pretty accepted and comfortable as an American in Dublin. After being in Ireland for a few months, I realized part of the reason the Irish are pro-American: Bill Clinton was in office at the time and had helped put together the 1998 Good Friday Agreement. This huge deal was a major breakthrough in ending three decades of sectarian violence in Northern Ireland. Additionally, I was from Boston, which I was informed is considered the "twenty-seventh county."

The Irish perceptions of Americans that I encountered were, for the most part, over-whelmingly positive. However, I discovered an American stereotype when an Irish student said to me, "Oh, so you're American? Do you own a gun? Do you see a therapist?" Apparently, after watching American talk shows, he thought guns and therapy defined the quintessential American.

I discovered another interesting cultural hurdle when I had returned from studying abroad and two of my Irish friends came to visit me at school in the fall. They were astonished at the difference between their sprawling university in the middle of Dublin and my small, perfectly landscaped liberal arts college in suburbia. I was actually good-naturedly accused of going to school at a "holiday camp"! Unsure of how to respond to this, I laughed and explained that my school wasn't extraordinary, but actually fairly typical for the U.S.

Planning Your Return

Believe it or not, planning to leave for your abroad destination also involves some preplanning for your return to your home university. Even though your return may be as much as a year away, at the very least, you need to complete the following two tasks before departing.

Preregistering for classes

Complete the preregistration process for the term you'll be entering when you return from your studies abroad, if necessary, before you leave. Consider which courses you'll need to take when you return. Some universities will offer their study abroad students the opportunity to preregister for the courses they'll be taking upon their return. You may complete the preregistration paperwork the semester before going abroad, and study abroad office staff or an academic adviser then actually registers you for classes during your home university's regular registration period.

If your school has an online course registration system, then you probably can register for classes from your abroad location during the semester before you return, as long as you have Internet access. (Be sure to check.) Just make sure that you know the date(s) for registration at home. When you're in a remote location without Internet access, you may also be able to register via snail mail, or you may be able to register once you return to the States. Some departments at some schools often save a few places in certain courses for students returning from abroad.

Making sure you have a place to live

Where are you going to live when you return from your studies abroad? You need to make housing arrangements for on-campus or off-campus housing before you depart. Check to see what the procedure is for returning to on-campus housing. You may need to designate a friend who you know will be on campus during the housing process to serve as your proxy and choose your housing for you. (Pick someone you trust!) Some study abroad and housing offices send on-campus housing preference forms to you while you're overseas, or you may be able to complete these forms before you depart and place them on file in the housing office. If you plan to live in off-campus housing, you may need to sign a lease and pay a deposit before you go. If you currently live in an apartment, finding someone to sublet your apartment while you're away is your responsibility.

Part IV
Leaving Home and Going Abroad

The 5th Wave   By Rich Tennant

"I think I'll have the Cocoa Puffs shepherd's pie."

In this part . . .

You have a lot to accomplish in the weeks leading up to your departure from the U.S. and arrival on foreign soil. I talk about all the paperwork (passports, visas, airline tickets) that needs to be in order before you leave and alert you to things you need to think about regarding money and budgets while abroad. Packing and unpacking can be two of the most overwhelming and monumental tasks, but let me help you fill that luggage, catch your flight, and settle in as painlessly as possible!

Chapter 12

Getting Ready to Go

*O*nce you're accepted by a study abroad program and you decide to go away, you need to focus on all the details of preparing to leave the country. Waiting until the last minute to get ready to go is a huge mistake; giving yourself time to make all your predeparture plans is best. The more organized and prepared you are for your study abroad adventure, the easier making the transition to a new place will be for you. When you're able to anticipate what to expect during this transition, you can get off to a much less stressful start.

Although this chapter gives you an idea of what you need to accomplish before boarding a plane for a foreign country, make sure that you also pay close attention to any predeparture instructions provided by your home university, study abroad office, or your university abroad. If your home university's study abroad office holds a predeparture meeting at the end of the semester before you go abroad, make sure you attend and listen for advice that your study abroad director or former study abroad students have to offer.

Putting Together the I.D.'s You'll Need

When traveling outside of the United States, you must carry a passport with you. A passport, which is issued by the country where you're a citizen, is the only identification document that is recognized throughout the world that will verify your citizenship. A few places in the world, including Canada, Mexico, and some Caribbean countries, used to allow U.S. citizens to enter their countries without a passport. Now, however, given the increased security measures that are being taken throughout the world, traveling outside of the U.S. without a valid passport is not such a good idea. Additionally, some countries also require you to have a visa before they'll allow you to enter. A *visa* differs from a passport in that it specifies how long you may remain in the country and is issued by the country you're visiting.

Getting a passport

A valid U.S. passport is the best proof of U.S. citizenship, and getting one means that you must prove that you are a citizen. To do that, you need to submit an application for one to a passport agency along with other documents that prove your U.S. citizenship, including:

- An expired U.S. passport
- A certified copy of your U.S. birth certificate
- A Certificate of Naturalization
- A Certificate of Citizenship
- A Report of Birth Abroad of a Citizen of the United States

U.S. Immigration requires you to prove your U.S. citizenship and identity when you reenter the United States, so need your passport to be able to pass through U.S. Immigration upon your return.

Applying for a passport

You can apply for a passport at over 5,000 designated passport acceptance facilities nationwide, including many post offices, clerks of court, other state/county/township/municipal offices, and a growing number of public libraries and public colleges and universities. To search for passport acceptance facilities, go to www.iafdb.travel.state.gov/. Unless you're renewing a passport (see "Renewing a previous passport" section later in this chapter) obtained after you turned 18, you must apply in person with a completed Form DS-11, Passport Application, at a passport agency.

Complete the form, but do not sign it until you're in the presence of an official who can process your application.

When you apply for your passport, you must present the following documentation along with your application form:

- *Proof of U.S. citizenship:* This evidence can be in the form of either a certified copy of your birth certificate or a previously issued passport.

  If you were born in the United States, you must produce a certified copy of your birth certificate (certified with the registrar's signature and raised, impressed, embossed, or multicolored seal) when you get your first passport. Certified copies of birth records can be obtained from the bureau of vital statistics in the city, state, county, or territory where you were born.

  If you cannot obtain your birth certificate, you may submit a notice from a state registrar stating that no birth record exists, accompanied by as much secondary evidence as possible. Secondary evidence may include a baptismal certificate, a hospital birth record, notarized affidavits of relatives having personal knowledge of the facts of your birth, or other documentary evidence such as an early census, school records, family Bible records, doctor's records, and newspaper files.

If you were born abroad, you can use a Certificate of Naturalization, a Certificate of Citizenship, a Report of Birth Abroad of a Citizen of the United States of America (Form FS-240), or a Certification of Birth (Form FS-545 or DS-1350).

✔ *Two Photographs:* Submit two recent (taken within the last 6 months), identical 2-inch by 2-inch photographs of yourself. Passport Services encourages photographs where you are relaxed and smiling. Passport photographs may be either black and white or color, as long as they are clear, front view, full-face, and printed on thin, white paper with a plain, white or off-white background. Photographs need to be portrait-type prints taken in normal street attire without a hat and must include no more than the head and shoulders or upper torso. Dark glasses are not acceptable except when worn for medical reasons. Head coverings are acceptable only if they are worn for religious reasons.

Newspaper, magazine, and most vending machine prints cannot be used in passports. The easiest and most reliable way to get the necessary photos is to go to your local grocery store or copy shop, or any store that handles photo developing. Most of them offer passport photos cheap.

✔ *Current identification with your signature and photograph:* When applying in person, you must satisfactorily prove your identity to the person accepting your application. The following list items explain:

- *What's acceptable:* Generally, the following are acceptable documents to use to establish your identity: a Certificate of Naturalization or Citizenship, valid driver's license, government-issued identification card, or previous U.S. passport. These all need to contain your signature and identify you by physical description or photograph.

- *What isn't acceptable:* Social Security cards, temporary driver's licenses, credit cards, any expired identification documents, or documents that have been altered or changed are not acceptable to use for proof of identity.

✔ *Passport Fee:* The fee is $85.00 if you are 16 years of age or older. This fee includes a $30 execution fee. The passport is valid for 10 years. Applicants under age 16 pay $70 for their passports. This includes a $30 execution fee. The passport is valid for five years. You may pay by check, bank draft, or money order, payable to Passport Services. You may also pay in cash (exact change only) at a passport agency and at some (but not all) post offices and clerks of court offices.

Meeting your personal passport deadline

Apply as early (before traveling abroad) as possible for your passport. The normal processing time is four to six weeks, but the wait can be even longer during the peak travel season (March to August). According to the U.S. Department of State, processing your application and returning your passport takes an average of 25 business days from when a passport agency receives your completed passport application.

When you need your passport more quickly, you can request expedited service. When you do, the passport agency processes your application within three business days of receiving it for a fee of $60 per application in addition to the regular passport fee. When you pay the $60 fee to expedite your application, make sure that you submit a complete and accurate application. That way you'll receive expedited service without any questions asked. You can expect to receive your passport within two weeks if you paid for expedited service and two-way overnight delivery. If you're leaving within two weeks, you must go in person to the nearest passport agency to apply.

The State Department recommends that when you plan to spend an extended time abroad, making sure that your close relatives in the U.S. also have valid passports available is a good idea. That way, if you contract a serious illness or experience some other type of emergency, someone can travel to be by your side without delay.

Carelessness is the main reason passports are lost or stolen. You may need to carry your passport with you frequently because you need to cash traveler's checks or the country that you're in requires you to carry it as an identity document. When you must carry your passport, hide it securely on your person. Don't leave it in a handbag or in an exposed pocket. Whenever possible, leave your passport in the hotel safe rather than in an empty hotel room or packed in your luggage. Leaving a copy of your passport — or at the very least, your passport number and the date and place of the passport's issuance — with your parents before boarding that plane to go abroad is another good measure to take, as is carrying a copy with you when you're traveling. If you happen to lose your passport, having a copy can speed up the replacement process. Keep this copy of your passport separate from the passport itself.

Renewing a previous passport

When you want to renew your passport, you may be eligible to apply by mail if your previous passport was issued on or after your 16th birthday and was issued within the past 15 years. Obtain Form DS-82, Application for Passport by Mail, from an office authorized to accept passport applications, from your travel agent, or from the Internet at www.travel.state.gov. Make sure you completely fill out, sign, and date your application. You must enclose your previous passport, two identical 2 x 2 (recent, within the past six months) photographs, and the $55 passport fee. (The $30 execution fee is not required for applicants eligible to apply by mail.) Mail the completed application and attachments to the National Passport Center. The address is listed on the application. When requesting expedited service, don't forget to include the $60 expedite fee.

When you receive your passport, sign it right away and then fill in the personal notification data page. (For the emergency contact, write in pencil the name, address, and telephone number of someone who is not traveling with you.) Your previous passport and other documents that you may have submitted will be returned to you with your new passport.

Amending your passport

If you change your name, you must amend your passport. Fill out Form DS-19, Passport Amendment/Validation Application and submit it along with proof of the name change (a marriage certificate, divorce decree, adoption decree, or certified court order) to the nearest passport agency. This service doesn't cost anything, except when expedited service is requested.

Replacing a lost or stolen passport

Whenever your passport is lost or stolen while you're in the U.S., apply for a new passport by completing Form DS-64, Statement Regarding Lost or Stolen Passport.

Whenever your passport is lost or stolen while you're abroad, you need to report the loss immediately to local police and the nearest U.S. Embassy or Consulate. If you can provide information contained in your passport, the consular officer will facilitate issuance of a new passport. Carrying two extra passport-sized photos with you is another good idea in case your passport is lost or stolen.

If your U.S. passport is mutilated or altered in any way (other than changing the personal notification data), you may render it invalid, cause yourself much inconvenience, and expose yourself to possible prosecution under the law.

Finding more information

Additional passport information can be obtained from the National Passport Information Center (NPIC). Callers can dial 1-900-225-5674 to receive passport applications, additional information about passport emergencies and applying for a U.S. passport, and to check on the status of a passport application. Automated information is available 24 hours a day, 7 days a week. Operators can be reached from 8:30 a.m. to 5:30 p.m. Monday through Friday, excluding federal holidays.

The cost of this service is 35 cents per minute for the automated system and $1.05 per minute for live operators. This service also includes an optional number, 888-362-8668, if you have blocked 900 numbers from your phone service.

You can get more information about passports online at `www.travel.state.gov/passport_services.html`.

Getting a visa

Some countries require U.S. citizens to obtain an additional entry document called a visa. A *visa* is your abroad destination's way of officially giving you permission to enter the country for a specified purpose and a limited time — for example, a three-month tourist visa. They may document your visa by stamping a page in your passport or they may give you an official document that includes a photograph (in which case, you may need to provide them with passport photos).

Whether you need a visa is largely determined by the length and purpose of your stay. Visa requirements vary widely from country to country. The nearest embassy or consulate of the country or countries in which you'll study and/or travel has the most accurate and up-to-date visa information for you. You can also try the following online source: `www.travel.state.gov/foreignentryreqs.html`. Furthermore, you can check with your study abroad program to see what the visa requirements are.

Your study abroad program may provide special letters or documents that must accompany your visa application, so start the visa process as early as possible.

You'll probably need to request a student visa or residency permit. Getting your visas before leaving the U.S. is advisable because you may not be able to obtain visas for some countries once you've departed. You need to apply directly to the embassy or nearest consulate of each country that you plan to visit. Most visa applications require a fee. Some of these fees can be significant, so remember to figure them into your study abroad budget.

Department of State publication M-264, Foreign Entry Requirements, gives entry requirements for every country and tells where and how to apply for visas and tourist cards. You can order it at `www.pueblo.gsa.gov`. The State Department updates this publication annually, but there is always a chance that it may not reflect the most current requirements. This information is also online at `www.travel.state.gov/foreignentryreqs.html`.

Some countries will neither allow you to enter nor place a visa in your passport when your passport is valid for only another six months or less. Check your passport's expiration date once you've been accepted into a study abroad program. If you already have a passport, but it expires during the time you're abroad, apply for a new one before leaving to avoid this visa issue.

If you need additional visa pages before your passport expires, you can obtain them by submitting your passport to a passport agency. Extra visa pages are added without charge.

If countries that you plan to visit while you're abroad require only a tourist card, you can usually obtain one from any number of places, including the country's embassy or consulate, airlines serving the country, or the port of entry. You'll probably have to pay a fee for the tourist card.

Another must-have: The ISIC

The International Student Identity Card (ISIC) is an important and valuable travel document to have while studying and traveling abroad. Endorsed by the United Nations Educational, Scientific, and Cultural Organization, it was developed to provide traveling students with a document that is accepted worldwide as proof of their status. Realize that your regular university student ID won't be recognized in other countries.

The ISIC qualifies you for a number of discounts. Many international airlines offer special fares to ISIC cardholders. Other discounts range from cheaper insurance coverage, hotels and rental cars to special rail or bus passes to reduced or free admission to museums, theaters, concerts, and cultural sites.

Also, by having an ISIC you're granted supplemental health insurance coverage, which includes hospital stays, accident-related medical expenses, emergency evacuation, accidental death and dismemberment, repatriation of remains, passport protection, and baggage delay insurance. The emergency medical evacuation coverage is particularly important, because most private health-care plans don't provide this coverage. You want to have a way to make it back home in case your illness or injury cannot be treated overseas. Because of the need for medical evacuation coverage, many study abroad offices and programs either offer their own overseas insurance or require the ISIC.

Another benefit of the ISIC includes access to a toll-free help line for assistance while you're traveling. The help line provides a range of emergency medical, legal, and financial services, including locating a doctor or lawyer, replacing lost or stolen documents, and arranging travel in the event of an emergency.

When you receive your card, you also get a handbook that provides information on all its benefits and uses.

In 2003, the card costs $22 and is valid for 16 months — from September 1 through December 31 of the following year. You can still use the card when you get back to the U.S. for special student discounts on airlines, lodging, international phone calls, and international money transfers.

The card is issued by STA Travel. You can pick one up at all STA Travel offices and also at many U.S. colleges and universities. Check with your study abroad office to find out whether they have them. For more information, check out STA Travel's Web site at www.statravel.org or call 888-268-6245.

Being Your Own Travel Agent

Studying abroad and traveling go together like peanut butter and jelly. Part of the fun of studying and traveling abroad is acting as your own travel agent. If you've never had to do this before, it really is a great learning experience that you'll benefit from for the rest of your life. Part of being your own travel agent also entails figuring out how cheaply you can travel on your student budget. In this section, I get you started with the basics of running your own personal travel agency.

Booking (and recovering from) your flight

Things start getting exciting when you begin making travel plans and when the reality that you're actually packing up and moving to a far-off place starts sinking in. Something about booking plane tickets starts to make your adventure more real, changing the hypothetical into the actual. You'll have an exact date and time of departure and the countdown can begin!

When you're going abroad with your home university or other U.S.-based program, your initial travel plans may be taken care of for you. The program may arrange a group flight not only to and from your study abroad destination but also transportation from the airport to your new home. The cost of this kind of group flight typically is included in your program fee.

You may, however, need to make your own travel plans when you're directly enrolling in a foreign university or when your program requires you to make your own travel plans. Please be sure to make these arrangements as soon as possible (as soon as you know you're going), particularly when you're traveling in the summer or close to the holidays when air travel is busy.

Regardless of whether you're taking a group flight, find out from your program staff what, if any, arrangements have been made for the arrival of students in your host country before ever finalizing your travel reservations. Often a meeting place and time are established so that program staff can greet students upon their arrival.

Be aware that many countries list a round-trip ticket as one of their entry requirements. When making your initial flight reservations, you may not know when you want to return home. When that's the case, a round-trip ticket with a *flexible return date* is preferable. If this option doesn't work out, you'll have to pay a fee to change your return flight, because it's still cheaper to buy the round-trip ticket than it is to buy two one-way tickets.

When estimating return dates for flights home, always schedule your return trip after the exam period ends at the school you're attending abroad and try to think about how much time you'll need to pack up or travel once exams have ended.

Shopping for flights

When making travel plans, shop around! Plenty of good airfare deals are out there. A few points of comparison to consider when looking for flights are

- *Price:* Obviously, you want the least expensive ticket you can find, but be careful that you're not doing this at the expense of making your journey miserable and more difficult than it has to be. Traveling is tiring, and you don't want to arrive in your host country frazzled.

- *Number of connections:* Getting lower fares sometimes means that you need to fly through a few cities. My advice is to keep connections to a minimum. The more direct the flight, the better. Layovers make you even more exhausted and stressed out, particularly when you end up not making one of your connections.

- *Airline:* Some airlines are more comfortable for international flights than others. Ask around. You may also want to take into account any frequent flyer miles that you already have or can earn when booking a flight.

- *Fees for changing your return ticket:* The cheaper this fee is, the better. You also want to make sure that changing your return ticket is going to be relatively easy and hassle free.

- *Departure and arrival airports:* Fly in and out of airports closest to your home and study abroad destinations. Extending car trips or trips on trains and buses before and after your plane ride just to save a little bit of money usually is not worth the hassle and stress and only increases your level of exhaustion.

If you are planning to travel on your own after your study abroad program ends, you need to investigate fares that enable you return from a location that's different from your point of arrival.

If your airline ticket is lost or stolen, contact the airline, travel agency, or other agency where you purchased the ticket. If you bought your ticket from an airline, you usually must fill out a claim for a lost ticket and then buy a new one. Eventually (and it can take up to six months), you'll be refunded the cost of the replacement ticket, minus a fee.

Whenever you have special requests while booking a flight, remember to make them at the time you make your reservation. If you have long legs and would be more comfortable in an aisle seat, or if you're a vegetarian and need a special meal, the best way to guarantee that your needs will be met is making them known when you book your flight.

Scheduling for a smooth transition

You *will* experience jet lag if you're flying to different time zones. When traveling long distances, you can expect your body to adjust to a new time zone at the rate of about 1 hour per day. In other words, if you go to a time zone six hours ahead of where you live in the U.S., adjusting to your new time schedule will take you six days.

You need to think about dealing with jet lag not only when you arrive at your new home, but also when you make your travel plans. Consider the following:

- ✔ If you cannot sleep on a plane, avoid an overnight flight — although doing so is not always possible.

- ✔ You can minimize jet lag by scheduling your arrival at your destination at roughly your usual bedtime, according to the clocks in the time zone to which you're flying.

- ✔ Arrive early enough to be able to adjust to the time difference. Don't arrive the day before classes begin and expect to be able to function normally.

Conquering jet lag

When you arrive at your study abroad destination, feeling as though you're in a fog after hours and hours of travel is normal. Try the strategies that follow for adjusting your body to the new time schedule as quickly as possible:

- ✔ If you're taking an overnight flight, don't stay up late the night before, and don't sleep in. Thus, don't save packing until the last minute! Before your departure, consider going to bed earlier for a couple of days when you're traveling east or later when you're traveling west.

✔ Although the first day is the hardest, force yourself into the new time schedule when you arrive. Taking a nap may be tempting, but don't do it, regardless of how tired you are. Stay up until a reasonable bedtime so that you can sleep through the night as much as possible.

✔ What many people think is jet lag is actually dehydration. The air on airplanes is exceedingly dry. Force yourself to drink as much water as possible, but avoid caffeine and alcohol.

✔ Airlines feed you all the time on international flights, so pay attention to when you'll be eating at the place you're going to. If it is a reasonable mealtime there, then eat. If it's one in the morning there, try not to eat. Whenever you land first thing in the morning, eat, because doing so will jump-start your day. Getting on a new eating schedule as quickly as possible is important.

✔ Bring snacks with you on the plane. Airlines don't serve you meals based on what time it is at your destination. When you're trying to change your eating schedule, you need to be able to eat based on what time it is at your destination, and not necessarily when the airline crew serves dinner. Stopovers are another good reason for bringing food with you. If you're stopping at another airport to connect with another flight, bringing your own food can save you from having to convert your money to local currency just so you can buy a drink or a snack.

✔ If you're compelled to take sleeping pills for an international flight, try them out ahead of time! Don't take them for the first time ever on an international flight. Showing up in another country completely out of it can get you robbed or overcharged. Melatonin, an herbal medication that can be bought over-the-counter at health-food stores, may be a better option. It can also be used to induce sleep when you get to your destination. Some studies have shown that taking 1 to 3 milligrams of melatonin at bedtime for several days after arriving at your destination may decrease jet lag.

✔ Wearing comfortable clothing can make you more comfortable and thus may aid sleeping on the plane. Flying, after all, is not a fashion show. An eye mask and ear plugs may also help, especially with the ever-present crying baby. You may also want to consider bringing along a neck pillow.

✔ Move as much as possible while on the plane. Do in-flight exercises recommended in the airplane magazine. Blood doesn't flow as well in a constricted space, and airplane seats are highly constricting. Get up and walk around. Fidget. Your feet may swell during the flight, so wear shoes with laces so you can loosen them.

Exploring other places while abroad

Because talking about airplanes and making travel plans is so much fun, I also want to discuss other modes of transportation and searching for accommodations, two parts of the puzzle that you're likely to need to explore in your new country or continent.

Traveling by train

Many countries have highly efficient rail systems, and trains are the most widely used method of transportation. If you're planning to spend a few weeks traveling around your continent using trains, consider buying a rail pass in the U.S. prior to your departure. You can save a substantial amount of money this way. Rail passes, such as the Britrail Pass or Eurail Pass, can be obtained through most travel agents or ordered online. These passes usually offer unlimited travel for a specific amount of time. Just as airlines offer special airfares for students, rail systems offer special rail passes for students.

If you're planning to explore only one or two countries at a time, a Eurail Pass can be a more expensive option. Rail systems often discount student fares or offer rail passes good for unlimited travel within a country for a specific amount of time. I traveled around Italy for three weeks using one Italian Rail Pass that cost a total of $50 (U.S.).

Taking the bus

Although trains take you between most major cities, you may need to rely on buses to travel to more remote and less metropolitan locations. Bus and train stations usually are located near each other. Failing that, each kind of station usually provides good directions so that you can get between the two. Some stations also have popular bus/train route timetables available.

Don't forget you can probably use the Web to find bus and train information, including routes, schedules, and fees.

Cruising in cars

If you intend to drive while abroad, check with the embassies or consulates of the countries you're visiting to find out what they require in terms of driver's licenses, road permits, and auto insurance.

Whenever possible, obtain road maps of the countries that you plan to visit before going. You can also buy road maps in local bookstores in your host country.

You need to have a valid driver's license to be able drive while abroad. Some countries may recognize your current U.S. driver's license, but others may make you obtain an International Driving Permit. Before leaving, you can pick up an International Driving Permit at a local office of an automobile association. The U.S. Department of State has authorized AAA (American Automobile Association) and the American Automobile Touring Alliance to issue International Driving Permits to people who hold valid U.S. driver's licenses. You must be at least age 18 to apply for an International Driving Permit, have a valid U.S. driver's license, and provide two passport-size photographs.

In some countries, car rental agencies won't let you rent a car unless you're at least 25 years old. Car rental agencies usually provide auto insurance, but in some countries, the required coverage is minimal. When renting a car overseas, purchase coverage that is at least equivalent to the insurance you carry at home.

In general, your U.S. auto insurance will not cover you while abroad. However, check with your insurer to find out whether your policy applies when you drive to countries neighboring the United States (Canada or Mexico). Even when your policy is valid in these countries, it may not meet their minimum requirements, which means you may be under-insured for a country and need to purchase additional insurance on either side of the border.

I really don't recommend driving while abroad, if you can help it. First, you need to realize that when you're planning to travel by car, renting one, filling it with gas, and insuring it for the period of time you plan to drive it is expensive. Second, you need to know that every country has different — often extensive and confusing — rules of the road. To find out more about international road travel, try checking with the Association for Safe International Road Travel at www.asirt.org.

Finding accommodations during your explorations

Safety should be your primary concern when choosing places to stay while on the road. Stay in larger, reputable places that have some sort of a security system. Safety experts recommend booking a room somewhere on or between the second to seventh floors (in other words, above ground level), which are high enough to deter easy entrance from outside yet low enough for fire equipment to reach.

Roughing it in a youth hostel

When traveling before, during, or after your study abroad experience, you probably want to consider staying in a youth hostel. Hostels are not the most luxurious accommodations ever, but they are significantly less expensive than hotels and can range from dormitory-style rooms to private rooms. Likewise, you may be required to observe curfews, bring your own bedding, limit your length of stay, or adhere to other restrictions.

Always remember to bring your own towels when staying at youth hostels.

Many countries also have student hostels, which are restricted to use by university students. Student hostels usually offer more conveniences than youth hostels, such as food service, and provide a great way of meeting other international students. You may need to have a valid ISIC to prove your student status.

Hostelling International publishes an annual guide to worldwide hostels. It's published two volumes: Europe and The Americas, Africa, Asia and the Pacific.

If you're planning to stay in hostels while traveling, investing in an International Youth Hostel Pass is a good idea. Your membership card is valid at any Hostelling International–affiliated hostel worldwide. Some, but not all, hostels require this card when you make a reservation. Others charge extra money for nonmembers. All hostels that belong to the International Youth Hostel Federation (IYHF) display the tree-and-hut logo, meaning they meet the standards set by the IYHF, which carries out regular inspections.

Making your reservations for accommodations in advance always is a good idea, particularly during busy travel seasons and when you're going to a popular destination. Hostelling International has an International Booking Network (IBN) that enables you to make reservations up to six months in advance at more than 500 hostels in more than 50 countries. Book your accommodations online at www.hostelbooking.com or directly with a hostel via letter, fax, telephone, or e-mail.

More information is available at www.iyhf.org.

Looking at other options

Other affordable options for accommodation when you travel include bed-and-breakfasts (B&B) and budget hotels. Getting recommendations for places to stay from other students who have traveled abroad is always helpful; make sure that the B&B or budget hotel you choose is certified by some sort of traveling or hotel association. Other good sources to check for possible ideas on accommodation are travel guidebooks that target college students, but remember that if you're using a guide, one hundred other people probably are too, and these published places may tend to get booked up more quickly.

Using travel Web sites

Travel Web sites abound on the Internet. As is true with most things on the Web, you must realize that not all information out there is credible or reliable. If you're accustomed to using a particular site for booking travel and have had good experiences with it, there probably isn't much of a reason to switch sites, so keep using the company.

When purchasing travel tickets online, be sure to protect your credit card and use only secure sites.

General travel sites through which you can book flights, accommodations, and car rentals include:

- www.budgettravel.com
- www.cheaptickets.com
- www.expedia.com
- www.travelocity.com
- www.orbitz.com
- www.trip.com

For information on inexpensive accommodations, visit:

- www.hostels.com
- www.travlang.com

For information on discounted travel by plane, train, bus, and ferry, try:

- www.transitionsabroad.com/listings/travel/index/shtml
- www.istc.umn.edu/Travel/travel/default.html

- www.routesinternational.com (links to airlines, trains, ferries, and buses)
- www.etn.nl (European Travel Networks discounts in 185 countries)

Web sites and agencies that focus on student travel include:

- www.statravel.org: STA Travel is the world's largest student travel organization. Its Web site is an excellent source for student travel information, catering exclusively to student travelers. STA operates in more than 400 locations in 17 countries worldwide, specializing in low-cost, flexible student airfares, rail passes, budget hotels, travel insurance, work-abroad programs, and tours. You also can sign up for a free monthly e-mail newsletter that keeps you posted on sales and other special offers. STA also publishes a fairly low-priced student travel magazine, called *Break,* which provides travel advice and ideas on fun destinations to visit.

- www.usitnow.com: USIT offers a full range of services similar to those provided by a travel agent, but it also has developed products and services specifically for student and youth travelers. Like STA Travel, USIT discounts plane, bus, and rail fares, insurance policies, and budget accommodations. It also provides a global support network that can help students wherever they may be. USIT specializes in student and youth work exchange programs by offering all the information, administration, and support needed to work around the world.

Squaring Away Insurance, Wills, and Taxes

There are details you probably don't pay too much attention to while you're living in this country. For instance, how often do you think about travel and property insurance? Taxes? Voting? Well, you probably want to give certain administrative details like these a bit of thought before you depart. I'll explain why in this section. Remember that while you're abroad, life at home doesn't stop. Although you're off in a different country, you still have certain civil, financial, and legal responsibilities in the U.S. Making prior arrangements and plans to take care of those responsibilities makes your life easier, and you'll have fewer things to worry about while you're abroad.

Protecting yourself: Travel and property insurance

Unfortunately, while traveling or attending school abroad, bad things can happen. You can lose things. You may have personal items stolen. Baggage sometimes gets lost. Trips sometimes are canceled or delayed. For these reasons, being covered by travel and property insurance is a wise idea. The travel insurance plan that you choose may even provide some emergency medical care while you're abroad. (For information on health insurance, check out Chapter 18.)

Checking your existing insurance policies is a good starting point. For instance, if you have homeowner's, renter's, or personal property insurance, it may already cover the loss or theft of your luggage or personal items while you're abroad. So you may not need travel insurance, when you're already adequately covered by other insurance policies. When you have a fully refundable airline ticket, you may decide that you can live without trip cancellation or interruption insurance. Some credit-card companies also provide travel insurance, especially when you've used their services to purchase the ticket for your trip.

Before deciding on a travel insurance plan, do your homework and be careful about buying (or duplicating) coverage that you may already have. Ask your study abroad office whether it recommends any particular plan. Find out whether your parents have a reliable property insurance vendor. Compare a few different insurance options. Carefully investigate all the plans you're considering and always read the fine print! See what written guarantees a plan offers and, especially where travel insurance is concerned, check any agreements insurance vendors may have with any companies (in other words, travel agents and airlines) that are involved with your travel plans.

Traveler's insurance plans can protect you by covering the financial costs when:

- ✔ You become seriously ill or injured.
- ✔ An airline, cruise line, or tour operator goes into financial default.
- ✔ Natural disasters or strikes that impede travel services occur.
- ✔ A terrorist incident happens in a foreign city within 10 days of your scheduled arrival in that city.
- ✔ You're quarantined, served with a court order, or required to serve on a jury.
- ✔ You're directly involved in an accident en route to departure for your trip.

Designating power of attorney

Before leaving for your studies and travel abroad, make sure that you organize your will (if you already have one) and insurance documents.

Giving a family member or trusted friend power of attorney while you're abroad is an excellent idea. Having your power of attorney enables the person you designate to act on your behalf in case a legal document requires your signature while you're away and prepares you to handle any emergency that may happen while you're away.

Power of attorney is especially important when you receive financial aid. Checks that you receive to cover educational costs must be endorsed by you before they can be deposited, so providing someone with your power of attorney can be helpful when completing and signing these and other financial aid forms (your FAFSA is one) that you need to complete by certain deadlines.

If your home university has a student legal services office on campus, check with its staff to find out whether they have a power of attorney document available. You can also give someone power of attorney by simply writing what duties that person is allowed to perform on your behalf and having that paper notarized.

Arranging to vote

If elections are scheduled in the U.S. or your hometown while you're away, you can still vote by completing an absentee ballot. However, to be able to vote by absentee ballot, you must be registered to vote before you leave home.

Contact local election officials or the town hall to ask about absentee voting and whether you need to have your ballot notarized at a U.S. Embassy or Consulate.

Dealing with taxes

When you plan to be away from the U.S. during the spring semester and therefore will miss the April 15 tax deadline, you can request an automatic extension of the deadline for filing federal, state, and local tax returns. If you want to file your taxes from abroad, your family needs to send you all the paperwork, or you can go to the nearest U.S. Embassy or Consulate to get forms. The U.S. Embassy and Consulate are sometimes able to find someone who can help you complete the forms.

Chapter 13

All the Right Stuff: Taking What You Need

*O*nce upon a time, I thought I was a master packer. Two days before I had to get on that plane to Dublin, I thought differently. My bedroom looked like the aftermath of a tornado. The contents of my closet and drawers were in assorted piles on my bed and floor. In the middle of this mess were two empty duffel bags. I thought, "How is all this going to fit in there?" I knew it wasn't. I'd have to find a way to part with some of what I thought were necessities. But how was I going to do that? I was going away for an entire year! I needed all this stuff . . . or so I thought.

Packing is quite possibly the most daunting and difficult task you'll encounter when preparing to study abroad. You're going away for a semester or a year, but you can pack only two bags, each subject to airline weight limits of as little as 40 pounds or as many as 70 pounds, to take with you. You're probably used to packing up an entire car or two with all your worldly possessions in tow on your way back to college at the end of every summer. But now you don't have that luxury; you're going abroad (unless, of course, that means you're driving to Canada or Mexico). Every cubic inch of space you have in those two suitcases counts! So you must ask yourself, "Can I live without this?" regarding just about every single item you want to put into one of those two suitcases.

The Golden Rule of Packing

Before I get into the nitty-gritty of packing, I'll introduce you to my golden rule of packing. I spent many hours packing, unpacking, and repacking before learning this rule. I wish I had known it while I tried to pack my duffel bags for Ireland. Although it isn't a magic formula, I think that if you keep it in mind as you begin packing for your adventure, your experience will go a bit easier. Okay, here ya go. Drumroll, please. Here's my golden rule of packing: *Don't take too much stuff.* Sounds altogether too simple, right? Well, it is! However, the sad fact is: The majority of travelers (like me) break this rule, and all of them live to regret it.

Let me explain why this is such an important rule.

- ✔ **Heavy, bulky luggage is hard to carry.** Never take more than you can carry, all by yourself, at one time. Pack what you plan to take, then carry it around the block two or three times and go up and down a flight of stairs. If you can't make it, you've overpacked.

- ✔ **Too much stuff slows you down.** Airports turn into nightmares, and so will public transit, when you must walk through long corridors with more stuff than you can comfortably carry. When your aim is always to travel light, you can move more quickly (and run, if need be) to catch trains and buses, and you'll be more likely to have a free hand when you need it.

- ✔ **Heavy bags can mean a heavy heart.** The lighter you travel, the more fun you'll have. You'll also be less tired and less likely to set your luggage down, leaving it unattended and at risk of being stolen.

So how do you manage this feat? How do you pack light for a months-long trip? It isn't impossible — I promise. Following these rules can help you keep your urge to overpack in check:

- ✔ **Reduce your load.** Set out all the clothes you plan to take, and then put half of them back. Most people tend to take far more clothing than is necessary. Remember that you probably wear your favorite outfits over and over, and being abroad won't change that!

- ✔ **Pack only what you *need*.** Don't bring things just because you *may* need them. If something unexpected comes up, chances are slim that you won't be able to borrow or buy what you need. You will not study abroad forever, so this is only a temporary separation from your belongings. Your stuff will be here when you get back! Before you know it, you will be reunited with that spectacular but impractical pair of blue sequined pants.

No student has ever complained about packing too little, but plenty of them have cried over packing too much.

Finally, if a second Golden Rule for packing exists, it's this: Pack in advance. Waiting until the last minute significantly increases your chances of forgetting something and of feeling stressed out and rushed. Packing a week before you're scheduled to depart is ideal.

Finding the Right Luggage

Luggage is certainly not the most exciting part of going abroad, but it is necessary. When you're going abroad, good quality luggage is a must! Whether you're heading out to a store or simply climbing the stairs to your parent's attic to choose your luggage, I've written this section in order to help you find luggage that will work for you!

Adhering to baggage guidelines

First off, you need to remember that all airlines have baggage guidelines. Go to your airline's Web site or call its customer service number to find out what those guidelines are. With international flights, you typically can check two bags, and your airline will impose luggage size limits. Ask your airline what the maximum total dimensions of your luggage should be. One carry-on bag (total dimensions cannot exceed 45 inches) is usually allowed, but it must fit under the seat. In addition to size dimensions, many airlines also have weight limits (usually 40 to 70 pounds).

If your luggage exceeds size and weight limitations, most airlines charge you an extra fee. This limitation shouldn't be an issue, because you just don't need that much stuff.

Whenever you're worried about exceeding the baggage allowance limitations, measure the height, width, and length of your bags when they're all packed, and use the bathroom scales to check their weight.

Choosing your luggage

You want to invest in luggage that is of good quality, making sure that it offers plenty of space, is made of durable material, has wheels, and is easy to carry. I found my canvas duffel bags, with wheels and shoulder straps, worked very well. A small carry-on bag that can double as an overnight bag for weekend trips also is a good idea.

Don't buy the lowest priced luggage you can get your hands on if you want it to last for a long time. Also, because you're packing the luggage for a trip that will last one month or longer, buy luggage that has at least 5,000 cubic inches of storage space (you can find this capacity information on the luggage tag).

Luggage comes in many varieties. If you're looking for a travel backpack, I devote an entire section later in this chapter to picking the perfect pack. The classic suitcase often falls into the wheeled luggage category. Suitcases with durable wheels and reinforced handles (that usually retract) are great for whizzing through airports and train stations. The convertible luggage category includes wheeled bags with hidden shoulder straps that allow you to convert the bag into something you can carry on your shoulder. And then there is the duffel which you usually carry using straps, but larger sized duffels may offer wheels to make transporting them easier.

Other suggestions to keep in mind when choosing luggage:

- Luggage with multiple storage compartments and pockets makes it easy to organize packing and to secure items.
- Compression straps on the inside of the luggage are helpful in holding down clothing.
- Don't worry too much about the weight of the empty bag in the store. The weight of your bag is primarily determined by what you put in it! Think of it this way: What is another pound or two when you are already packing 40+ pounds of stuff in your bag?
- Wheels should be securely fastened to your suitcase by durable hardware. In-line skate wheels often work best.
- Zippers should pull smoothly and not catch on corners.
- While leather is the most expensive material for a suitcase, it is also the most durable. Ballistic nylon is the most popular material in high-quality luggage today. It's durable and has a stylish, high-tech look. Other popular, durable materials for luggage include high-denier fabrics, canvas-like nylon, and parachute nylons.
- Hardside suitcases adequately protect items inside the case but are more likely to receive dents and scratches during baggage handling. Softside suitcases allow more flexibility and therefore can better absorb and withstand rough baggage handling, and they protect fragile items that are packed carefully just as well as a hardside case does.

Picking the perfect pack

You also may want to invest in a backpack (not the kind you use at school) if you plan to travel extensively. Look for good backpacks in an outdoors or sporting goods store.

When considering a backpack, remember the following:

- Don't buy a backpack (or any piece of luggage, for that matter) that is bigger than you! Make sure your backpack is proportional to your body size. Experts say to limit yourself to a pack that has a capacity between 2,800 and 4,000 cubic units.

- As with most major purchases, you need to shop around. Be patient and give yourself enough time before your departure to check out a few stores and try out a number of styles.

- High cost does not necessarily mean equally high quality. Just because the backpack is the most expensive one in the store doesn't mean that it's the best one and will satisfy all your requirements. Unless you plan to do quite a bit of backpacking during the course of your lifetime, a moderately priced backpack ($85 to $180) probably is just fine. You don't want to be stuck with a $400 backpack that collects dust in the attic after this one trip.

- Backpacking is neither a fashion show nor a fashion statement. Don't buy a backpack because it's available in your favorite color. Don't refuse to consider a backpack because you don't like the looks of it; it may suit your needs perfectly, and you may be able to order it in a different color. Comfort is your number one priority here, not aesthetics.

- Test your backpack in the store to get a good fit. You want to make sure that you can easily carry at least 25 to 30 pounds in your pack. Most stores that sell packs have weights you can put inside the pack to determine how well you're able to carry it. Buy your backpack at a store, not online or through a catalog.

- Whenever possible, get a pack that qualifies as a carry-on. Carry-on size requirements vary by airline, but a good rule of thumb is to make sure dimensions do not exceed 45 inches (see earlier section on "Adhering to baggage guidelines"). You save time when you don't need to check and claim your pack in airports.

A backpack that has zippers that open around the pack (like a typical school backpack) is more efficient. When you have access to the stuff in your pack only via an opening at the top, you spend too much time unpacking and repacking just to locate a single item.

Make sure your backpack doesn't have any protruding rods that are part of the frame. You wouldn't want them getting caught or stuck on anything. However, make sure that it does have padding on the hip belt, shoulder straps, and back, which definitely makes carrying your pack much more comfortable.

Remember to put your name, address, and telephone numbers inside and outside of each piece of luggage. Use covered luggage tags to prevent strangers from learning your identity or nationality and buy luggage locks to secure your belongings. While these days airports don't allow luggage to be locked when it is checked, locks are still handy when traveling on trains or buses or for securing your items in hostel lockers.

If you notice that many other people's luggage out there happens to resemble yours, try tying a particular color ribbon on your bag so you can easily pick it out at luggage carousels.

Deciding What to Bring

Deciding what you absolutely cannot live without and what can stay at home is often an agonizing process. Use logic when packing. Do your research on the climate of your study abroad destination. If you're going to be at your study abroad destination during summer months, for example, leave the heavy winter coat at home. In addition to climate, think about events you'll be attending, and so on. Also, pay attention to your host university or study abroad program's suggestions on packing. They're the experts on your host country's climate and culture and the things you need to live there.

Some other variables to keep in mind when packing are

- When are you going to get to your final location?
- Are you getting off the plane and going right to your new home to settle in?
- Does your program have a tour or orientation program planned so that it may be a few days before you arrive at your final destination?

Pack everything you need for those first few days at the top of your suitcase so you have easy access to it. If your program is a study tour, and you won't be settling anywhere for any considerable length of time, you'll constantly be carrying whatever you brought, so limit yourself to a moderate-sized bag and a small carry-on bag in which you can keep valuables and critical travel documents (passports, airline tickets, and so on.).

Ask other students who have already studied abroad with your program for their advice about what you need to take and what you can leave at home.

Wondering about wardrobe

Clothing takes up the most space in your suitcase when you pack to go abroad, and you want to choose it carefully. Remember that safety abroad begins with what you pack. You want to dress conservatively to avoid drawing attention to yourself, and try to look as unlike a tourist or an American as possible. Don't wear tennis shoes or sneakers (In other countries, sneakers are much different than what we wear in the U.S.). Baseball hats are a dead giveaway that you're an American, as are sweatpants. Wearing black is usually safe. Also, wear skirts that are of a conservative length (knee length). In other words, aim to blend in, and avoid wearing expensive-looking jewelry or clothing. *Note:* Clothing that is too casual for where you're studying can signal that you're a tourist.

Here's a list of things to remember when packing clothing for your trip abroad:

- Clothes need to compliment each other so you can easily mix and match them for a wide variety of outfits. Dark (black, navy, purple, green) or neutral (all browns and shades of gray) colored clothing is not only easy to interchange, but also tends to hide any dirt or stains you inevitably acquire along the way.

- Try packing clothes made of fabrics that require little care. Wrinkle-free and cotton-knit blend clothes are most convenient and are extremely easy to pack, thus creating more space in your suitcase because you can tightly roll items that won't wrinkle. I also recommend rayon/polyester/spandex blend clothes for traveling. They are good for multiple seasons, take up little room in luggage, are almost impossible to wrinkle, and dry relatively quickly after being washed.

- Avoid packing anything that requires dry cleaning because it's too much of a hassle. Put dresses, suits, and shirts in plastic bags (dry-cleaning bags) to cut down on wrinkling. If your suitcase has a garment cover designed to accommodate hanging items, use it.

- Waterproof clothing is a great idea, particularly when you're headed for a rainy climate or any region where you'll be studying during the wet season. At the very least, bring a raincoat and a pair of waterproof shoes. A travel raincoat takes up little space and is easily rolled up so you can even carry it around in your school bag. You'll be more comfortable and less likely to overheat if you have a raincoat made of a breathable fabric.

- If you're traveling to a cooler climate, be aware that dressing in layers is key! Layering clothes is more effective than hauling around bulky sweaters or coats.

- Pack a change of clothes in your carry-on luggage just in case your luggage gets lost during your travels.

- If you know that you will not be able to use a clothes dryer at your study abroad destination, remember that jeans and bulky clothes take forever to dry.

- Pack heavier items, like shoes, at the bottom of a suitcase. Wear the pair of shoes that would take up the most space in a suitcase while you're on the plane. Put your shoes in shoe bags (or thoroughly clean the soles) before packing them so your clothes don't get dirty. Stuff small items such as socks or travel-size toiletries inside your shoes to save space.

✔ Consider packing your clothes in plastic bags sorted by type of garment (In other words, have different bags for shirts, pants, undergarments, and so on). This enables you to easily find what you're looking for without taking everything out of your bag and then having to repack.

Packing your personal items

Here are a few tricks of the trade for packing nonclothing items:

✔ Remember that soap, toothpaste, and other toiletries can be purchased when you arrive at your destination, so you can just bring a few travel size bottles to get through the first few days. Don't take up valuable space in your suitcase with full-sized bottles.

✔ Pack toiletries in resealable plastic bags, because changes in pressure on airplanes often cause these items to leak (and sometimes even explode) during flight.

✔ Pack small breakable items between clothes, which provide enough protective cushioning that these items can be sent safely in your checked-in luggage. I suggest that you pack fragile items inside a few socks for extra cushioning and then place them inside a shoe.

✔ Face it, you'll return home with more stuff than you had when you went abroad. So leaving space in your suitcase to account for these extras is a good idea. You can also pack a collapsible or expandable bag to carry items you purchase on the return leg of your trip. Packing all of your purchases in one bag will help you get through Customs more quickly.

✔ If you take a camera, don't forget to register it (see next item) and be sure to buy a lead-lined film bag. Contrary to posted airport claims, some X-ray devices ruin film.

✔ Register imported items, such as portable tape or CD players, cameras, watches, and so on, with U.S. Customs before leaving the States. Unregistered foreign-made items are subject to duty charges when you reenter the U.S., unless you can prove ownership prior to your departure (such as by showing the receipt). Take the items to Customs services at the airport and fill in a registration slip. When you reenter the U.S., show Customs officials the slip.

✔ Guidebooks can take up lots of space. If you have more than one guidebook and want to save some space, consider ripping out pages that you don't think you'll need. When I traveled through Europe, I ripped out pages of my guidebook that I knew I wouldn't need and then tore out the pages that applied to a location whenever I left it bound for another.

✔ Airlines don't always allow you to carry musical instruments in the cabin of the plane. If you intend to take one with you, it may need to be checked. Insure the instrument and make sure your name and address are on it and on the case.

Checking out a checklist

This suggested packing checklist is by no means exhaustive or the last word on what you do and don't need to pack. Your study abroad program or home university study abroad office may also provide you with relevant packing information.

✔ **Basic items**

- Luggage (I.D. tags)
- Weekend travel bag/day pack
- Money belt/neck pouch (can be worn inside your clothing, safer than a fanny pack)

✔ **Documentation**

- Passport
- Visa or other immigration documentation
- Insurance information (health, property, travel insurance)
- Traveler's checks
- Small amount of currency of study abroad destination
- U.S. dollars
- Plane tickets
- International Student Identity Card
- Emergency contact information
- Any relevant health information you may need to enter the country, such as an immunization record and/or proof of HIV/AIDS testing

✔ **Clothing**

- Easy care clothing items
- Layers of warm and cool clothes for weather changes
- Waterproof jacket and shoes
- Comfortable walking shoes or hiking boots
- A variety of socks (thin cotton, thermal, and wool)
- Underwear
- Hat, gloves, scarf, and mittens if you are studying in a cold climate
- One nice, more formal outfit
- Trousers
- Tops
- Swimsuit

✔ **Healthcare items**

- Prescriptions

- Spare glasses or contacts

- First aid kit (include frequently used items in your medicine cabinet)

- Adhesive bandages

- Sunscreen and sunglasses

- Tweezers

- Scissors

- Nonprescription painkillers (aspirin, ibuprofen, acetaminophen)

- Anti-diarrhea medicine

- Malaria pills (if needed)

- Water purification equipment (if needed)

✔ **Academic items**

- Dictionary in English and your country's native language

- Your home university's study abroad office contact information

- Your major adviser's and dean's contact information

- Any course information/credit transfer paperwork

- Program materials, which may include handbooks, course registration information, or directions to your new home sent by your program

- Photocopies of important documents

✔ **Miscellaneous**

- Camera, film

- Battery-operated alarm clock

- Extra batteries

- Watch

- Sewing kit

- Towel and washcloth (for travel)

- Travel guides, maps

- Book to read on the plane

- Travel journal

- Gifts if you'll be staying with a host family

- International phone card (with access number to the U.S. from your host country)
- Sunglasses
- Earplugs

Remember not to pack any sharp items or anything that could be used as a weapon in your carry-on bag.

Packing for Short Trips While Abroad

You're probably going to explore your host country during your free time on weekends while you're abroad. In packing for these short trips and perhaps a week or two of backpacking, strive to travel as light as possible. Don't forget your passport, ATM card, and travel tickets.

When you're going away for just a weekend, a small bag (think school backpack or messenger bag) with a single change of clothing and pajamas does just fine. Remember to pack the proper gear whenever you're spending an extended amount of time outside.

When you're taking your backpack to travel around for weeks on end, you still want to pack as little as possible and leave room for souvenirs you collect along the way. Here are a few ways to create space in your pack:

- Do your own laundry as you travel. You can pack fewer clothes by bringing along a small packet of laundry detergent, washing and rinsing clothes in a sink at night, and then hanging them up to dry.
- Don't pack a full-sized towel. Getting by with only a hand towel for a few weeks is possible.
- Unless you're planning to attend a fancy dinner party, take only one pair of shoes: sneakers or waterproof hiking shoes.
- Sacrifice the umbrella and just pack a raincoat with a hood.
- Don't pack excessive amounts of makeup. Just bring the bare necessities with you.
- Make sure all toiletries you bring are travel size.
- Most hostels don't allow sleeping bags, so don't waste the space. Bed linens are either included or cost only a nominal fee.
- Don't go overboard with souvenir purchases.

Saying "no" to shipping

Whenever possible, avoid shipping any of your belongings abroad. Doing so is an expensive idea, times two, because whatever you ship to your abroad destination at the beginning of the semester, you must ship back home at the end. Fees for shipping baggage back to the U.S. generally are higher than the cost to ship packages from the U.S. The cheapest way to send packages is by surface mail through the U.S. postal service, but this method can take anywhere from six to ten weeks.

Shipping items abroad also is fairly risky because damage caused to packages shipped abroad is quite frequent, and so is theft.

You may also encounter unusual Customs regulations in your country abroad that limit what you can send or receive. Your package from home may be held at the Customs office, and you may have to pick it up and pay a fee. Students often find that they must pay large amounts for packages of personal items from home. When shipping packages, students and parents typically declare a high value on the contents for insurance purposes. However, to avoid unnecessary Customs tax, your packages need to be labeled as "used personal items with no commercial value." When shipping baggage home to the U.S., you can be charged storage fees while waiting for Customs clearance.

Chapter 14

Settling In and Enjoying Your New Home

So, you've made it! All the planning has paid off; you've endured a long plane ride and landed in the country that will be your new home for the next eight weeks or months. Now what? It may seem like everything should just start happening or magically fall into place now that you've arrived, but that is hardly the case. You have to hit the ground running, working through your jet lag and organizing and orientating yourself in whatever amount of time you have before classes begin.

Pulling the Cart with the Horse: First Things First

As soon as you arrive and set your bags down in your new home, the first thing you need to do "phone home!" Your parents want to know that you arrived safely and in one piece. So phone or e-mail home within hours of arriving, so you can then focus on settling in.

The day of the week that you arrive on affects the number of things that you can immediately accomplish. Many cities and towns shut down during weekends, so when you arrive on a weekend, you can catch a bit of a breather and do some leisurely unpacking. Two things that you need to do, regardless of when you arrive, include:

- ✔ Take the time to get to know your roommates or other students who share your living space. Don't play those silly icebreaker games from your first year of college; going out for a pint with them, having dinner together, or chatting in the common room works well.

- ✔ Learn how to place an emergency phone call (fire, police, ambulance).

During the first few normal business days in your new home, make your way through these basic tasks:

- ✔ Change more money.

- ✔ Find your way from your accommodations to the university. Scout out where the international student office is located, introduce yourself, and see whether the staff has any information for you.

- ✔ Familiarize yourself with your environment by walking around the city, catching the bus or train (finding out transportation schedules between home and school), and taking a campus or city tour. Ask your roommates or other students which routes are safest or quickest for everyday travel.

- ✔ Find out where the closest convenience store, supermarket, self-service laundry, and post office are located.

- ✔ Open a bank account (check out Chapter 16 for more on banking while studying abroad) and get a cell phone, if you've determined that you need either one.

Venturing Forth: Finding Food and Shopping

I guarantee the first time that you head to the supermarket will be an adventure. Taking a friend, especially someone who's a local, makes the task easier, and so does discovering the ins and outs of the supermarket before you ever go. Where are prices and quality best? Do you have to pay in cash, or do stores take credit cards? Are prices fixed or open to negotiation? When is the supermarket busiest (don't go at these times in the beginning, because doing so can increase your stress level)? You need to set aside a good chunk of time and make sure you have plenty of patience. If you go to the store alone, watch how others shop and take note of things such as payment, weighing produce, and bagging groceries. Although navigating a supermarket that you're not used to, especially one that requires you to function in a different language, is not easy, it can be fun.

Finding the right shop or the right kind of food in any place new to you often comes down to luck and experience. For example, I spent an entire month thinking that Ireland sold only whole milk before discovering where skim milk was located in my neighborhood supermarket and what it was called. Even when you're in an English-speaking country, food items may be known by different names. Furthermore, you may not be able to find food items exactly like they are produced in the United States, so aim for close approximations.

Your favorite convenience store may be within walking distance of your accommodations, but I caution against making it the place where you buy most of your food. Convenience stores are notoriously more expensive than supermarkets — there goes the sightseeing cash.

In addition to groceries and staples, make sure that you take time to scout out nearby fast-food or *take-away* restaurants and places that offer home delivery. Let's face it — you're not going to want to cook for yourself all the time! If you're a pizza fiend, you may have a hard time finding U.S.-quality pizza abroad (unless you're in Italy). I was very disappointed that I couldn't get a decent piece of pizza in Dublin. So stick with local food — like fish and chips in Dublin — or try the other classic take-away options like Chinese, Indian, or Thai.

Communicating with Home

Before going abroad, make sure to decide with your family and friends how to communicate with them while you're abroad. You can choose between regular postal delivery (the snails are slower overseas), telephone, or e-mail. Each has its own merits and some disadvantages, and one means may be more available to you than others.

Snail mail

As you probably have already discovered as a college student, not much is better than walking to your mailbox and finding a card or letter there amongst all the bills. Receiving mail via postal delivery becomes even more cherished and exciting when you're abroad!

Letters are economical. They cost less than phone calls, and you can write them from anywhere. If you're not someone who writes pages and pages, consider postcards! They're easy to write and can be written while at a park or café, on a train, or from your hostel bed while on the road. Letters and postcards also tend to be more personal and can make great keepsakes. My grandmother and parents, for example, collected all the postcards I sent while I was abroad, chronicling my adventures in Ireland and the rest of Europe.

Pack your address book! If you don't already have one (because you keep everything in your PDA or on your computer), make one before you leave. You may even want to make a photocopy of your address book and keep it separate from the original, just in case you lose it.

To help guarantee that you receive letters while you're away, give your friends and family self-addressed, stamped (with the proper amount of postage) envelopes before you leave.

Of course, the major downside to letter writing is that snail mail is just as the name implies: slow. Sending letters back and forth can take a long time, usually more than a week for an airmail letter to get to you from the States. International postage is more expensive than domestic postage, but if you limit it to letters or postcards, you won't break the bank.

Mailing packages while abroad is expensive and unwise. Surface mail is less expensive than airmail, but when using either of them, be sure to

- ✓ Allow plenty of time for delivery.
- ✓ Expect your package to be opened and searched during its journey.
- ✓ Avoid sending send money or valuables.

In some places, it's smart to avoid receiving packages altogether. The fact of the matter is that not everyone is honest. Your package may be searched and something stolen from it in the process. And if your package just "disappears," it usually can't be tracked once it leaves the U.S. unless you use a not-so-fast and very expensive international express service.

Phoning home

Nothing, I repeat, nothing is like a phone call home when you're studying abroad. But my Sunday afternoon phone calls to home were what made me the most homesick when I was abroad. In fact, when I arrived in my host country, I called to let my parents know that I had arrived safely, but then I instituted a two-week moratorium on phone calls to home, so that I could adjust and cut down on homesickness.

Besides, phone calls can be quite expensive while you're abroad — for you and for friends and family who may be calling you. In most foreign countries, domestic and international phone calls are very expensive, and phone bills are not itemized. Phone service, meanwhile, may be poor with frequent static, echoes, delays, and disconnections.

You may find that where you're staying doesn't have any phone access at all, or you may have to share a public phone with an entire dorm of students. So expect restricted access to a phone while abroad.

Options for making phone calls

If your family doesn't already have an international calling plan, you may want to invest in one. Usually, an international calling plan gives you low rates on calls from your home to a specific country or region for a nominal monthly plan fee (typically $3 to $5 per month) plus the reduced per-minute rate for each call.

You may want to do some research on international calling rates before going abroad — call your local long distance carriers for information. I set my parents up with an international calling plan before I left — since I seem to be my parent's one-stop shop for technical support (the DVD player, computer, broadband connection, and so on). Although I wasn't able to figure out the most affordable way of calling home until I got to my destination, my parents at least were all set to call me. If your parents are calling you, you're not the one paying for the call, but it's a good idea to keep your eye out for special deals from the long-distance carriers as you're preparing to go abroad.

Calling cards may be an affordable option for calling home while you're abroad because you may be able to dial direct from where you are to your home. Check with your service for rates and a list of country access numbers before you leave. Then you just enter the access number for the country you're calling from, and then the phone number you're calling and your calling card number. Most calling cards have special access codes that enable you to reach a U.S. operator, which may be a welcome relief when you're still working on your language skills.

In many countries, particularly Australia, New Zealand, and throughout Europe, these cards can offer amazing deals and prices as low as 3 cents per minute to the U.S.

You can also buy phone cards in the country you're visiting. These cards have a specific amount of money or time on them (in other words, 60 minutes). You dial an access number, input the code on the back of the card, and make your call. When you run out of minutes or money, you simply throw away the card and go buy a new one. Some countries also have public phone centers where you can place a call and pay for it when you're done.

A brief word about cell phones: They are increasingly popular all around the globe, but making international calls on them usually is incredibly expensive and therefore extremely unwise.

Phone tips

Follow these hints when making or receiving phone calls while abroad:

- Don't forget time differences. Family members will be glad to hear from you, but not at 4 a.m.

- Never call the U.S. directly when staying with a host family because of the cost and lack of itemized billing.

- Be sure to give friends and family the correct country and city codes for your location if you want to receive calls from the U.S.

- All international calls originating from the U.S. start with 011 and are followed by a country code and then possibly a city code before the actual phone number.

- Don't hang up after a call when you need to make another one; press #, instead, and you can avoid separate access charges for each call. If you dial a wrong number, don't hang up, but rather press the * key, which enables you to start over.

- Shield the phone keypad when entering your calling card number so no one can see it and use it. In countries where touch-tone service is not available, your long distance company may have voice-activated service and dialing. If that's the case, make sure no one is listening when you say your calling card code aloud.

Sending a fax

You may need to send documents or information to someone in a hurry, so don't forget about faxing. It is cheaper than long-distance calling but more expensive than e-mail.

E-mail

E-mail has become the main mode of communication for most of the world. It's great for battling homesickness, staying connected to friends, and making plans to visit other friends who are studying abroad, but keep your daily use to a minimum. You have too many other things to do while you're abroad.

E-mail solves a number of practical issues while you're abroad by:

- ✔ Eliminating the time difference problem.

- ✔ Reducing amounts you'd otherwise spend on telephone calls.

- ✔ Saving time when getting courses approved or registering for classes back home.

- ✔ Serving as a way to send important or emergency information to you. (On September 11, 2001, the telephone network went haywire, but the Internet stayed up and running.)

However, e-mail is a drain on your time. Fight the temptation to sit at a computer all day and catch up with friends and family at home. Set a self-imposed daily or weekly e-mail limit and stick to it so that you don't sacrifice a real study abroad experience for a virtual one. Being in your host country can be like exploring another world — don't waste it.

The good news about this e-mail conundrum is that accessing e-mail may be more difficult while you're abroad. The rest of the world is not as obsessed by e-mail and the World Wide Web as the U.S is. You're likely to find yourself in a situation where you don't have the 24-hour-a-day, 7-days-a-week Internet access you're used to with DSL, Ethernet, or cable-modem connections.

Internet capabilities and availability depend upon where you are, but in general, you can expect limited access and delayed responses. Many programs and universities provide students with computer access, but only on a limited basis. You may find yourself waiting in long lines at university computer labs or libraries just to check your e-mail. And once you finally get on a computer to check e-mail, you may be booted off by a student who has a paper to write — academics take precedence in university facilities. Be forewarned that many universities abroad charge students for e-mail usage, either in a flat fee or per minute.

Internet cafés are popular places to check e-mail or surf the Web, but they cost money. Ask local students about the least expensive places to go.

If you're not sure what e-mail accounts you can access while you're abroad, set up a free Web-based account through Hotmail or Yahoo before going abroad; you can access either from virtually anywhere.

Computers

If you currently own a desktop, you're not going to pack it up and ship it to your abroad location. It just isn't practical, and buying a laptop for one semester or year abroad is just plain silly.

If you already own a laptop, you may want to take it with you. However, you need to realize that you'll use it more for schoolwork than for e-mail. Contracting with an Internet service provider while abroad can be time-consuming and expensive, and besides, you may not even have a telephone hookup in your dorm room. The nice thing about having a laptop is that you don't have to rely on public computing facilities at your university. You can write papers and do work at home. You may just need to use university facilities to print your paper before handing it in.

If you plan to take a laptop, make sure that you can run it on the voltage common to the country where you're studying. Nowadays, almost all laptops have built-in converters in their power supplies that enable you to switch between 110-volt (standard in the U.S.) and 220-volt (standard in most other places in the world). If your laptop doesn't, or if you need a different voltage, consider investing a chunk of money in a good voltage converter designed for the place you're visiting. Paying more for a good converter means you'll pay less in repair bills if the higher voltage fries your machine!

In many developing countries, voltages fluctuate and you may experience frequent power outages. Investing in a voltage regulator/uninterrupted power supply may help. Another way of dealing with power surges and fluctuations is making sure your battery is always charged. The battery can handle fluctuations, so you can work undisturbed on your laptop.

Printers, on the other hand, are much more sensitive to fluctuations in power. In most cases, saving your work to disk and printing it out at a university computer lab or Internet café is best. If you absolutely must have a printer, you may want to wait until you're overseas to buy one that's designed to work in your host country.

Always take your laptop as a carry-on when you fly. Do not check it like you would regular airline baggage or ship it overseas. If you check it, your laptop may arrive in several pieces. If you ship it, you may be charged substantial customs duties for "importing" it into the country. Always keep your laptop's documentation with you, including a receipt that proves where and when you bought it. Don't forget that you probably will be required to prove that the computer works at airport security.

You can, however, get along just fine without a computer. I did. Believe it or not, professors with some programs at some universities don't mind when your work is handwritten. If you're without a computer and want to type your paper (because you type faster than you write), find out when the computer lab is open and ask whether you can reserve a computer in advance.

Get up early whenever you know you need to use computers at school. I guarantee that you'll have a much easier time of getting a computer to use if you get to the computer lab when it first opens in the morning.

Recording Your Experiences

Part of settling in and getting up and running in your new home is devising a way to remember the time you spent abroad when you're back in the U.S. I found that keeping a journal and taking photos were two of the best ways to document my time abroad. Journals and cameras are easy to throw in a backpack and carry around with you and are fairly inexpensive ways of transporting memories and sights — since you can't bring the Trevi fountain or gondolas home with you.

Start using your journal and camera shortly after you arrive abroad so you get into the habit of documenting your experience!

Keeping a journal

Before I went abroad, the last time I'd kept a journal of any sort was in second grade, when diaries with locks and keys were all the rage. Or maybe it was in third grade, when I had to keep a journal for creative writing. At any rate, my journal skills pretty much started and ended in elementary school.

If you've never kept a journal, I'd say that while you're abroad is a good time to start. You're going to experience plenty of thoughts, feelings, observations, realizations, and memories, and a journal is the perfect place to keep track of them. A journal helps you remember what you've seen and experienced in a different way than photographs can.

Writing things down improves your memory! Detailed entries enable you to go back and relive a moment.

On a deeper level, a journal may help you process your time spent abroad. Another benefit of keeping a journal is that doing so can inspire you in the future. Maybe you'll want to clean up a few pages for publication (does your study abroad office need any brochures written?) or find some use for your entries in a course project or essay when you're back at your home university.

Two of the more important things to remember about keeping a journal:

- You don't have to be a Pulitzer Prize–winning writer to keep a journal.

- It's your journal; do what you want with it! No rules apply, so make it enjoyable.

Those two things said, I give you some ideas in the next few sections about what you can do with your journal, in case you need some inspiration. This information is neither exhaustive nor essential; it's merely intended to give you a boost. Besides, you may already be an avid journal writer with some creative ideas for your study abroad journal.

Practical considerations

When considering the kind of journal you're going to keep, make sure that you:

- **Buy a durable journal.** Get something with a hardback cover. If you intend to sketch or paste things into your journal, you may want to get an artist's sketchbook with a heavy cover.

- **Choose just the right size.** Your journal needs to be big enough for you to write in comfortably but small enough to take anywhere. (Remember: You don't need to take it with you to every tourist site or on every hike. You can certainly write in it at the end of the day.)

- **Pack your journal in a resealable plastic bag.** Because you'll be traveling, keeping your journal in a waterproof bag and using waterproof ink are good steps to take. If you're artistically inclined, pack your art supplies in a sealed bag, too.

- **Include your identity.** On the inside cover, write your name, address, and phone number in case you happen to lose it.

- **Keep it in a safe place.** If you don't want others reading your journal, that is.

Because you probably won't have constant computer access, don't even attempt to keep a journal electronically. It just isn't practical to travel with either.

A journal made of acid-free paper lasts longer.

Using your journal to chronicle your travels

One reason I'm grateful that I kept my study abroad journal is that it helps me remember all the places I traveled. Whenever you do an extensive amount of traveling during weekends and breaks from school, you'll want to remember everything you did and saw when you get home. You can also use your journal to help you remember what's in all the photos you take.

Record all your exotic destinations and describe interesting people, adventures, and mishaps you encounter in your travel journal. I guarantee you'll notice new aspects of your personality when traveling. You may recognize your fun or free-spirited self or discover an adventuresome and mischievous side.

Travel journals are also a great place for jotting down itineraries, intentions, and expectations. Writing entries the night before you depart on a trip can express your hopes and desires: "I hope for a gorgeous weekend in the west of Ireland with no rain," or "I plan to see all the art I studied in Art 101 during my three week tour of Europe's museums." Try writing down a list of ten places and things you want to do on your trip. Your travel journal is also great for:

- Jotting down suggested destinations you may hear about during your travels so you can remember them when planning a future trip.

- Noting any apprehensions you may be working through. (My friends and I are backpacking for two weeks, but we haven't made a single hostel reservation!)

- Venting some of the stress of your travels. If you don't manage stress while traveling, you may feel pretty miserable. When you happen to miss a connecting flight and lose a whole day of planned travel as a result, write about it and what you've learned from the situation. How would you do it differently next time?

- Pouring out your thoughts and frustrations. Your journal is a better source for this than a traveling companion with whom you must get along for a number of days or weeks.

You can bring your travels to life in a myriad of ways by including:

- Overviews/thumbnail sketches of your current location

- Dates, times, and weather observations

- Where you're staying

- With whom you're traveling

✔ The names of other interesting travelers or locals you meet

✔ Observations about local cultures or languages

✔ Things you like or dislike about your current location

✔ What you ate and where

✔ Attractions, sights, and museums you saw

✔ Souvenirs you purchased

✔ Cool pictures you took

✔ Interesting things you discover

✔ Favorite works of art you saw

✔ Sketches (if you're artistic) of neat places, people, or things

Providing endless details about what you saw, felt, smelled, or touched can help you remember later.

When your destination is someplace you've already visited, you can note what you remember about it and how it's changed or stayed the same.

Journaling 101

Many options for journal writing exist. What you write in your journal depends largely on what study abroad memories you're trying to capture. Journals aren't only for writing. Feel free to paste drawings, pictures, post-cards, poems, quotes, or newspaper/magazine clippings in your journal. I often printed out e-mails from friends at home and glued them into my journal (good for those times when you feel homesick).

Your study abroad life may be a little hectic depending on where you're living, so you may want to think about what type of atmosphere is most conducive for your writing. Do you need the peace and quiet of your room? Do you need music, candles, or tea and cookies to focus? Maybe you'd prefer to take your journal with you to a coffee shop or nearby park. Generally, you need a place where you can remain undisturbed until you're finished writing.

Notice things about your new home that make you happy and write them down. You can look at the list when you start to feel frustrated with your abroad location, and it helps you remember the positives. Or you can refer to it when you're struggling with the adjustment back home.

Look for beauty, tastes, and sounds that you can't find at home or any-where but where you are right now (for example, the taste of a perfectly poured Guiness, how Venice sounds at night, and so on). Make a note of them. You can also compare and contrast different aspects of places, things, and situations.

Try titling your entries. Simple titles work, such as "Weekend in London". It may make it easier to find certain entries as you're paging back through them at some point.

Lists are a quick and fun way to record your experiences! Try ideas such as "Top ten things I like about being abroad," "Top five things I miss about home," or "Favorite places that I've visited."

What you don't need to worry about when writing in your journal is

- **Adhering to a strict journal-writing schedule.** You don't have to write every day. Write when you have something to say or report or have feelings to express. Whenever you feel inspired. This shouldn't feel like homework.

- **Making sure your grammar is precise.** You don't even have to write in full sentences. Write in fragments. Practice writing in a stream of consciousness, writing down whatever pops into your head.

- **Being overly dramatic.** Exaggerate if you feel like it. Use humor. Keep track of funny things people say.

- **Making mistakes in your journal.** You don't have to erase things or use correction fluid; just cross out what you don't like and move on.

Creating a post-abroad journal

You can also keep a journal of your experiences and feelings upon your return to the U.S. Doing so is a good way to reflect on your experiences abroad. Try asking yourself any of the following questions:

- What are the three most important things I learned about myself? About my host culture?

- If a student were to ask me for advice about living in my host country, what would I say? How did I acquire all this wisdom? (Through trial and error? Just by living there? Did someone else give me a valuable piece of information along the way?)

- How do I view the U.S.? What do I like or dislike about it?

- How do I describe the world I'm living in now? How does it differ from the world I just left?

- How can I apply what I discovered while I was away to my life at home?

- What are my resources? Who will listen to my stories and look at all my photo albums?

- Do I want to get more involved in international activities on campus?

Photography

Taking pictures of people, places, and things that you find interesting, unusual, thought provoking, or simply striking is an important way of documenting and remembering your time abroad.

You're more likely to flip through a photo album than reread every page of your journal when you return home. You're also more likely to want to share your photos with other people than you are your journal. Showing people photos is a great way of narrating your experience.

Photography 101

You don't have to be Ansel Adams to chronicle your experiences abroad with a camera. If you're concerned about taking exquisite photos or want to develop a hobby as a photographer while you're abroad, try taking a photography course the semester before you go.

Take your camera's instruction manual with you in case of technical difficulty. Manuals often provide helpful photography tips, too.

Keeping a journal to perfection

Try some of the common journal techniques in the list that follows. These are merely suggestions, and they may or may not work for you. Don't feel as though you need to subscribe to any particular journal-keeping method. You can use all, none, or some of these. The choice is yours.

✔ **Topic Method:** Choose something you did or saw (maybe even discovered in class?) and just write about it for ten minutes or until you've reflected on everything you wanted to write about.

✔ **Flow Chart Method:** Pick a shape and draw it in the middle of your journal page. Write your main subject within that shape. From that shape, you can branch off into other shapes that contain thoughts related to your main idea. This technique is good for organizing your thoughts and thinking about related ideas.

✔ **Idea Box Method:** At a loss for what to write? Draw a small box on a journal page

and then fill it up with thought-provoking topics you pick up from magazines, newspapers, and books you read or movies you see. Even better, keep running lists of topics to think or write about or questions to ponder during those times you have writer's block. For example, ask yourself:

What have I learned today?

What are my current life and personal goals? Have they shifted since I left the U.S. and began living in another culture?

What activities do I most enjoy in my new country? Why?

If I could travel anywhere this weekend, where would I go? Why?

What cultural differences am I struggling with?

What makes me homesick? What makes me feel less homesick?

✔ **List Method:** If you haven't had much time to write and you aren't traveling or exploring much lately, then why not take a moment to make a list of events that occurred in the past week or month, even if they seem mundane. (For example: "I've become a slave to the library because I have a term paper to write; made dinner with flatmates Wednesday night, but it was a disaster, and we ordered pizza; I really like the poetry class I'm taking....")

✔ **Reflective/Descriptive Writing Method:** Step back into a meaningful moment in time within the past day or week and vividly describe and detail your feelings, reactions, and viewpoints about events in your life and the world. (For example: "Feeling adventurous, I decided to skip class for the day and take the train an hour south of the city to go hiking with a few friends. We packed a picnic lunch and got on the 8 a.m. train. We arrived, looked at the mountain and wanted to turn back, but the next train home wasn't for hours, so we decided to take on the challenging climb....")

✔ **Storyboard Method:** This method is ideal for the artistically inclined who like to add pictures or sketches to their journals to relay emotions or events. Be creative. Use colorful pencils. Choose to add some narration, or let the pictures speak for themselves.

✔ **Imagination Method:** This method is great for those stressed out and homesick times when you need to use your imagination to relax. Write about a relaxing place. The more descriptive you are when writing about this place (and the place can be real or fictitious) — how it looks, sounds, feels, and smells — the better. Using this method can serve as a platform to writing short stories, songs, or poems. Another idea is to imagine yourself somewhere back home, in your dorm room, bedroom, or the dining hall with your friends. Write down what it looks like and how it feels to be there.

First rule of photography while abroad: Take pictures of whatever you want! Photography is such an inexpensive way of making memories. So shoot with reckless abandon.

Another basic idea to remember: Photography is an art form, so be creative. Take pictures at different angles. Get on your hands and knees. Lie on the ground. Climb a few feet. Take a picture of a famous statue with you or some friends in front of it making silly faces. Take pictures of strangers whenever it captures the moment (make sure it's okay with them).

You can never take too many candids, especially of the friends you make while abroad. Candids make great memories, and I guarantee that they'll mean more to you than photos of buildings and landscapes. Pack your camera with you wherever you go and not only when you go on trips. Take your camera with you to everyday activities, like meeting in the pub after classes. You remember the times and people better when your photos capture everyday expressions and things you did with your friends.

Take pictures of *postcard sites,* because doing so is cheaper than buying postcards. Don't be afraid to personalize the photo by putting yourself into it or taking it from a different angle. But don't get too caught up in taking pictures of famous buildings and statues. Write down names of the landmarks you take photos of, because after awhile they all start to blend together. At the end of your time abroad, take the time to walk around where you've lived and take pictures of your favorite places — the ones that weren't important to you when you arrived may now be very meaningful. If it's important to you, take a picture, even when the subject of your photo seems ordinary.

See Chapter 17 for more information on the legal issues surrounding photography in some countries.

Take pictures that express the way you feel rather than pictures that are documentary in nature. In short, capture your emotional memories. And remember to take pictures of change. Seasons and landscapes change frequently. Don't forget to take pictures of changes of appearances — especially yours. (My hair color changed a few times while I was abroad.)

Finally, if you have a digital camera, take advantage of technology and send pictures back home to your family and friends via e-mail.

When traveling, you may want to opt for a disposable camera in place of a nice 35mm or digital camera you'd rather not lose or have stolen.

Assembling albums and collages

I returned home with more than 15 rolls of film. One of my first projects (after unpacking) was to meaningfully organize all my photos. Sitting down to more than 200 photos may seem a little daunting, but it is also a fun (though time-consuming) project. Resist the urge to sweep all your developed film into a quasi-neat pile under your bed or into a box at the top of your closet, thinking that you'll deal with it later. Later you'll forget places you went and people's names.

Framing your favorites

Don't leave your favorite photos buried in an album! Frame them so you can look at them every day! You can also enlarge your favorite photos to 5 x 7 or 8 x 10 sizes and put them in larger frames. Making a collage is a way to frame a large number of photos. And you don't have to be an artist. Buy collage frames, or if you're feeling slightly more artistic, just buy an empty 8 x 10 frame and cut and paste your pictures onto a piece of cardboard in any way that suits you. More collages are often better than one, for that matter.

At a minimum, you need to write the where, when, and who on the backs of your photos. These days, most cameras have automatic time stamping, so the question of when a photo was taken may not be an issue for you.

If you're interested in a higher level of organization and preservation, I'd suggest putting your photos into an album. You still want to label the backs of your photos or opt for an album that provides space for writing descriptions on each page, so you can easily reference essential information about your photos. Another option is buying labels to add captions to your pictures.

If you want to create a more extensive or detailed photo journal when you get home, consider listing simple or descriptive phrases to create a simple narrative without worrying about sentence flow.

Remember the Five Ws: Who? What? When? Where? and Why? Who is in the photograph? Who took it? What was happening? What story does the photo show? Where was the photo taken? When was the photo taken? Why was this moment special? The following suggestions may help your photos tell the entire story:

✔ Use adjectives — especially those describing sound, smell, color, and feelings.

✔ Include thoughts that the photograph doesn't necessarily show. How did you feel? What was going on in the world at that time?

✔ Record the circumstances surrounding the photo. If you return to this album 20 years from now, what do you want to remember about this photo? If your children or grandchildren read this album 20 years from now, what do you want them to know?

Chapter 15

Driving on the Wrong Side of the Road and Other Cultural Differences

In This Chapter

▶ Coping with culture shock

▶ Fitting in

▶ Dealing with minority issues

Right now you probably feel so excited about going abroad that you can't imagine being homesick or frustrated with a new culture that is not your own. You may even think about never coming home! However, the reality of the situation is that you are going to a strange place where you may not speak the language or have any friends. You are bound to have minutes, hours, or days where you want to pack up and go home, because, for example, you miss speaking English, your dorm doesn't have an elevator and you have to walk up four flights of stairs with all your groceries, or you can't find chocolate chips anywhere in your new city.

While you may not stay abroad long enough for your new country to feel totally like a second home, you will adjust. At times you may get frustrated and impatient with your new culture, but being aware of the potential for culture shock and having strategies to deal with it are good ways to keep yourself from being swallowed up or completely overwhelmed.

Adjusting to Life in Another Culture

First of all, what is culture? Robert Kohls, who has extensively studied and written about cross-cultural experiences, defines *culture* as the "total way of life of a particular group of people" — everything from the food they eat and the language they speak to their customs and attitudes. For example, jeans, baseball hats, fast food, Coca-Cola, and MTV are all considered part and parcel of culture here in the U.S.

Taking stock of what's familiar: American culture

When preparing to live in a different culture, you need to think about your own culture, recognize the American values you subscribe to, and develop an awareness of the cultural values you may be taking abroad with you. The following list presents 13 common cultural values that Kohls (the guy I just mentioned) has identified as being uniquely American. See whether you recognize any of these in yourself; while Americans see these values as positive, you may end up in a culture that interprets these values as negative.

- **Personal control over the environment:** The future is not up to Fate. Each person is the captain of his or her own destiny. One must take the initiative to make improvements in his or her own environment. Man can control Nature.

- **Change:** Change is positive; it means development, progress, and improvement. (Other societies value stability, continuity, tradition, and a rich and ancient heritage.)

- **Time and its control:** Time is valuable. Time is money; money is time. Americans are obsessed with being on time and doing things on time; time must be used wisely. Some foreigners think we are controlled by our wristwatches.

- **Equality/egalitarianism:** Equality is a cherished American value. It is a civic and social goal. All people have been "created equal" and should have an equal opportunity to succeed in life. Rank, status, and class mean very little; everyone should be treated in the same manner.

- **Individualism and privacy:** Everyone is unique. The word *privacy* doesn't even exist in many languages or has a negative connotation, suggesting loneliness or isolation from the group. Privacy, or having some "me-time," is necessary and desirable in the U.S.

- **Self-help:** Americans take doing things for oneself very seriously. The self-made man or woman is an American ideal.

- ✔ **Competition and free enterprise:** Competition brings out the best in us. Because Americans value competition, they devised an economic system to go with it — free enterprise.

- ✔ **Future orientation:** Americans always look toward the future and place less value on the past. Traditionally, Americans have hoped that the future would bring even greater happiness, and thus direct all energy toward realizing a better future. The present is just a stepping stone to a better future.

- ✔ **Action/work orientation:** "Don't just stand there; do something!" Action is superior to inaction. We think that it is a shame to waste time or to sit around doing nothing. Hence the workaholic culture that is prevalent here.

- ✔ **Informality:** Americans are one of the most informal and casual peoples in the world. Casual attitudes prevail in the way we greet people and dress for work.

- ✔ **Directness, openness, and honesty:** Americans believe honesty is the best policy, whether delivering good news or bad news. We tend to be blunt and "not beat around the bush."

- ✔ **Practicality and efficiency:** In making decisions, Americans tend to err on the realistic side, giving practical concerns the highest priority. We try not to be overly emotional, subjective, and sentimental. Rational, objective assessment or judging a situation on its own merits is preferred.

- ✔ **Materialism/acquisitiveness:** By most standards, Americans are materialistic. We collect more material objects than most people would ever dream of owning. We value innovation and newness, always wanting to have the latest cutting-edge gadgets.

Given these American cultural characteristics, you can probably understand why other cultures stereotype us as outgoing, friendly, or informal; obsessed with hard work; always in a hurry; lacking class consciousness or disrespectful of authority; and wealthy, extravagant, or wasteful. You may view some of these characteristics as positive or as negative, unfair, and misleading.

You know that every American, possibly yourself included, does not fit the previous description. The most important thing you can do while abroad is avoid reinforcing negative stereotypes with your behavior. Make sure unjustified American stereotypes can't be applied to you!

Confronting the unfamiliar: Culture shock

Moving to another country can often be traumatic and full of the unexpected. You most likely will feel overwhelmed, particularly if this is the first time you've traveled or lived outside the U.S. The rules change when you go abroad, and you need to realize that you have arrived in an environment where many of your assumptions about life no longer apply. You have suddenly been cut off from all your familiar cultural cues and patterns.

In your new country, you may encounter difficulties with language, housing, money, transportation, food, or health. You may notice yourself growing increasingly frustrated with riding on a confusing public transportation system that is never on time, chatting with people who don't completely understand every word you say, or going to restaurants with menus you can barely read. You feel like an outsider, and you may even feel slightly depressed. This psychological disorientation is commonly referred to as *culture shock* and it is an inevitable part of studying abroad.

Culture shock cycles through feelings of disorientation and accommodation. Your feelings may run the gamut from "I hate this place" to "I never want to leave." At the beginning of your stay abroad, you may often feel uneasy because you cannot predict what's going to happen in a social situation — like when you extend your hand in greeting and the person grabs you and kisses you three times instead.

You can't prepare for culture shock in any way — sorry — you just have to deal with it as it arises. You may experience culture shock right after you arrive. Or you could wake up one morning six months later and suddenly think, "Get me out of here now!" The best thing you can do is be flexible. Roll with the punches! Don't just be prepared to learn what you don't know, but to unlearn a few things, too. Also, be sure to check out the section later in this chapter on how to cope with culture shock.

The American way is not the only way. Your view of the world and yourself is about to change. You may begin to appreciate your own country more or you may start to become critical of American ways.

Four phases of cultural adjustment

Adjusting to another culture takes time. While living abroad, you go through a constant cycle of being dumbfounded by your new surroundings and then accepting and adjusting to them. Be aware that you may cycle through four distinct phases of cultural adjustment during your time abroad.

Stage 1: Initial euphoria and excitement

This first stage of euphoria is also referred to as the *honeymoon stage*. Everything is new and exciting; new sights, sounds, and smells preoccupy you. You travel around the town or city you're staying in to see all the sights. You find your new culture and friends intriguing. The similarities between this culture and your own seem very interesting. You wake up each day wanting to learn and feeling like you can handle absolutely anything. You don't think you'll have any problems adjusting.

Stage 2: Culture shock! Irritation and/or hostility

The euphoria and novelty of your study abroad situation has worn off. You become hyperaware of the differences between the new culture and your home culture. What you initially considered cool and exciting is now boring, annoying, or inconvenient. In fact, you may become outright irritated or hostile toward your host culture. And at this stage, small problems quickly grow into major catastrophes!

Don't panic or book a ticket home yet! This is a normal part of the integration process that everyone goes through when they go to a new culture. Recognize that any of the following are symptoms of cultural stress:

✔ Feelings of anger, frustration, fatigue, irritableness, or depression.

✔ Feelings of rejection, isolation, or loneliness.

✔ Hostility or a superior attitude toward host nationals. "Why are they so weird?" You complain about and criticize everything.

✔ Major concern over small health problems.

✔ Frequent eating/drinking (especially alcohol).

✔ Loss of appetite or concentration. You can't get any work done.

✔ Homesickness. Craving things from home. Strong desire to hang out exclusively with Americans or in American places. Huge phone bills home.

Stage 2 eventually goes away, and you learn to cope, progressing to Stage 3. (Make sure to read the section "Coping with culture shock" for ways to cope with Stage 2.)

Stage 3: Gradual adjustment

Gradually, your sense of humor returns and you gain perspective on your experience. Things begin to seem less forbidding and more comfortable. You adapt to your new surroundings and are familiar with your new culture's logic, values, and social cues. You no longer feel isolated and begin to enjoy parts of your new culture. You still occasionally experience highs and lows as you adjust.

Stage 4: Adaptation

Getting to the adaptation stage is the ultimate goal of studying abroad (although it may be difficult to achieve in only one semester), and when you do, it makes working through the culture shock worth it. The foreign country you live in now feels like home. You have no problems living and working to your full potential. You're confident, able to communicate, and enjoy your experience. In fact, you may not fully realize how well you've adapted until you head home and encounter reverse culture shock, which I discuss in Chapter 20.

Coping with culture shock

There is no sure-fire way to deal with and alleviate culture shock. But recognizing that, as a foreigner in a new country, you are particularly vulnerable to it is a good place to start from. Culture shock is a learning experience and leads to broader perspectives, deeper insights, more tolerance, and appreciation of both your home culture and your new culture.

Try the following strategies for coping with culture shock:

✔ **Expect the unexpected:** Always expect change, differences, ambiguity, mini-crises, and inconveniences (long commutes and lost luggage) — and don't panic!

✔ **Arm yourself with knowledge:** Be able to recognize culture shock and learn as much as possible about your host country both before and during your stay. Take pre-departure and orientation materials seriously. Don't ignore this advice!

✔ **Be persistent with language skills:** Speak as much as possible in your new home and take the initiative to study vocabulary and grammar in your free time.

✔ **Don't marginalize your host culture:** Joking about what you may perceive as stupid or backward about the host nationals is tempting when you're feeling frustrated, but avoid this negative behavior. Remember the problem isn't with "them," but with you.

✔ **Don't spend all your time with Americans:** This is a good way to get stuck in Stage 2: Irritability/Hostility. You feed off their negative perspectives. The more host national friends you make, the more comfortable you begin to feel in your new home.

✔ **Laugh at yourself:** Maintain a healthy sense of humor at all times.

✔ **Keep an open mind:** Remind yourself why you went abroad.

✔ **Stay healthy:** Get enough sleep, eat good food, and try to exercise regularly.

✔ **Keep busy:** Don't sit around being negative or critical — go out and do something to experience the culture.

✔ **Pursue your interests, hobbies, or favorite sports abroad:** Joining a group, club, or sports team at your host university allows you to maintain a familiar interest while meeting host country students at the same time.

✔ **Don't isolate yourself:** If you're feeling out of sorts, seek out other people. Talk to other members of your program who may be feeling the same way or visit your program director.

> ✔ **Keep in touch with family and friends at home:** Send some e-mails or snail mail letters and use the telephone. Interacting with home may help you feel less far away.

> ✔ **Remember basic stress management strategies:** How do you cope with stress at home? Do you run? Spend time with friends? Read a book? Try using one of your stress-reducing strategies to deal with culture shock.

Common panic points

Abroad students can often "make mountains out of molehills" (no, not me!) and begin to panic when events or situations fall short of expectations. While being in a foreign place and having to deal with the unexpected or changing plans is unsettling, it is part of the learning experience. If something doesn't turn out the way a returned study abroad student told you it would or the way the program guide described it, adjust to what your current situation is and ask questions as needed. Resist frustration and generalizing about your new home and host nationals.

Common things abroad students panic about include the following:

✔ Your flights were delayed and you lost your luggage.

✔ No e-mail or phone connection in your room.

✔ Your housing is a big disappointment. You have a long commute to school and are always running into class at the last possible second. Your dorm seems a little on the dirty side. Your bed is uncomfortable.

✔ You thought you'd have plenty of time to travel and explore, but you're swamped with schoolwork.

✔ You don't know what schoolwork you're supposed to be doing. There's no syllabus, only a reading list of 200 suggested books.

✔ No one understands you when you speak the native language.

✔ Speed and efficiency seem to be unheard of: It takes forever to register for classes, get access to computer labs or libraries, obtain a student I.D., or make an appointment at the student health center.

Knowing that these panic triggers, along with many I haven't listed here, are out there may help a little bit. Know that whatever you're feeling panicked about has probably happened before to another study abroad student. A solution is out there, and it may be as simple as taking a deep breath and learning to accept the situation for what it is. Also, don't be afraid to ask for help, advice, or clarification from natives, professors, the international students office, or your home university study abroad office.

When in Rome, Do as the Romans Do

Social customs vary from culture to culture, so it's virtually impossible for me to construct a list of social guidelines that works all over the globe. You can figure what behavior is and isn't appropriate in your new home by observing local students in your dorm, classes, or other places on campus. If you live with a host family, notice how they dress and interact with one other.

You don't need to change your entire personality and identity to fit in while abroad. In general, if you are friendly, respectful, and courteous, you'll do just fine. Remember you're a sort of guest in your host country, so you should get by if you act as though you're a guest in someone else's home. Host nationals also realize that you're an outsider and grant you some leniency regarding things you don't readily understand.

It's fine to politely ask questions about local customs and ways of behaving. Most people appreciate that you are trying to learn about their culture and lifestyle and are willing to help you adjust.

Talk the talk

You may be afraid to use the native language because you're not completely comfortable with it; maybe you hesitate when putting together sentences, stumble using the correct tense, or often pause to determine the correct vocabulary. Most people are flattered by your attempts to use their native language and may even help you out by correcting your sentences!

Try to avoid using slang expressions you learned before your arrival because slang expressions are unique to a particular culture. You may have learned Spanish that is frequently used in Mexico, but you are now studying in Spain, so the idiomatic expressions you know could be meaningless or inappropriate in Spain. Any slang expressions that you learn in your host country should be okay. Also, know whether you should use the "familiar" or "formal" forms of address. If you are uncertain, err on the side of being too formal.

In case your foreign language teacher has never mentioned this, do not, under any circumstances, attempt to translate American idiomatic expressions into the native language. Most likely the idiom will sound like complete nonsense when translated, but even worse, it could turn into an inappropriate or offensive comment.

Avoid personal questions and politics

Americans have a fairly open and sharing culture. It is not difficult or out of the ordinary for us to talk about ourselves. However, in other countries, talking about oneself may be considered rude, as could asking personal questions. It is best to let your host lead the conversation when engaging in "small talk." On the other hand, don't be offended if natives from your host country ask questions that are considered rude or strange in the U.S. You may be asked how much money your father makes, which president you voted for in the last election, whether you own a gun, or how much your parents paid for their house. These kinds of questions are considered normal in some cultures.

You may be surprised at how well-educated your abroad counterparts are in politics and international relations (some pay more attention to American politics and policy than Americans do!). As the token American in the crowd, you may be unknowingly roped into a political debate. Don't feel as though you need to falsify your own political views, but be aware of your audience — you may want to tone down your statements or make sure you can rationally defend what you say. Try to avoid offending people as much as possible, if only so that you don't get classified as an arrogant American who thinks everyone must agree with the United States or with you personally.

Mind your Ps and Qs

Always strive to be as polite as possible. That way, no one can ever fault you for not being polite enough. Remember many cultures have more formal social customs than the U.S. does, so spend more time on social niceties than you may at home. For example, be ready to offer a formal word of greeting to whomever you meet on campus, on the street, or in stores. Familiarize yourself with the appropriate expressions of gratitude in response to hospitality.

Be wary of making jokes

Ever seen the late night British comedies on PBS and wondered at the rather dry, witty British humor? Every country has a different sense of humor, and it is often quite different from the type of joking around Americans are used to. In fact, many will not appreciate our jokes. Some cultures are quite literal and frequently misconstrue comments that we intend as humorous.

Go easy with the snapshots

You are going to want to document your time abroad with a camera. But be careful about including random people on the street or who just happen to be in front of a monument or building in your photos. The people you snap pictures of are human beings and not creatures in a zoo! Use tact and discretion in photographing strangers; it is always a good idea to politely ask permission before taking someone's picture.

Negotiate market prices effectively

In some cultures, haggling over price is expected in the marketplace. Figure out in which circumstances bargaining is appropriate so you don't run the risk of insulting merchants or appearing ignorant. If you're unsure whether bargaining is appropriate in a given situation, you can let the merchant know you like a particular item but that it is a bit outside of your price range. If the merchant wants to bargain with you, this gives him or her the opportunity to offer you the item at a lower price; if the merchant is not of the bargaining sort, then you can politely end the conversation and move on.

Respect personal space

Every culture has a different perception of personal space: how far away to stand or sit when conversing and how to shake hands or wave goodbye. Physical contact may not be especially appreciated or understood by someone unfamiliar with the American culture; a cheerful pat on the back or a hug may be embarrassing or uncomfortable in certain cultures. Use restraint until you learn what level of familiarity you should adopt. On the other hand, your host culture may have very little personal space — women — and even men — may walk arm in arm with each other or kiss each other in greeting. You don't need to initiate greetings this way if this may make you uncomfortable — but do try not to shy away when a local grabs your arm or kisses you on the cheek. They may not understand your reservation.

Managing Minority Issues

Attitudes toward gender, race, ethnicity, and sexual orientation vary from culture to culture. Inevitably you will encounter or observe ways your host country handles diversity issues that may slightly or dramatically diverge from the way issues are handled and viewed in the U.S. You may find your new culture's opinion of particular minority groups disturbing or upsetting. The best thing to do in this case is to remind yourself that this is a learning experience. You're not only learning about another culture, but you're probably noticing new things about your own cultural identity by comparison.

When planning to go abroad, take the time to consider your own cultural identity and values in terms of gender, ethnicity, and sexual orientation and what potential differences may arise between your cultural values and views and those of your host country. Perhaps you will fit more easily into a cultural group while abroad than you do at home. As much as possible, refrain from setting unrealistic expectations about how you will be perceived by the host culture. Realistically, living abroad involves challenges unique to particular minority groups.

Gender roles: Back to the Dark Ages?

Coming from a country where so much attention and effort has been given to the equality of the sexes and women shattering the glass ceiling, you may find your host country's treatment or view of women disappointing or disturbing. Or perhaps you will be surprised that your host country is more advanced than the U.S. in the way it treats women. Growing up in the U.S. has given you a perspective of gender roles that may differ from your host country's expectations of male and female roles. Realize that host nationals view you in light of the gender constructs that prevail in the host culture. This can occasionally make you feel uncomfortable, particularly during the beginning of your stay.

Before departing, try to understand the gender roles in the culture to which you are traveling. Remember that what may be appropriate and friendly behavior in the U.S. could bring you unwanted attention in your new country.

Check out Chapter 17 for safety tips for women.

Perceptions of American women

The American pop culture that manages to find its way to other countries hasn't exactly helped the image of the American woman (think Baywatch, Jerry Springer, and Brittany Spears). In fact, TV, movies, and advertising have created a distorted stereotype of the cheap and easy American woman. Furthermore, in some places throughout the world, American women maintain a lifestyle that sharply contrasts with traditional behavior for women.

With these things in mind, realize that simple things, such as a smile, a hairstyle, or the way you carry yourself or make eye contact, can have different interpretations abroad than they do at home. Body language reflects cultural differences: U.S. students often report that people do not understand that their familiar way with strangers is a gesture of friendship.

Behave conservatively until you figure out the most appropriate way to act in your new home. Ask for advice from a local friend. Respecting the social rules helps your relationships with host nationals.

Check out the following resources for additional information on women travelers:

- *Half the Earth: Women's Experiences of Travel Worldwide,* edited by Miranda Davies et. al., published in U.S.A. by Routledge and Kegan Paul.

- *Women Travel: Adventures, Advice and Experience,* edited by Natania Jansz and Miranda Davies, published by Prentice Hall, New York (1992).

- *A Journey of One's Own: Uncommon Advice for the Independent Woman Traveler,* by Thelia Zepatos, published by The Eighth Mountain Press, Portland (1992).

- www.journeywoman.com: Online travel magazine for women.

Harassment happens: What you can do

You probably rarely experience men whistling or hooting at women (unless the guys are drunk). However, believe it or not, this type of behavior is common in other cultures. While abroad, you may notice men staring at you or making comments as you walk down the street. Ignore it as best you can. This behavior isn't necessarily culturally acceptable, but you're getting this attention because you're foreign.

If you encounter uncomfortable situations and behaviors, try using one of the following tactics:

- Gain control of the conversation. You start asking the questions. Initiate rather than react. Change the subject to something neutral, like literature or history. Maintain a gracious sense of humor.

- Be direct and specific. Tell the other person that you want him or her to stop whatever is making you uncomfortable. Stay calm, serious, and use body language that coincides with your words. Don't giggle, smile, or apologize! This could undermine your message.

Cultural differences never excuse verbal or physical abuse. If you find yourself in such a situation, try to remove yourself from it as quickly as possible, confront the person, or ask others (your program director, other women, or local authorities) for help.

Playing the dating game

If you want to date, have fun, but first find out the "dating rules" from a local friend. Always keep in mind the differences between your culture and your host culture; therefore, you should be more cautious about dating than you are in the U.S. In some cultures, the American notion of casually dating several people at once is unheard of. In some places, if you date, you are in a relationship; thus, dating two people at once is cheating!

Americans are much more accustomed to having close friends of the opposite sex than other cultures are. For example, American women used to having male friends may not realize that just being seen with a man, talking with a man, or going out with a man has a different "meaning" than intended. Always ask yourself, what do my actions mean in the culture I am in? Is that what I intend? If not, change your behavior so that you don't send unintended messages.

Keeping your guard up

You want to have fun and experience life while abroad, but be sure to understand and respect the inherent differences between your culture and theirs. Check out the following dos and don'ts.

To ensure a smooth and safe experience,

- Do respect the culture, whether you agree or disagree — you are not there to change it or start a feminist movement; you are there to learn about the culture.

- Do try to integrate into the community. This includes making friends with local women, interacting with men according to the local customs, and dressing and acting according to local customs.

- Do stay in control of yourself and situations at all times; you need your senses to protect you, so stay sober and alert.

- Do practice the buddy system, particularly in social situations. Have at least one other person whom you trust with you to help you in problematic situations (such as someone spiking your drink). Traveling in groups is always a safe idea.

- Do develop an awareness of any potential safety issues when you go somewhere for the first time.

- Do say "no" to any invitation you don't want.

- Do trust your gut: Pay attention to that little voice in your head that says, "Something isn't right," and remove yourself from the situation. If you're offered a ride and you feel some anxiety, decline the offer. If you're in a place that makes you nervous, leave. If your instincts send you warning signals, listen to them.

To avoid any possible mishap,

- Don't give your address to someone you don't trust.

- Don't go to a secluded area (or even be alone in your room) with a man whom you don't know well.

- Don't make judgments about your safety based on another person's appearance or financial status. Remember that looks can be deceiving!

✔ Don't behave like you do in the U.S. Experience a different way of life, assimilate into your new home, and join the community.

✔ Don't think that you are giving up yourself by conforming to local customs. Instead, realize that you are expanding your horizons. You may appreciate the choices you have as an American female when you return home!

Sexual orientation

Attitudes and tolerance toward gay, lesbian, bisexual, and transgender (GLBT) students vary from country to country as they do within the U.S. While some countries may afford GLBT students more privileges and legal protections than the U.S. does, other countries are less accepting and may pose greater challenges than you experience at home.

Realize that homosexuality may have a different definition in your host country than it does at home. Cultures vary in terms of what they consider appropriate behavior and how they understand sexual identity. In spite of a global trend in support of GLBT rights that has brought the issue of homosexuality to the public's attention in many countries, GLBT people are still met with harassment and violence in some places. Basically, the level of acceptance varies based on the set of social norms in each country, city, or neighborhood.

While U.S. study abroad offices/programs are welcoming and inclusive of GLBT perspectives, in-country staff members and faculty may be part of a different cultural climate. Depending on how you're received by the program office abroad, you may need to look outside your program for support or GLBT community information.

In order to help ease transitions both before you go abroad and before you return home, I provide the following tips to get you started.

Before you go

Before you go, you need to do two things: reflect and learn.

Think about how your identity as a GLBT person may affect your study abroad experience. How will you choose to act on your GLBT identity while abroad? Does your right to be GLBT in the U.S. conflict with your destination's religious or cultural values and traditions?

If you are "out" at home, you are leaving a support system of friends and family; some GLBT students have described being abroad as a second coming out. You may need to reestablish your identity overseas. See whether you can find information on the support systems (meeting places and organizations) available in your host country before you go abroad. When possible, talk with other people who have gone abroad as GLBT students, especially if they studied in your host country. When you get settled in your new home, seek out other GLBT students from the host country who can act as a resource for you.

Find out about laws related to sexuality in your host country. Homosexuality is still illegal in some countries and may even carry consequences as serious as the death penalty. For safety's sake, you may need you to hide your sexual identity. Are you willing to hide your sexual orientation? If not, you may want to reconsider where you study. Research the country's laws on age of consent and traveling with print or other materials on sexual orientation.

The legal system in your host country may not protect victims when issues of sexual orientation or other behavior are involved.

GLBT students need to gather as much information as possible regarding the social climate and behavioral norms in the host country. As I mention in the section on gender, behavioral signals that mean one thing in the U.S. may mean something different in your new home. For example, in the Middle East, hand-holding among males is a custom of special friendship and respect and does not imply homosexuality.

Things such as eye contact, a smile, or a touch may be grossly misinterpreted in a foreign culture, and depending on the situation, the consequences can be serious. Physical harassment, assault, and rape are very real issues that everyone needs to consider when interacting in foreign cultures, because of the distinct possibility that behavior will be misunderstood.

Before coming home

If you choose to come out while abroad, this is bound to affect your return to your life in the U.S. Be aware before you come back home of the ways you may have changed. Reintegrating yourself into friend and family relationships may be difficult and you may need to seek out a supportive community. You may have to come out all over again when you return home. Keep in mind that family and friends may dismiss your sexual orientation as a temporary change because of your time abroad, instead of acknowledging that this is part of your identity. Check out Chapter 20 later in this book about reentry shock.

For more information on GLBT issues around the globe, check out www.indiana.edu/~overseas/lesbigay/index.html for an extensive bibliography, GLBT organization list, and links to GLBT Web sites. Other good resources that provide sections on issues of interest to GLBT travelers include Let's Go and The Real World Travel Guides.

Race and ethnicity

Definitions of race and ethnicity vary from culture to culture. Undeniably, racism exists abroad, just as it does at home. You may experience different obstacles or privileges because of your race or ethnicity than you do at home. Or you may suddenly find yourself in a culture where you're no longer part of a minority group, but instead belong to the majority. Another possibility is that people from your host country will not think you are American until you tell them — and this can be an advantage or a disadvantage, depending on how you look at it. African Americans studying in South America are often assumed to be from Brazil or Cuba, and Asian Americans are often assumed to be from the country where their parents or grandparents are from.

In the past, myths about how minority students are treated abroad have prevented members of different ethnic groups from venturing overseas. However, a recent push among U.S. colleges is encouraging minority students to study abroad. Study abroad programs here in the U.S. are striving to be more reflective of the diversity in this country and are making an extra effort to attract various ethnic groups. As a result, the number of minority students spending a semester or year away from home is quickly increasing.

Information on student abroad experiences relating to diversity is far from abundant, although many universities are collecting data on this issue. In the meantime, if you're trying to evaluate a potential study abroad opportunity, pursue the usual channels for information: program reviews in the study abroad office, returned students, as well as members of your ethnic group at your home university.

Additionally, if your home university has advisers for various ethnic groups, they may have heard of good study abroad programs for minorities. Another resource is academic departments on campus, such as the African studies department and the Chinese, Japanese, or Spanish departments. Ask potential study abroad programs if they have had minority students study on their program. If so, is it possible for you to get in touch with them? Furthermore, what kinds of support does your program offer to minority students studying abroad?

Seek out your ethnic community in your host country. They can provide invaluable support, help you find your way around, and explain social/cultural norms.

Remember that you are studying abroad to understand a new culture, not change it! Do not expect to be able to fight racism all by yourself and alter what could be deeply entrenched racial prejudices in your host country.

Some helpful resources include

- *Diversity Issues in Study Abroad.* A compilation of Brown University student comments from countries around the world. Web site www.brown.edu/Administration/OIP/files/links/.

- *Go Girl! The Black Woman's Guide to Travel and Adventure* by Lee Elaine (editor), published by Eighth Mountain Press.

- *The Chronicle of Higher Education* and *Transitions Abroad* often publish articles regarding minority students and study abroad. "Top Ten Reasons for African American Students to Go Abroad," *Transitions*, July/August 1998. "Students of Color Abroad," *Transitions*, July/August 1995.

- "The Participation of Historically Underrepresented Students in Study Abroad Programs: An Assessment of Interest and Perception of Barriers" by A. Carroll. (Master's thesis, Colorado State University, 1996.)

- "Asian American Students: Study Abroad Participation, Perspectives and Experiences" by Thuy Doan. (Master's thesis, University of Minnesota, 2002.)

Dealing with disabilities

If you think that your disability prevents you from spending a semester or a year abroad — think again! Increasing numbers of students with disabilities are embarking on study abroad adventures as part of their college experiences.

Good places to seek information regarding study abroad for students with disabilities include your home university's Disabled Student Services office as well as Mobility International USA (MIUSA). MIUSA works to help people with disabilities pursue opportunities in international exchange and development programs. Check out their Web site www.miusa.org, which is loaded with resources for students with disabilities, including links to a network that connects students interested in study abroad with returned students.

Realize that the Americans with Disabilities Act (ADA) does not apply overseas, although some countries may have similar legislation. Consult your study abroad program or study abroad director at your home university to find information about how your host country views people with disabilities.

Here are some suggestions for students with disabilities preparing to study abroad. The list is not all-inclusive, and you may need to consider other issues based on your individual disability, preferences, or host country.

Before leaving the U.S., notify your host university or study abroad program of any modifications you need for housing, note taking in class, mobility around campus, and so on.

✔ If you use a wheelchair, bring extra tire tubes and repair tools and consider using tubeless tires (for more information, contact a local medical supply or bike repair shop).

✔ If you usually use an electric wheelchair, you may want to bring a manual wheelchair for use in some types of terrain or if you won't be able to regularly recharge the electric one. Or consider bringing a portable motor that can be easily installed on a manual wheelchair.

✔ Be sure to bring the necessary electrical adapters and converters to recharge equipment batteries.

✔ Bring extra prosthetics, braces, or any other adaptive equipment you cannot live without.

✔ If you usually use crutches, you may want to bring a manual chair for days when you're out and about for extended periods of time.

✔ Try to predict, as much as possible, difficult access situations prior to departure so you have time to create strategies or backup plans for dealing with them.

✔ If you use a hearing aid, bring plenty of extra batteries.

✔ If you are deaf, you may want to make a habit of carrying a notepad and pencil with you at all times for ease of communication.

✔ If you use a guide dog, check with your host country about quarantine and other regulations for bringing a pet into the country.

✔ Learn key phrases in the host country language so you can communicate important needs regarding medication, equipment, or accessibility issues.

✔ If you think you may need medical help while abroad, know how to contact appropriate professionals who speak a language you know (or consider using a translator).

✔ Identify and contact disability-related organizations in your host country prior to departing or soon after you arrive (MIUSA/NCDE may be able to help you locate this information).

✔ Carry a letter from your primary care physician explaining your current medical condition, including what medications you take, the correct dosage, and why you take them.

✔ Secure travel and medical insurance that covers preexisting conditions.

✔ Be aware of your bathroom needs — possibly bring a change of clothing in your daily pack for emergencies.

✔ Talk with returnees (whether they're disabled or not) from your host country/program to get information on disability access and attitudes.

> ✔ Bring egg crate pads for sitting or sleeping if you are concerned about pressure sores (These will come in handy on long plane, train, or bus rides).
>
> ✔ If you are blind, have someone orient you to your new environment, alerting you to dangers such as large potholes or manhole covers missing in streets.

Many U.S. college students have learning disabilities, including dyslexia and Attention Deficit Disorder (ADD). If you have dyslexia, provide a written diagnosis from a medical professional. If you require modifications such as extended exam periods, be sure to discuss your needs with your study abroad program or university abroad well in advance of your arrival overseas and confirm any arrangements when you begin classes.

Know that many countries and universities overseas are suspicious of learning disabilities, even dyslexia, and many regard ADD as a manufactured "American" disorder. Some universities abroad may be reluctant to make modifications such as extended exam periods. In addition, be aware that Ritalin and other ADD medications are considered controlled substances in many countries, so you will not be permitted to bring more than a month's supply into your host country.

Check out the following resources for additional information on traveling with disabilities:

> ✔ The Americans with Disabilities Act (ADA) at www.ada.gov.
>
> ✔ *Rights and Responsibilities: A Guide to the Americans with Disabilities Act (ADA) for International Organizations and Participants.* Includes information on disability rights law for international exchange advisers. You can find it at www.miusa.org/publications/rr.htm.
>
> ✔ *A World Awaits You (AWAY).* A journal that discusses international exchange for people with disabilities. Highlights personal experiences of people with disabilities who have participated in international exchange programs. To receive a free copy of this journal, send an e-mail to clearinghouse@miusa.org.

Chapter 16

Money Makes the World Go 'Round

*I*n the U.S., students often attend colleges where tuition, miscellaneous fees, and room and board are all included in each semester's bill. A student's out-of-pocket expenses are usually for books and going out with friends. Although the actual cost of tuition is usually lower at non-U.S. schools, many expenses may not be included in the program fee but are unavoidable (like laundry) and are part of living on your own and studying in another country.

For some students, the study abroad experience is the first time they have to carefully manage their finances. The dormitory and dining hall model is pretty much unique to the U.S. In other countries, students pay their rent weekly or monthly and are responsible for feeding themselves. No 24-hour, all-you-can-eat dining halls outside this country. Isn't that shocking?

The Burden of Budgeting

Do yourself a favor, and try to figure out a budget for your semester or year abroad before you leave. If you've never made a budget before, now is a great time to start practicing for what happens when you enter the real world after college graduation.

Budgeting for living in a foreign country can be tricky, primarily because you don't currently live there and you've probably never lived there before. How are you supposed to know what things cost? Well, because prices and exchange rates regularly fluctuate, you will never know exactly what things cost while sitting at your desk trying to figure out a budget for three months from now. But you can estimate.

The best way to collect information on the cost of living in your host country is to use resources you're already familiar with: students who have already spent time in the country you're going to, international students or professors at your home university who are from your host country, the study abroad office, the international student office at your host university, or your program office if you're going with a U.S.-based program. Another place to check is the admissions office at your host university; admissions offices typically keep statistics on cost of living for students.

Always contact the abroad university or program directly for the most up-to-date information on costs. Exchange rates fluctuate, and what is included in the program fee can change from year to year. So the fees listed in last year's catalog or study abroad guide may no longer be accurate.

Determining your expenses

I created a list of expenses that are likely to come up after you decide to study abroad. Using all the resources available to you, see which ones you can collect estimates for to help you make your budget.

Academic fees

The following fees may not be included in what you are charged for tuition.

- ✔ **Administrative fees:** For creating ID cards, administering exams, registering for classes
- ✔ **Books and other supplies:** Goggles for science labs, paints for art classes, photocopies of supplementary readings, and lab fees
- ✔ **Use of facilities:** Including labs, libraries, and gym
- ✔ **Computers:** Use of Internet, charge for a university e-mail account, paper for printing

Room and board

Your living arrangements while studying abroad may vary considerably from what you're used to. Now you may pay one lump sum for room and board per semester and never have to think about these fees until next semester's bill arrives. While you're abroad, you may have a more true-to-life experience in which you need to pay rent on a regular basis, budget for utilities, and prepare your own meals.

- ✔ **Rent:** Do you pay rent weekly or monthly? Some university halls of residence require students to pay rent, just like an apartment. If you're living in university-operated housing, do you have to pay extra to be there during vacations or holidays? Keep in mind that some dormitories abroad charge monthly or semester activity fees. You may also have to pay for rented sheets and towels.

- ✔ **Food:** If you have a meal plan that covers most of your daily meals, then you don't have to worry about food expenses on a regular basis. If you have a meal plan that only covers a few meals a week, or no meal plan at all, what will it cost you to prepare your own meals on a weekly basis? (You won't be able to eat out all the time — it will get too expensive!) Do you have special dietary requirements?

- ✔ **Utilities:** The cost of heat, water, electricity, phone, or cable may not be included in your rent.

- ✔ **Security deposits:** You may have to pay one month's rent as a security deposit that will be put towards you last month's rent or refunded to you when you move out. You may also need to pay key deposits. Ask your study abroad program or host university how they handle these fees; they may be paid on your behalf.

- ✔ **Residence permits:** Do you need a permit to have certain telecommunications equipment in your place of residence? (For instance, telephone, television, or cable modem connection.)

Transportation

While you're abroad, you may have to figure out how you're getting to school each day and budget for trips around your host country or region.

- ✔ **Round-trip transportation from the United States to the host country:** Usually the cost of a round-trip flight, although you may have to take a train or bus from the airport to your final destination.

- ✔ **Commuting costs:** How are you getting to and from school every day? Bus? Train? Walking? Are you going to buy a bicycle to ride to school?

- ✔ **Program-related travel:** Field trips to other cities or museums; if you're on a program sponsored by a U.S. institution, they may plan weekend adventures in nearby towns or cities, the costs of which may not be included in the program fee.

- ✔ **Optional travel:** Are you planning on traveling during vacations, holidays, or on long weekends?

Travel documents

Before you leave, you'll need to invest in several different travel related documents that will get you in and out of your host country.

- ✔ **Passport fee:** If you've never applied for a U.S. passport before, you have to pay a $55 passport fee and a $30 execution fee. If you're renewing a passport, you only have to pay $55, provided that the passport you're replacing

  - Was issued when you were 16 or older

  - Was issued in the last 15 years

  - Is not damaged

  - Is submitted with your application

  If you need to expedite a passport application, you get slapped with a $60 charge.

- ✔ **Visa (if required):** Processing and visa fees vary.

- ✔ **Immunizations (if required):** May be less expensive at college student health centers.

- ✔ **International Student Identity Card:** For current fees, see `www.counciltravel.com/idcards/isic.asp`.

Insurance

You're going to want to protect yourself against situations that may be out of your control, like accidents, theft or illness.

- ✔ **Health insurance:** You don't want to incur expensive medical costs in case of mild or serious illness while abroad. Make sure you take your American health insurance with you or subscribe to a new plan that covers you while abroad. See Chapter 12 for more information on health insurance.

- ✔ **Accident insurance:** Usually paired with health insurance, covers expenses incurred as a result of an injury. Makes allowances for accidental death or dismemberment.

- ✔ **Traveler's insurance:** For lost or stolen personal property.

Personal expenses

Here's where you can cut corners to save money if expenses are starting to add up!

- ✔ **Staying in touch with friends and family:** If you want to stay in touch, you need to pay for postage, phone calls, or Internet café fees.

- ✔ **Gifts and souvenirs:** You don't have to be extravagant; aim for simplicity and cultural relevance. And check out the list of things you can and cannot bring/send home in Chapter 19.

✔ **Admission to cultural sites and events:** You will probably be frequenting museums, theatres, or concerts more often than you do at home because you'll have "once-in-a-lifetime" chances to see certain exhibits or events (such as seeing the Mona Lisa at the Louvre or ballet in Vienna).

✔ **Luggage:** If you don't already own sturdy luggage that easily rolls through an airport, do yourself a favor and invest! Make sure you bring an everyday backpack to use at school. And if you're going to be doing extensive traveling, you may want to invest in a sizable traveling backpack, which is easier to carry around than a suitcase on wheels.

✔ **Clothing:** You'll probably want or need to buy some clothes while you're abroad. You may have to buy clothes that are suitable to the country's climate before you leave or while you are there. Remember to budget money for laundry and dry cleaning.

✔ **Personal care products:** Besides items like toothpaste and soap, you will most likely buy a few electronic items in your host country, like a hairdryer or an alarm clock because electrical standards vary throughout the world. Remember that toiletries such as contact lens care products and name-brand hair care items can be very expensive outside of the U.S. A good rule to follow: If a product is expensive here, it is probably more expensive abroad, so you may want to either bring some extra with you or plan these expenses into your budget.

Budgeting cautiously

When preparing your abroad budget, overestimate rather than underestimate. Think of how excited you'll be if you return with money left over! Or if you can go out to a really nice dinner that last week before you leave or buy the sweater you've had your eye on for a few weeks. But underestimating your budget is only going to cause problems — so don't be stingy here. You don't want to run out of money or have to go without food while you wait for money to be transferred from the States.

Tending to Spend in a New Legal Tender

Studying in another country means that you need to familiarize yourself with an unfamiliar currency. And if you travel to other countries while abroad, you'll probably become familiar with several different currencies. This is part of your experience; try not to be frustrated with the new bills and coins and be patient with yourself as you get adjusted to the new currency.

Many currencies use coins for denominations under $5 and paper money for $5 and higher. While the largest coin generally used in the U.S. is the quarter, the coins you are spending abroad are worth more than that! You may wonder where your money is going if you're always at the ATM. You may be carelessly spending those coins, so pay attention!

Looking before you leap to exchange your money

You can easily find out the latest exchange rates in your abroad destination on the Internet at www.xe.com/ucc or any other currency exchange Web site. Also, exchange rates can be found in major newspapers. Remember that exchange rates change on a daily basis.

Always keep your original exchange receipts. You'll need them to document the fact that U.S. dollars you may want to "buy back" at the end of your stay were yours from the beginning.

If you feel better arriving at your destination with some local currency already in your pocket, you can exchange U.S. dollars for foreign currency before you depart; just find a local bank that provides international services. But make sure to take care of this a week or two in advance of your departure, because sometimes banks need to order the currency you request. This is actually a good alternative to changing money at airport exchange bureaus, where rates may not be as good as at a bank. So for convenience and to save a little money, change enough money to get you through your first few days abroad, but not so much that you're carrying large amounts of cash around!

Another good reason to have some local currency on hand when arriving at your abroad destination is that you may need to travel for many hours by plane or train to get to your destination. You will have to wait to claim your checked luggage. Are you going to want to stand in yet another line to change money? Also, after traveling for so many hours, you may need to buy something to satisfy thirst or hunger.

While abroad, you can exchange U.S. dollars for the local currency at banks and exchange bureaus. Keep in mind that exchange rates vary slightly or significantly, depending on where and when you change money. In general, banks are going to be the best bet for good rates. In Europe, railroad stations offer decent exchange rates, and in Asia you can sometimes find the best exchange rates at hotels.

When you are settled in your new home, take the time to shop around for the best currency exchange rate in your area. Then, after you've exchanged money from U.S. dollars to foreign currency, stop thinking about the foreign currency in terms of U.S. dollars. Doing the conversion all the time can be confusing.

Another important thing to remember is to not exchange too much money toward the end of your stay abroad. Change only as much money as you need. In some countries, strict currency restrictions limit the amount of foreign currency that can be changed back into U.S. dollars, particularly if the original exchange receipts have been misplaced. Also, if you change foreign currency back to U.S. dollars, you'll be losing money a second time through fees or low exchange rates.

Never, ever exchange currency on the black market. Do not accept offers from people who approach you on the street to exchange money or from private vendors in airports and railroad stations. This is illegal in most countries. Many countries arrest people caught exchanging money on the black market and punish them with time in prison.

The power of plastic: ATMs and credit cards

Most major credit cards are accepted worldwide and some travelers find it convenient to travel with nothing but a credit card. And the increasing availability of automated teller machines (ATMs) has made it unnecessary to carry foreign cash with you from country to country.

Visa, MasterCard, and American Express are the most widely accepted and easy to use cards. For more information, try www.visa.com, www.mastercard.com, or www.americanexpress.com. If you do not currently have a credit card and want one, make sure you apply six to eight weeks before your departure in order to receive it before your trip.

Benefits of having a credit card while abroad include:

✔ Using them for emergency situations or major travel expenses.

✔ Accessing your money, regardless of the time of day.

✔ Getting the best exchange rates.

✔ Eliminating the need to carry large amounts of cash around with you.

✔ Replacing them easily if they're stolen or lost.

Additionally, you can sometimes use your U.S. banking debit/checking account card while abroad. Check whether your bank is part of an international network and whether you can use your ATM card to obtain cash in the local currency from your bank account in the U.S. Generally, the exchange rate is favorable because it's the same one the banks get when exchanging money.

In order to use ATMs abroad with credit or debit cards, your PIN code usually should be no longer than four digits. Make sure you can remember your PIN easily, because some places may require it for credit card purchases.

Be sure to memorize the numbers of your PIN as well as the letters; some ATMs have number pads without letters.

Before you go, call your credit card or bank customer service number to

✔ Find out whether your host country has ATMs on your network (for instance, the Cirrus network).

✔ Verify that your PIN works.

✔ Find out whether cardholders with your credit card have special privileges or discounts when abroad.

✔ Get customer service phone numbers that work from a location outside of the U.S. Often, the 1-800 customer service phone numbers on the back of your credit card will only work from the U.S.

Photocopy the front and back of all your credit cards before you go abroad. Take two copies with you and pack them separately (in a different bag) from where you carry your credit cards. If you travel while abroad, you can leave one of these copies at your abroad residence and take one with you. Also, leave a copy of your credit cards with someone at home. Having copies of credit card numbers allows you to have them replaced fairly easily and quickly.

You also need to figure out how to pay at least the minimum balance on your credit card while you are abroad. Consider the following options:

✔ If you will have Internet access, sign up for online bill payment. This means you can view and pay your bills online, usually by linking your credit card payments to your U.S. checking account. (Just be sure the checking account will have adequate funds!)

✔ Arrange to have your credit card bill sent to your address abroad and take some personal U.S. checks with you for paying them. Just be aware that this may not be the best method because of how long it could take for mail to travel back and forth between you and your credit card company.

When using credit cards abroad, be aware of your credit limit and do not exceed it. Exceeding your credit limit could lead to confiscation of your credit card. Furthermore, in some countries, Americans have been arrested for innocently and unknowingly exceeding their credit limit. Sign up for online account access with your credit card company so you can monitor the charges on your card.

Traveler's checks

Traveler's checks are another safe way to carry money abroad and are particularly useful in countries where ATM access or credit card use may be limited or unavailable. When lost or stolen, traveler's checks can be easily and quickly replaced.

Traveler's checks allow some flexibility in currency. You can purchase them in U.S. dollars as well as other major currencies, such as Euros and Japanese Yen. American Express Traveler's Checks tend to be the most widely accepted option, but most banks and travel agencies also sell traveler's checks.

You can cash traveler's checks in banks, exchange shops, hotels, or train stations. Like changing money, exchange rates and fees charged to cash the checks vary from place to place, so shop around for the best deals.

Keep the following tips in mind:

✔ Record the serial numbers of your checks. Keep the numbers separate from the checks; you would don't want to lose the serial numbers and the checks together or you have no way of replacing them. Leaving a copy of the serial numbers in the States with your parents is a good idea.

✔ Record the customer service numbers of the company that issued your traveler's checks (remember that U.S. 800 numbers usually don't work from overseas), so you can contact the issuing company for instructions on how to get them replaced if they are lost or stolen.

✔ You need your passport to cash traveler's checks. Keep your traveler's checks and passport in separate places so that you don't lose them at the same time. If someone picks up or steals your passport and traveler's checks, they will have no problem cashing them.

✔ Countersign your traveler's checks only in the presence of the person who cashes them.

✔ Don't carry all your traveler's checks with you at one time. Only carry what you need and leave the rest in a safe place.

Personal checks

You probably can't cash personal checks abroad, so don't rely on them as a way to get money. Three exceptions to this rule apply:

✔ Some credit cards offer check-cashing privileges, but find out whether this is available to you before going abroad.

> ✔ Your study abroad program (if it's a program with a good number of students) may arrange for local banks to cash their students' checks.

> ✔ Local banks usually cash personal checks from the U.S. if you have opened a checking account there. Of course, it takes one to two weeks for the check to clear and you are charged a fee for cashing the check.

Cash

I recommend that you avoid carrying large amounts of cash while you are abroad. If your cash is lost or stolen, you can do nothing to replace it. When you go to school or shopping or out with friends, take only the money you need for the day. Carrying a large amount of cash can attract a thief if she spots you sorting through your money while you pay for something.

If you are going to be abroad for an entire academic year, I highly recommend opening a bank account for the year. Set up an account with one of the larger banks in your host country because they will tend to have more ATM facilities and international banking options. Not only will you be able to cash personal checks, but you can also easily transfer money from an account in the States. When setting up your bank account, make sure you request a checking account, or what the bank offers that is equivalent to a checking account.

Transferring Money from Pennsylvania to Your Pocket

If you run out of money or an emergency comes up while you're abroad, you can get money from home in several ways. If you notice you're running out of money, try to get replacement funds before your balance dips down to nothing, so you don't have to starve or lapse in paying your rent.

If you have a bank account abroad, make sure to go to the abroad bank and request the correct sort codes and address for wiring money. Your U.S. bank can't send money without this information.

If you have an emergency, use one of the following options:

> ✔ **Wiring money:** In major cities, companies such as Western Union (www.westernunion.com) or American Express have a fairly easy time wiring money to you as cash or traveler's checks. Keep in mind that although this service may be fast, it is also expensive.

✔ **Postal money orders:** A family member or friend can purchase an international postal money order from a U.S. post office and send it to you, provided your host country has entered into an agreement with the United States Postal Service for the exchange of postal money orders. For under five dollars, you can purchase international money orders valued at up to $700 to 30 countries. Additional countries are regularly added, so check the USPS Web site for updated information: www.usps.com/money/welcome.htm. Postal money orders are less expensive than wiring money, but are not as fast. They take as long to get to you as an airmail letter or you can send your money order using Global Priority Mail or Global Express Mail. The money orders can be cashed at the post office locations of the destination country.

✔ **State Department assistance:** This service is only for emergencies. If you as a U.S. citizen suffers a financial emergency abroad and can't use a commercial service, someone in the U.S. can get money to you with the State Department's help. The State Department service establishes a trust account in the your name and sends the money overseas. They charge a $30 processing fee.

Upon receiving the funds, the State Department authorizes the appropriate U.S. Embassy or Consulate abroad to disburse the money. They can only disburse funds during normal office hours, not during weekends or local holidays when the Embassy or Consulate is closed. You must contact the Embassy or Consulate to arrange to receive the funds. The funds are normally disbursed in the foreign country's currency.

Whatever method you choose for transferring money in an emergency, be sure that the person sending the money provides the service with his name, address, and telephone number, as well as your name and overseas location. Otherwise, the transfer may be significantly delayed.

Keeping Your Money to Yourself

To keep your money as safe as possible, follow these precautions:

✔ Exchange money only in banks or authorized exchange bureaus.

✔ Keep a record of credit card and traveler's check numbers as well as customer service phone numbers in your country.

✔ Carry only as much money as you need for a day.

✔ Only bring credit and ATM cards that you plan to use. Leave the others at home.

✔ Do not flash large amounts of money when paying a bill.

✔ Make sure your credit card is returned to you after completing a transaction.

✔ Use the same precautions when using ATMs that you use at home. Withdraw money from ATMs inside banks or other buildings. Take a friend to the ATM with you and at night, only use well-lit ATMs. Be discreet when entering your PIN.

✔ Don't leave your purse or backpack unattended, even for a second. Wear purses across your chest rather than dangling off your shoulder. If carrying a backpack, keep money on your person; a waist pouch or money belt may be the safest way to carry money, especially when worn under your clothing.

✔ Keep the doors and windows of your dorm room or apartment locked.

If your money — or any of your possessions for that matter — is lost or stolen, immediately report this to the local police. Request a copy of the police report for insurance claims and in case you need to explain where your sources of funds have gone. After reporting losses to the police, be sure to contact credit card and traveler's check companies, banks, the U.S. Embassy if your passport is gone, and your airline company if you've lost plane tickets. And if your insurance company covers personal property loss, get in touch with them, too.

Thinking Again about Working Abroad

Studying abroad is not cheap. Although you may save money on tuition, you probably need more spending money per semester than you would if you were at your home university. Remember, in your new home, you'll want to go out with your new friends, try native cuisine at restaurants, sightsee, travel, and shop.

But I strongly caution you against trying to work while you're abroad. Your time away is precious and limited. Trust me, you don't want to spend it working. Use your time and energy for school and making new friends. If you're afraid you won't know what to do with yourself without a job, don't be. Take advantage of social and cultural opportunities available, join clubs at school, or take on a new sport.

Working toward study abroad

Because the chances of working abroad range from difficult to impossible and unrealistic, begin saving for your abroad adventure well in advance. Consider the following money saving tips:

✔ Work extra hours during the semesters before you leave.

✔ Summer is a great time to save money: Take on an extra summer job or live a little bit more frugally the summer before you leave. (Do you really need that new CD?) Live at home that summer to save money.

✔ If you spend your time at an unpaid internship, try to spend a few hours a week making money during the semester or take on a part-time job in the summer in addition to your internship.

If you insist: Some hints about working abroad

However, if you absolutely must work while abroad, the following sections present a few things to keep in mind.

Getting a work permit

In addition to your visa or residency permit, a work permit is usually required. Research work permits before you leave to go abroad. You can start your research by using the Internet or visiting the foreign embassy or consulate of your host country. Sometimes you can get a work permit before leaving the U.S., depending on the laws of the particular country. You can usually obtain a work permit after you arrive in the foreign country and apply for it at the same time as you apply for a residency permit or visa.

The Department of State cannot help you obtain visas or work permits.

Paying your U.S. taxes

U.S. citizens must report their worldwide income on their Federal income tax returns. Living or earning income outside the United States does not relieve a U.S. citizen of responsibility for filing tax returns. However, U.S. citizens living and/or working abroad may be entitled to various deductions, exclusions, and credits under U.S. tax laws, as well as under international tax treaties and conventions between the United States and a number of foreign countries. Working abroad can be an education in itself!

For information on taxes and locations of IRS offices overseas, contact any office of the IRS. IRS offices have copies of Publication 54, Tax Guide for U.S. Citizens and Resident Aliens Abroad; Publication 901, U.S. Tax Treaties; Publication 514, Foreign Tax Credit for Individuals; and Publication 520, Scholarships and Fellowships. During the tax-filing period, you can usually obtain the necessary Federal income tax forms from the nearest U.S. Embassy or Consulate.

You can also use the Internet to get forms and publications electronically from the IRS at www.irs.gov.

Knowing what to do about foreign taxes

If you earn any income while you're overseas, you're subject to the tax laws of that country. You should check the rules and regulations with that country's embassy or consulate before you leave the United States, or consult the nearest U.S. Embassy or Consulate abroad.

Staying longer to work a bit

Just as summer is a good time to save money to go abroad, you may also find it a good time to *stay* abroad and earn money, especially if your spring semester ends in mid-June. You'd arrive home looking for a summer job, but most summer jobs are already gone by mid-June because most colleges here finish in mid-May.

If you're considering staying abroad for the summer and working for a few months, make sure to do your research and get the appropriate work permits. Work permits can take a while to be issued, so don't wait until you've finished your exams and are ready to start working to get a work permit. Specify the amount of time you plan to work, as this could save you some money and get you a short-term work permit.

Also make sure that the job is worth your time. If you are living in a very expensive city such as Tokyo, London, or Dublin, everyday living expenses may eat up everything you earn.

You can also think about staying abroad an extra month or two to do some volunteer work. If you're living in a major city, you can easily find agencies in need of volunteers. Just be sure to volunteer on a project or in an environment where you feel safe.

Chapter 17

Staying Safe Abroad

· ·

In This Chapter

▶ Figuring out how to get around like a native

▶ Staying away from sticky legal situations

▶ Getting through extremely dangerous situations

· ·

Safety probably isn't your first concern, although it may be your parents'. However, if you're not safe, you'll have a hard time enjoying your experiences. Safety abroad really boils down to common sense and following many of the same rules and precautions that you follow at home. Keep in mind that your level of safety depends on where you study abroad. Some places are safer than others and some may be safer than where you study in the U.S. I felt as safe in Dublin as I do in Boston. If you currently study in a rural area where you don't worry much about dorm safety, walking home at night, or locking your car doors when you go to the grocery store, then studying abroad in a sprawling metropolis may seem less safe than staying home. But safety is all a matter of perspective, where you're coming from, and what your experiences have been.

Familiarize yourself with the laws of the country you're visiting before you leave or shortly after you arrive. Ignorance is never an excuse for not knowing the law.

The State Department, the authority on safety abroad, has a very helpful Web site for at www.travel.state.gov.

Remembering Street Smarts

The first step to staying safe is becoming familiar with the area in which you live and go to school. Ask other students, campus security, your program director, or the International Student Office for local safety information.

✔ Find out which areas of your town or city are safe and unsafe during the daytime and at night. Avoid dangerous areas where you could become the victim of a crime.

✔ Don't use shortcuts, narrow alleys, or poorly lit streets.

✔ Try not to travel alone at night.

✔ Keep a low profile and try not to stand out as a foreigner or tourist. In most places, wearing tennis shoes, baseball hats, jeans, or sweatpants are dead giveaways that you're American. Observe the local standards of dress — and don't hang a camera around your neck.

✔ Never, ever discuss travel plans or personal information with strangers.

Aim to blend in. Speak the language of your host country instead of English. Also, speak softly. Americans tend to speak loudly and this attracts attention. Don't frequent American hangouts like McDonald's — pickpockets can linger around looking for unsuspecting American students.

Warding off pickpockets

When you're out and about in your host country, pay attention to your surroundings just as you would in any public place. Remember that crowded elevators, festivals, market places, subways, train stations, tourist sites, and marginal areas of cities are prime locations for thieves and scam artists. Beware of strangers who approach you offering bargains or to be your guide.

Petty theft is rampant in many countries, and foreigners are almost always a favorite target. Pickpockets often have an accomplice who jostles you, asks you for directions or the time, points to something spilled on your clothing, or otherwise distracts you by creating a disturbance as the pickpocket runs off with your money. Wear the shoulder strap of your bag across your chest and walk with the bag away from the curb to avoid drive-by purse-snatchers.

A child or even a woman carrying a baby can be a pickpocket. Beware of groups of vagrant children who create a distraction while picking your pocket.

If you're confronted by a thief, don't fight back. Just give him what he asks for. Give up your valuables. Your money and passport can be replaced, but you cannot.

Use the following tips to keep yourself safe on the streets:

- ✔ Try to seem purposeful when you move about. Even if you are lost, act as if you know where you're going. Consult maps very discreetly.

- ✔ When possible, ask directions only from individuals in authority.

- ✔ Avoid public demonstrations and other civil disturbances.

- ✔ Learn a few phrases in the local language so that you can signal your need for help, the police, or a doctor.

- ✔ Make a note of emergency telephone numbers you may need: police, fire, your hotel, host family, roommates, program director, and the nearest U.S. Embassy or Consulate.

The U.S. Embassy is available to help you if you're the victim of a crime. Every embassy has an officer on call 24 hours a day to assist in an emergency and help you get in touch with medical care or police.

Staying safe aboard public transportation

As a student studying in a foreign country, you are probably not going to have access to a car. Wherever you're going, you'll likely be relying on your own two feet or public transportation to get you from place to place.

The consular information sheets on the State Department Web site, www. state.gov/travel, list whether a country has a pattern of tourists being targeted by criminals on public transport in the "Crime Information" section. Even if your area isn't listed, always carefully watch your belongings while you travel.

Taxis

In cities, taxis are often the safest way to travel at night, but remember to keep your wits about you. Take only those taxis clearly identified with official markings. Beware of unmarked cabs or drivers soliciting passengers in train stations or airports: They may take advantage of you or take you somewhere you don't want to go. Never get into a taxi if someone is already in the backseat. Never put your bags in the taxi before you get in — the driver could take off with your stuff! Try to become familiar with routes to and from your destination so that taxis don't take the longest and most expensive routes possible.

When going out, always take enough money for a taxi home.

Trains and buses

Public transportation may be a new adventure for you and can be challenging and difficult until you get used to it. If you're intimidated by the rules and routes, take a friend with you to show you the ropes your first time out. If you do venture out on your own, carry a map of public transportation systems with you until you are comfortable getting where you need to go. Plan your routes ahead of time, and make sure you know the fares and how to signal the driver to stop.

Passenger robberies along popular tourist routes on trains and buses are a serious problem, but you can protect yourself. Take a look at the following list for some tips:

- First and foremost, never accept food or drink from strangers when traveling on trains and buses. Criminals have been known to put drugs in food or drink offered to passengers and then rob them while they're sleeping.

- Crime on trains and buses is more common at night and especially on overnight trains. You don't need to avoid such trips altogether, but do stay alert and in tune with your surroundings.

- Remember the following if you travel via train at night:

    • Lock your compartment.

    • If you are unable to securely lock your compartment, sleep in shifts with your traveling companions. If you're traveling alone, stay awake.

    • If you must sleep and are traveling alone, tie down your luggage, strap your valuables to you, and sleep on top of them as much as possible.

- Never be afraid to alert train authorities if you feel threatened in any way during your trip. Extra police are often assigned to ride trains on routes where crime is a serious problem.

In some countries, entire busloads of passengers have been robbed by gangs of bandits.

Memorizing the rules of the road

Road rules and conditions vary widely by country and region and likely aren't what you're used to.

If you rent a car for a road-trip, make sure to take a friend with you (and a mobile phone if you have one) and follow these tips:

- ✔ Don't rent something exotic (like an SUV); choose a car that you see on the roads in the country you're in.

- ✔ Fully insure the car for the duration of your trip and make sure you have contact numbers for roadside assistance.

- ✔ Keep good road maps on hand.

- ✔ Ask your rental car agency for advice on avoiding robbery while visiting tourist destinations.

- ✔ Where possible, ask that markings that identify the rental car as a rental be removed, otherwise you're an easy target for thieves who prey on tourists.

- ✔ Make certain that the car is in good shape and recently serviced. When possible, choose a car with automatic door locks and power windows.

- ✔ Get a car with air conditioning so you can drive with the windows closed. Thieves can snatch purses and bags through open windows of moving cars.

- ✔ Keep bags and purses out of sight locked in the trunk.

- ✔ Keep car doors locked at all times. Wear seat belts.

- ✔ As much as possible, avoid driving at night.

- ✔ Don't leave valuables in the car.

- ✔ Don't park your car on the street overnight. If you can't park in a parking garage or other secure area, select a well-lit area.

- ✔ Never pick up hitchhikers.

- ✔ Don't stop to help strangers or accept help from anyone except authorized roadside assistance. Criminals may pose as stranded motorists seeking help. Or they may flag you down, ask for assistance, and then steal your luggage or car. Usually they work in groups; one person preoccupies you by chatting while the others rob you.

- ✔ Never put yourself into a situation in which you feel uncomfortable or unsafe. If the area where you planned to park doesn't feel safe to you, drive away instead.

According to the State Department, victimization of motorists has been refined to an art in many places frequented by tourists, including areas of southern Europe. Where this sort of crime is a problem, U.S. Embassies are aware of it and try to warn the public about the dangers. In some locations, these efforts at public awareness have paid off, reducing the frequency of incidents.

Carjackers and thieves operate at gas stations, in parking lots, in city traffic, and along the highway — basically, anywhere there are cars. In extreme instances, criminals may attempt to get your attention with abuse, either trying to drive you off the road or causing an "accident" by rear-ending you and creating a fender bender. Or in some urban areas, thieves don't waste time on ploys: They simply smash your car windows at traffic lights, grab your valuables or your car, and get away.

The bottom line is that it is simply better to avoid driving in a foreign country. If you must drive, drive defensively, and keep an eye out for potentially criminal pedestrians, cyclists, and scooter riders.

Taking precautions when traveling

If you're studying abroad, chances are you're going to travel outside of your host town or country. Travel is exciting, but remember to be smart and safe about it.

Find out about the place you're planning to visit before you go. Pick the brains of your fellow students and other locals you trust, or buy an up-to-date guidebook that includes maps, descriptions of public transportation routes, lists of local embassies and police information, and suggestions for places to stay, eat, and visit. Familiarize yourself with local laws and customs, especially when it comes to dressing and socializing. You may also want to read the consular information sheets, public announcements, or travel warnings for countries you plan to visit. (Don't know what these are? Check out Chapter 4!)

Your travel itinerary can be a lifesaver, literally. Be sure to let a friend, family member, roommate, or your program director know your detailed itinerary, including names, addresses, and telephone numbers where you will be staying and the date when you'll return. Leave a copy of your passport, visas, and flight and ticket information with them as well, in case this stuff gets lost.

One of the best ways to stay safe is to establish certain check in dates when you call or e-mail to let someone know you're all right. If you do this, stick to those dates and times because if you miss a check in, your contact may assume that you're having a problem or are in trouble.

In general, I do not recommend traveling alone unless you're meeting someone you know at your destination and are just making the trip by yourself. For example, if you have an emergency or injury situation, you may not be able to find anyone who speaks your language or understands you well enough to help you. Alone, you become a target for thieves. Remember there is safety in numbers. If you're traveling alone, don't announce this information!

What you take with you may also put you in harm's way, so remember the following tips:

- ✔ Leave any valuables, including extra credit cards, large amounts of cash, and jewelry — even fake jewelry — at home. Thieves don't know the difference between real and fake jewelry until after they take it, so why risk your personal safety?

- ✔ Travel as lightly as possible and take items that you wouldn't be particularly upset to lose if they're stolen or lost in transit.

- ✔ Never leave your luggage unattended or accept packages from strangers.

- ✔ If you take prescription medication, make sure you have enough to last the duration of the trip, including extra medication in case you're delayed. Always carry your prescriptions in their labeled containers. Pills in unlabeled bottles cause suspicion.

Always be alert and aware of your surroundings. If you're unsure about local conditions, check with the local U.S. Embassy or Consulate for the latest security information.

Hotel/Hostel safety

When you leave your home base for an overnight trip, make arrangements to stay at hotels or hostels with good security and easy access to transportation. And don't go off with people who approach you in airports or train and bus stations and offer you a place to stay. Instead, look for accredited and reputable hotels and hostels — get tips from friends who have traveled before or consult a student travel agency.

When you arrive in your hotel room, check the locks on all the doors and windows and be sure to use them whenever you're in your room. Take a moment to read the fire safety instructions in your hotel room. Hopefully, a fire won't come up, but you should know how to report a fire and locate the nearest fire exit — just in case. Also, counting the doors between your room and the nearest exit could be a lifesaver if you have to crawl through a smoke-filled corridor.

Keep the following tips in mind whenever you stay in a hotel or hostel:

- ✔ If you feel uncomfortable, ask hotel security to escort you to and from parking lots and your room at night.

- ✔ Always check your peephole before letting people into your room.

- ✔ Don't get on an elevator if someone inside makes you uncomfortable.

- ✔ Do not leave money, passports, visas, or other valuables in your hotel room while you're out. Use the hotel safe, if available.

If you need directions from your hotel, your hotel concierge or another staff member can help. Remember to ask before you leave, but if you do find yourself lost, ask for directions right away. Generally, the safest people are policemen or someone working in a restaurant or shop. Getting the right information may save you from ending up in a potentially unsafe area.

Traveling to high-risk areas

Common sense dictates that you should avoid traveling to areas with a history of terrorist attacks or kidnapping. If you must travel to or through a high-risk area, the State Department advises the following precautions (in addition to travel precautions already discussed in this chapter):

- Discuss with your family what they would do in the event of an emergency. Make sure your affairs are in order before leaving home.

- Register with the U.S. Embassy or Consulate upon arrival.

- Leave no personal or business papers in your hotel room.

- Watch for people following you or observing your comings and goings.

- Keep a mental note of safe places, such as police stations, hotels, and hospitals.

- Avoid predictable times and routes of travel, and report any suspicious activity to local police and the nearest U.S. Embassy or Consulate.

- Select your own taxicabs at random. Don't get into a vehicle not clearly identified as a taxi. Compare the face of the driver with the one posted on his or her license.

- Refuse unexpected packages.

- Formulate a plan of action regarding what you will do if a bomb explodes or you hear gunfire nearby.

- Check for loose wires or other suspicious activity around your car.

- Be sure your vehicle is in good operating condition in case you need to resort to high-speed or evasive driving.

- Drive with car windows closed in crowded streets. Bombs can be thrown through open windows.

- If you're ever in a situation where somebody starts shooting, drop to the floor or get down as low as possible. Don't move until you're sure the danger has passed. Don't attempt to help rescuers and don't pick up a weapon. If possible, shield yourself behind or under a solid object. If you must move, crawl on your stomach.

Travel tips for women

Each country and culture has particular views of what is appropriate behavior for women. Although you may not agree with these views, tolerate them to avoid problems: "When in Rome, do as the Romans." Become familiar with the laws and customs of the places you plan to visit.

Women traveling alone can be more susceptible to problems in certain cultures. Don't forget that as a foreigner you stand out; a woman traveling alone can be even more of an oddity in some places. If you're a woman, I don't recommend you travel alone. Even if you're traveling with a group of females, you need to be careful. Here's how to keep yourself safe:

✔ To eliminate unwanted encounters with men while traveling, invent a convincing story as to why you're traveling without family members or a husband.

✔ If you're single, you may want to wear a wedding ring to reduce unwanted advances or even wedding proposals.

✔ If you ever feel as if you're being followed, step into the first available store or other safe place and wait to see whether the person you think is following has passed. Don't be afraid or embarrassed to ask for someone to double check for you to see whether all is safe.

✔ Always look and act with confidence. Looking as if you know where you're going may ward off potential danger.

Remember that fashion makes a statement, and that a statement may not always translate the way you want it to — not everyone interprets your style of dress the same way. What you consider casual clothing may be seen as provocative or inappropriate in other cultures. Observe the way local women dress or dress conservatively to save yourself some trouble.

Believe it or not, your clothes may actually put you in danger. Thieves may choose you over another potential target based on your style of dress or the amount of makeup or jewelry you're wearing. Others may single you out for harassment or even physical violence because they find your clothing offensive according to their cultural norms.

Avoiding Legal Difficulties

No doubt you'll enjoy your time abroad much less if you're spending it in a foreign jail. Avoiding this situation shouldn't be too difficult, however, as long as you educate yourself about the local laws and follow them, even if they're not what you're used to. You *can* be arrested overseas for actions that may be either legal or considered minor infractions in the United States.

Don't assume that as a U.S. citizen, you cannot be arrested in a foreign country! While visiting another country, you're subject to their laws. After you leave the United States, you're no longer covered by U.S. laws and constitutional rights.

The State Department's consular information sheets include information on unusual patterns of arrests in various countries.

Doing time for doing drugs

The State Department reports that each year, 2,500 Americans are arrested overseas. One third of these arrests are on drug-related charges. Many countries have mandatory drug-related sentences. A number of Americans have been arrested for possessing prescription drugs, particularly tranquilizers and amphetamines, that they purchased legally in certain Asian countries and then brought to some countries in the Middle East where they are illegal. If in doubt about foreign drug laws, ask the nearest U.S. Embassy or Consulate.

Drug laws vary from country to country, and many countries take drug offenses very seriously, which could have some unsavory consequences for you, such as serving a mandatory (and lengthy) prison sentence or even — gulp! — the death penalty. And you can count on some seriously unpleasant prison time, often served in solitary confinement, while your trial takes place.

You're responsible to know the drug laws in a foreign country. "I didn't know it was illegal" won't get you out of jail. Drug possession and trafficking amount to jail time in most foreign countries.

If you purchase prescription medications in quantities larger than considered necessary for personal use, you could be arrested on suspicion of drug trafficking.

There is very little that anyone can do to help you if you are caught with drugs. If you're arrested, an American consular officer cannot rescue you from jail! Just do yourself a favor and don't get involved with drugs while abroad.

If someone offers you a free trip and some quick and easy money just for bringing back a suitcase, say "No." Don't carry a package for anyone, no matter how small it may be. The police and customs officials have a right to search your luggage for drugs. If they find drugs in your suitcase, you will be held responsible.

Steering clear of other legal minefields

Although the biggest legal concern for U.S. students studying abroad is typically keeping out of drug trouble, here are a few other legal issues you should be aware of — some obvious, some not.

Possession of firearms

Stay away from firearms while abroad (this is the obvious one). Although your right to bear arms is protected in the U.S., this is often not the case in foreign locations. U.S. citizens most often encounter difficulties for illegal possession of firearms in the countries nearby: Mexico, Canada, and the Caribbean. Sentences for possession of firearms in Mexico can be up to 30 years. In general, firearms, even those legally registered in the U.S., cannot be brought into a country unless a permit is first obtained from the embassy or a consulate of that country and the firearm is registered with foreign authorities on arrival.

If you take firearms or ammunition to another country, you cannot bring them back into the U.S. unless you register them with U.S. Customs before you leave the U.S.

Photography

Be polite about photography. Always request permission before photographing people. In many countries, you can be harassed or detained for photographing such things as police and military installations, government buildings, border areas, and transportation facilities. If you see security in front of a building (policeman, soldier, and so on), don't take photographs without asking permission first. Such photos may be perceived as acts of espionage that can land you in jail.

Cameras are a good target for thieves and can make it obvious that you're a tourist. Take stock of your surroundings before whipping out your camera. Disposable cameras are a good alternative.

Purchasing antiques

As a student, I doubt that you're going to have the money available to purchase expensive antiques, but be aware that Americans have been arrested for purchasing souvenirs that were, or looked like, antiques and that local customs authorities believed were national treasures. This is especially true in Turkey, Egypt, and Mexico. In countries where antiques are important, document your purchases as reproductions if that is the case.

Getting help from the U.S. Consulate

U.S. Consulates are located in your abroad country to help you — in both emergency and non-emergency situations. Feel free to visit or call them. Even if they can't directly answer your questions or help you with a particular issue, they can tell you where to get an answer. (Realize that some issues are not within their jurisdiction, such as residence permits for your host country.)

If you plan to stay more than two weeks in one place, if you're in an area experiencing civil unrest or a natural disaster, or if you're planning travel to a remote area, register at the Consular Section of the nearest U.S. Embassy or Consulate. This makes it easier if someone at home needs to locate you or in the unlikely event that you need to be evacuated in an emergency. You'll also have an easier time obtaining a new passport should yours be lost or stolen.

If you run out of money overseas and have no other options, consular officers can help you get in touch with your family, friends, bank, or employer and inform them how to wire funds to you.

Should you find yourself in legal difficulty, contact a consular officer immediately. When necessary, consuls can transfer money from home for you and will try to get relief for you, including food and clothing in countries where this is a problem. If you are detained, remember that under international treaties and customary international law, you have the right to talk to the U.S. Consulate. If you are denied this right, be persistent. Try to have someone get in touch for you.

If you are arrested while studying abroad, you need to know what the U.S. government can and cannot do to help you.

The U.S. Consular Officer will:

✔ Visit you in jail after being notified of your arrest.

✔ Provide you with a list of local attorneys who speak English.

✔ At your request, notify your family and friends and relay requests for money or other aid.

✔ Ensure that your rights under local law are observed and that you're treated humanely, according to internationally accepted standards.

✔ Protest mistreatment or abuse.

Encountering anti-Americanism overseas

You're probably well aware by now that not everyone in the world loves Americans. Unfortunately, anti-Americanism abroad is a reality. Be aware that you will most likely be a member of an international university that exists to promote the free exchange and debate of ideas and opinions. You may find anti-American views in campus newspapers or even in the classroom. Don't feel threatened or take personal offense to these anti-American feelings. Your personal safety is not at risk.

The best thing you can do as an American abroad is to know your U.S. history and U.S. foreign policy. You could play an important part in educating others about your country! Many study abroad students, myself included, have found that abroad universities and students are usually very friendly to Americans.

The U.S. Consular Officer cannot:

✔ Demand your immediate release or get you out of jail.

✔ Represent you at trial or give legal counsel.

✔ Pay legal fees or fines with U.S. Government funds.

Handling Yourself in Situations of Extreme Danger

Most likely, you will have a safe, wonderful experience abroad like the vast majority of the students who have gone before you. Nevertheless, the best way to be sure you return from your trip safe and sound is to be prepared for anything. Please take the following advice seriously, read it carefully, then file it away, and get on with your good time.

Encountering terrorism

Terrorist acts occur at random, which means you can't completely protect yourself against them.

The best protection against terrorism is to avoid travel to unsafe areas with persistent records of terrorist attacks or kidnapping.

According to the State Department, the vast majority of foreign countries have good records of maintaining public order and protecting residents and visitors within their borders from terrorism.

Realize that most terrorist attacks result from long and careful planning. Terrorists look for defenseless, easily-accessible targets who follow predictable patterns. The chances that you, as a tourist traveling with a non-publicized program or itinerary, would be the victim of terrorism are slight. And many terrorist groups, seeking publicity for political causes within their own country or region, may not be looking for American targets.

Nevertheless, the following pointers may help you avoid becoming a target of opportunity. These pointers should be considered in addition to the tips already discussed for protecting yourself against becoming a victim of crime. The State Department believes that these precautions may provide some degree of protection, and can serve as practical and psychological deterrents to would-be terrorists.

✔ Schedule direct flights and avoid stops in high-risk airports or areas whenever possible.

✔ Try to minimize the time spent in the public area of an airport. Move quickly from the check-in counter to the secured areas. When you get to your destination, leave the airport as soon as possible.

✔ Avoid luggage tags, dress, and behavior that may identify you as an American.

✔ Keep an eye out for suspicious abandoned packages or briefcases. Report them to airport security or other authorities and leave the area promptly.

✔ Avoid obvious terrorist targets such as places where Americans and Westerners are known to congregate.

Getting through hijacking/hostage situations

Most likely, you will never encounter a hostage or hijacking situation while studying abroad. But if you are in a high-risk area, pay attention to warning announcements from the U.S. and check out www.state.gov/travel for tips on how to best manage a hostage situation.

The U.S. government will negotiate, but won't make concessions in hostage and hijacking situations — to do so would only increase the risk of further hostage-taking. When Americans are abducted overseas, the U.S. looks to the host government to exercise responsibility under international law to protect all persons within its territories and to bring about the safe release of hostages. The U.S. will work closely with these governments from the start of a hostage-taking incident to ensure that its citizens and other innocent victims are released as quickly and safely as possible.

Chapter 18

An Apple a Day: Staying Healthy While You're Away

In This Chapter

▶ Protecting yourself by planning ahead

▶ Keeping up your health

▶ Avoiding those nasty illnesses

▶ Making your food and water safe

Staying healthy while abroad is up to you. And when you get right down to it, is not terribly different from staying healthy at home. You still need to eat right and wash your hands, for instance, and your asthma will follow you wherever you go, but there are some differences, too. Healthcare varies widely in terms of availability and quality, and if you're going to a country where English is not the primary language, well, that's a whole different can of worms.

Change often can stir things up within your body — the stress of moving to a new place alone takes a toll — so it's important to be ready for whatever health problems may arise. Do your best to collect some information about the healthcare system in the region where you'll be studying. Good questions to find the answers to are

✔ What are the medical care facilities like?

✔ How do you pay for medical care?

✔ Do you have a legal right to medical services?

Although I spend most of this chapter talking about looking after your own health, you should also discuss with your family what to do in the event of a family emergency at home, such as illness or death. Believe me, it is much easier to have these hypothetical discussions before departing for a foreign country than during a stressful international phone call at 3 a.m.

This chapter is not intended to cause panic about the myriad illnesses and diseases out there. Most of you will go away and have no medical issues whatsoever. However, it certainly doesn't hurt to be aware of all the nasty things you could catch so that you know when to seek medical attention. When in doubt about your health, take the saying "better safe than sorry" to heart and get some medical care. Don't worry about looking like a hypochondriac; you want to be healthy and enjoy your experience abroad as much as possible.

Healthy Things to Do Before Departing

Make sure that you are in good health before you leave by having both physical and dental checkups. In addition to checking out your current state of health, ensure your future health by getting the required immunizations and finding out as much as you can about the health conditions in your host country. Let your doctors know where you plan to study so they can alert you to peculiar health conditions or precautions you should take. On-campus health services can usually provide you with accurate information about student health issues abroad.

Many study abroad programs require you to submit medical forms about your physical and mental health prior to enrolling. Additionally, take a copy of your medical and dental records with you, as well as the contact information for your doctors and dentist at home.

Minding your mental health

Realize that living abroad is, at times, stressful. Most likely, you will experience some sort of culture shock (see Chapter 15) as you adjust to your new home. If you are already dealing with unresolved emotional issues, culture shock can intensify these feelings. Make a point of discussing any emotional or mental health issues you have with your study abroad adviser, mental health provider, or other trained medical personnel before leaving home.

Before departing, you may want to investigate the availability of mental health services in your new home. Counseling can be difficult to find in many countries in the world. Check with your program or abroad university's health center to see what psychological counseling is available, should you need it. Once you arrive at your abroad destination, program staff and international study offices will be available to help with the adjustment cycle.

If you are currently taking medication for mental health issues such as depression or anxiety, keep taking your medicine when you arrive overseas. Do not assume that a mental health problem or an eating disorder will go away when you go overseas. Sometimes the initial excitement of being in a different place can make you feel overconfident, but when culture shock and everyday routines and problems begin to set in, your mental health can become even more fragile.

Coping with pre-existing medical conditions

Ongoing medical problems (such as allergies, asthma, and diabetes) require special attention. Take the time to figure out what precautions and preparations you need to consider to manage your health abroad. Bring a letter from your doctor explaining how your condition is being treated.

Not only can a doctor's letter bring whomever treats you abroad up to speed, but it can sometimes make explaining your medications to customs officials easier. Remember, while you may be tempted to stock up on medications before going abroad, your host country may have restrictions on how much you can bring in with you. Before departing, find out which medications and treatments for your condition are available in your host country. Your doctor can help you find this information and may also be able to give you the name of a reputable doctor in your host country.

Consider wearing a medical alert bracelet or necklace or carrying a card to identify your condition, so that in case of emergency you will receive the proper treatment.

Tackling prescriptions

Planning ahead for your health is particularly important where medications are concerned. If you take prescription medications regularly, consider the following tips and guidelines:

✔ If possible, bring a supply to last your entire time abroad. However, check to see whether your country has any restrictions on bringing prescription medications with you.

✔ Keep all drugs in the clearly labeled original pharmacy containers.

✔ Remember that foreign drugs may not closely resemble drugs here in the United States. Often pharmaceutical companies market drugs with different names or varying strengths in other countries. Therefore, your exact medication may unavailable to you abroad. Take a letter from your U.S. physician or pharmacist describing your medicines, the condition the medicine is treating, dosage, and any generic names for the medication.

✔ Carry copies of your prescriptions or a letter from a doctor to avoid problems with customs. Clearing more than a 30-day supply of drugs classified as narcotics through customs will be difficult. You need to bring a prescription with the narcotic drug's generic name and fill it in your host country.

✔ Some pharmacies abroad may not honor a prescription from the United States. In this case, take your U.S. prescription to your abroad school's health center and have them write a new prescription for the pharmacy in your host country.

✔ Protection against potentially hazardous drugs is nonexistent in some countries, increasing the risk of adverse reactions. The State Department recommends that you do not buy over-the-counter medications unless you are familiar with the product.

✔ If you have a medical condition that requires a syringe to administer medication, bring a supply of disposable syringes. Syringes are not available in all countries and are essential to protect yourself against HIV, hepatitis, and other illnesses.

✔ Be aware that some countries restrict the import of syringes as well as certain medications and contraceptives. Before departure, find out whether this applies to your host country.

✔ If you wear eyeglasses or contact lenses, pack an extra pair and don't forget to bring contact lens solution.

✔ Do not pack your medications, eyeglasses, or contact lenses in your checked luggage. Pack them in your carry-on so you're not without them if your luggage is lost.

Protecting yourself: Immunizations

Depending on current health conditions, some countries require certain immunizations in order for you to receive a visa or enter their country. You need to check whether your host country or countries you plan on traveling to have immunization requirements. Your country may also mandate an AIDS test for entry or to get a residency permit.

Even if your host country does not require immunizations, you still may want to get them. Be sure to discuss this with your doctor.

If you must present an official record of immunizations, an "International Certificate of Vaccinations" is the most common form used. You can find this form, issued by the U.S. Department of Health and Human Services, at your local health department, travel clinic, passport office, physician's office, or travel agency. The person who provides the immunization must fill out and date the form.

You may also want to update your basic childhood immunizations (diphtheria, polio, tetanus, and so on). If you're traveling to a developing country, frequently recommended vaccines include cholera, hepatitis A and B, typhoid fever, and yellow fever. And don't forget anti-malarial medicine if you plan to travel or live in malarial areas. To find out what vaccines you may need, check out the list of health resources later in this chapter.

Occasionally a required or recommended vaccine may be expensive or difficult to obtain in the U.S. Ask your host university or your study abroad program if they recommend obtaining these vaccines once you are abroad.

Insurance = Assurance

You must obtain adequate medical and accident insurance prior to heading out. At some point in your time abroad, you will probably need to show proof of health and accident insurance. Make sure you have coverage for medical evacuation, repatriation of remains, and life insurance. Medical evacuation back to the United States can easily exceed $10,000, depending on your location and how sick you are.

If you are currently covered by your family's health and life insurance policies, find out whether this coverage meets your program/abroad university's insurance requirements and is valid for the duration of your program abroad. Some study abroad programs and universities abroad may require you to purchase a mandatory insurance policy, regardless of any other insurance you may have. If you do get special overseas health insurance as part of your study abroad program or university abroad, make sure it covers pre-existing conditions. Many policies don't. If it doesn't, you need to purchase a supplement or a second insurance policy.

Students with an International Student Identity Card receive basic medical/accident insurance coverage for their travel outside the continental United States while the card is valid (check out Chapter 12 for info on getting this card). However, this coverage may not be adequate to meet every possibility, so you should check to see what additional insurance you may need.

If you have no insurance at all and your abroad program doesn't offer it, check with your home university's study abroad office for a list of insurers that offer overseas coverage.

Substance abuse

Views on drug and alcohol abuse differ around the world. In some cultures, alcohol is an accepted part of the culture. Binge drinking and drunkenness are common behaviors. Alcohol may be less expensive to buy, the drinking age may be lower, or the laws against public drunkenness are fairly lenient. In other cultures, public drunkenness is unequivocally frowned upon. Just because you are away from your home university and the U.S. laws regarding the use of alcohol, don't get carried away and fall into patterns of alcohol abuse. And be careful not to misinterpret how your new culture uses alcohol. Make sure to determine your program and university rules about alcohol and the consequences for alcohol abuse. Do yourself a favor and just drink responsibly. You find less variety of opinion on illegal drugs — they're generally not acceptable.

 If you currently attend a support group such as Alcoholics Anonymous, check on meeting availability and schedules in your host country. (Contact Alcoholics Anonymous World Services, phone 212-870-3400.)

 While drug abuse is never a good idea, impure drugs and rigid legal systems that impose severe penalties make using drugs abroad even riskier. Don't forget that the U.S. Embassy can do very little to bail you out of a drug charge. The U.S. government has no jurisdiction and little influence over the judicial systems in other countries.

Strategies for Staying Well

Realize that standards of sanitation vary throughout the world and may be better or worse than you're used to. As a result, you may have less resistance built up toward everyday germs in other places. In developed countries, like Canada, Australia, and Western Europe, health risks are about the same as here in the U.S. But in less developed parts of the world, such as Africa, Asia, or South America, health risks can vary widely from place to place.

No matter where you study, you can keep yourself safe and healthy by following a few simple rules:

- ✔ Wash your hands with soap and water. It's the best way to prevent catching and spreading germs.

- ✔ Get plenty of sleep. Don't allow yourself to get run down.

- ✔ Eat healthy, exercise regularly.

- ✔ Don't share cups and utensils with other people.

- ✔ Pay attention when walking or driving — car crashes are a leading cause of injury among travelers. Avoid traveling at night when possible. Always wear your seat belt.

- ✔ Use latex condoms to reduce the risk of HIV and other sexually transmitted diseases.

- ✔ Don't share needles with anyone.

- ✔ Never eat undercooked ground beef and poultry, raw eggs, and unpasteurized dairy products.

✔ Do not eat unpeeled fruits or vegetables.

✔ Stay in well-screened areas and use insect repellent to protect yourself from insects. Also, wear long-sleeved shirts and long pants tucked into boots or socks to keep ticks away when you're tramping through rural areas.

✔ Do not go barefoot in rural or undeveloped areas. Keep feet clean and dry or you risk contracting a fungal or parasitic infection.

✔ Don't handle animals (especially monkeys, dogs, and cats) to avoid bites and serious diseases (including rabies and plague).

Here are a few wellness items that have served thousands of travelers well and that you may want to carry with you:

✔ Insect repellent containing DEET (diethylmethyltoluamide)

✔ Over-the-counter anti-diarrheal medicine

✔ Iodine tablets and water filters to purify water in case bottled water isn't available

If you do become seriously ill or injured while abroad, make sure you contact everyone who may be worrying about you, including your family at home in the U.S. If you end up hospitalized or in an emergency medical situation, your first point of contact should be your program director, International Student Office, or Health Services at your abroad university. They can point you to a doctor who speaks English.

If you're having trouble locating medical help and can't get in touch with the people I just mentioned, a U.S. Consular Officer can help you locate the appropriate medical services and inform your family. If necessary, a Consular Officer can also assist in the transfer of funds from the United States. However, payment of hospital and other expenses is your responsibility.

Looking Out for Some High-Profile (and Not So Fun) Diseases

In many cases, the dangers to your health are the same as they are in the U.S. Other illnesses and afflictions are location-specific. Either way, it can't hurt to know about some of the major diseases that you may encounter at home or abroad. In addition to the illnesses I mention in the following sections, you may need to watch out for cholera, dengue fever, diphtheria, rabies, typhoid fever, yellow fever, and various worms and parasites. Just because you're away from home doesn't mean you're any more susceptible, but the distance from your regular doctor and your family may make an extended illness harder to deal with. Education is probably your best defense.

The CDC (Centers for Disease Control) and the U.S. State Department's Overseas Citizens Emergency Center can give you detailed health information about particular regions where you plan to visit or study. An excellent resource for detailed health information entitled "Health Information for International Travel" is available from the CDC.

✔ Centers for Disease Control
www.cdc.gov
1-800-311-3435

✔ Overseas Citizens Emergency Center
(202) 647-5225

✔ World Health Organization
www.who.int

✔ American College Health Association
www.acha.org
(410) 859-1500

✔ You can get a list of English-speaking doctors worldwide by contacting the International Association for Medical Assistance to Travelers
www.iamat.org
(716) 754-4883

Altitude illness

If your traveling itinerary requires mountain climbing or hiking to high-altitude destinations (above 6,000 feet), you should be aware of the risk of altitude illness. Susceptibility to altitude illness varies from traveler to traveler, and you can't really take a screening test to predict whether you'll get sick. If you've gotten altitude illness before, chances are you are suscepti-ble to it and will get it again. You cannot affect whether you'll get altitude ill-ness by training or increasing your physical fitness.

If you have a pre-existing medical condition, particularly involving your heart or lungs, consult your doctor before undertaking travel to high-altitude destinations.

Watch out for the following types of altitude illness:

✔ **Acute mountain sickness (AMS),** the most common form of altitude ill-ness, can occur at altitudes as low as 4,000 feet, but most often happens in abrupt ascents to over 9,000 feet. AMS usually begins at least 6 to 12 hours after arrival at a higher altitude. Symptoms include headache, extreme fatigue, loss of appetite, nausea, and vomiting.

✔ **High-altitude cerebral edema (HACE)** is a severe progression of AMS. In addition to the AMS symptoms, you can feel confused and be unable to walk a straight line.

✔ **High-altitude pulmonary edema (HAPE)** can occur by itself or in conjunction with HACE. You can experience increased breathlessness with exertion that fails to go away after several minutes of rest.

Altitude illness is easy to avoid. Simply learn the symptoms of altitude illness, and if you find you're suffering from them, do not ascend any further until symptoms disappear. Descend if the symptoms become worse. Planning a gradual ascent also helps you avoid altitude illness.

Never sleep at higher altitudes when you feel any of the symptoms of altitude illness.

You can get medications that prevent and treat altitude illness. When taken prior to ascent, medications speed recovery and aid in acclimatization if symptoms develop. You can also carry certain drugs in case of emergency. You should consult a doctor for more information.

Malaria

Malaria is a serious and sometimes fatal disease caused by a parasite carried by infected mosquitoes. It occurs in over 100 countries and territories, including large areas of Central and South America, Haiti, the Dominican Republic, Africa, the Indian subcontinent, Southeast Asia, the Middle East, and Oceania.

The World Health Organization estimates that 300–500 million cases of malaria occur per year and more than one million people die of malaria every year. The 1,200 cases of malaria diagnosed in the United States each year are, for the most part, found in immigrants and travelers returning from malaria-risk areas.

Symptoms include fever and flu-like illness: shaking chills, headache, muscle aches, exhaustion, nausea, vomiting, and diarrhea. Malaria can also cause anemia and jaundice because of red blood cell loss.

Symptoms typically begin ten days to four weeks after infection, although a person may feel ill as early as eight days or as late as a year later. Two kinds of malaria, *P. vivax* and *P. ovale,* can relapse; some parasites can hide in the liver from several months to four years after you were initially bitten by the infected mosquito. When these parasites leave the liver and start to attack red blood cells, you will feel sick.

Infection with one type of malaria, Plasmodium falciparum, if left untreated, can lead to kidney failure, seizures, mental confusion, coma, and death.

Doctors can diagnose malaria with a simple blood test and prescription drugs can cure it. The type of medication and length of treatment depend on which kind of malaria is diagnosed, where the patient was infected, the age of the patient, and how severely ill the patient is when diagnosed.

Visit your healthcare provider four to six weeks before traveling for any necessary vaccinations and a prescription for an antimalarial drug. Take antimalarial drugs on schedule and do not miss any doses.

Do everything you can to prevent mosquito and other insect bites.

- ✔ Use DEET insect repellent on exposed skin and flying insect spray in the room where you sleep.
- ✔ Wear long pants and long-sleeved shirts, especially from dusk to dawn.
- ✔ Sleep under a mosquito bednet if you are not living in screened or air-conditioned housing.

Seek immediate medical attention if you have traveled to a malaria-risk area and display fever or flu-like symptoms while traveling or up to one year after returning home. You may just have the flu, but better safe than sorry in this situation. Tell your healthcare provider that you have been traveling in a malaria-risk area.

Travelers' diarrhea

Experiencing some form of diarrhea is normal while you're adjusting to local food and water and it is usually quite mild. However, contaminated food and drink may cause more severe stomach or intestinal illness.

Diarrhea is often accompanied by nausea, bloating, urgency, and malaise. Fortunately, it usually lasts only three to seven days (although those can certainly feel like long days). It is rarely life threatening.

Travelers' diarrhea is caused by ingesting germs in food and water that you're not used to. Generally, your risk of infection varies according to where you eat: private homes are low risk, street vendors, high risk, so choose foods and beverages carefully.

The best way to treat diarrhea is to stay hydrated and wait it out.

- ✔ Drink lots of fluids, especially fluids with electrolytes. Fruit juices, soft drinks (without caffeine is better), and sports drinks (like Gatorade) are advised.
- ✔ Eat salted crackers.

✔ Avoid dairy products and water that you cannot guarantee is safe until you feel better.

✔ Avoid unpeeled fruits and vegetables.

✔ Don't eat or drink the same thing you know or suspect made you sick.

Seek immediate medical attention if you have bloody diarrhea, dehydration, a fever in excess of 102° F, persistent vomiting, or don't feel better in a few days. Doctors may prescribe antimicrobial drugs to shorten the length of illness and reduce all the yucky symptoms. Antidiarrheals, such as Immodium, can decrease the number of diarrheal stools, but can cause complication for persons with serious infections.

Tuberculosis

Tuberculosis (TB) is a pulmonary infection transmitted through the air, although to become infected, you would have to spend a long time in a closed environment with a person with untreated TB who was coughing up a lot of stuff. There is no danger of TB spreading via dishes, linens, or by food. However, it can be transmitted through unpasteurized milk or milk products.

As you may guess, your best bet is to avoid exposure to known TB patients. If you plan on working in hospitals or healthcare settings where you will encounter TB patients, consult infection control or occupational health experts. Furthermore, if you anticipate prolonged exposure to TB (for example, you will routinely come in contact with hospital, prison, or homeless shelter populations), you should have a tuberculin skin test before leaving the United States. If the reaction is negative, you will need to repeat the test after returning to the United States.

Most developing countries use the Bacille Calmette-Guerin (BCG) vaccine to reduce the consequences of TB in infants and children. However, the BCG vaccine does not necessarily prevent the adult forms of TB and is not always recommended for use in the United States.

If you become infected with *M. tuberculosis* organisms, doctors can treat you to prevent active TB. In this case, treatment of a latent TB infection requires at least two months of antibiotics. Active TB can also be treated with a longer course of antibiotics.

Tetanus

Tetanus, also known as lockjaw, affects the central nervous system and can result in death. It is caused by the toxin of the bacterium Clostridium tetani, which lives in soil and is distributed worldwide. This bacteria can cause the muscles to go into severe spasms, which can be so powerful that they tear muscles or cause compression of the vertebrae.

Tetanus incubates for 5 days to 15 weeks — although 7 days is the average. Tetanus often begins with mild spasms in the jaw muscles, neck muscles, and facial muscles and progresses to stiffness in the chest, back, abdominal muscles, and sometimes the laryngeal muscles (which then interferes with breathing). Irritability, fever, excessive sweating, trouble swallowing, drooling, and uncontrolled urination and defecation can also accompany tetanus.

Without treatment, you could die. With proper treatment, less than ten percent of tetanus patients die.

Tetanus can be controlled and reversed with an antitoxin and antibiotics. Penicillin is frequently prescribed, but if you are allergic to penicillin, other antibiotics can also cure tetanus.

Muscle relaxants will ease the muscle spasms. Bedrest with a non-stimulating environment is also recommended (dim light, reduced noise, and stable temperature). Support with oxygen may also be necessary.

Keeping up to date on your tetanus boosters will prevent you from contracting tetanus. A tetanus immunization provides protection for ten years. If you have been injured, especially if you sustain a puncture wound, you should receive a booster immunization for tetanus if your last immunization was more than ten years ago.

AIDS/HIV

AIDS and HIV infection, which is transmitted sexually and through contaminated hypodermic needles and blood supplies, occurs worldwide. In the United States, Australia, New Zealand, Canada, Japan, and Western European countries, the risk of transfusion-associated HIV infection has been virtually eliminated through required testing of all donated blood. Less developed nations may not adequately screen blood or biological products for HIV.

Risk of HIV infection to travelers is not determined by geography but by your sexual and drug-using behaviors. You are only at risk if you come into direct contact with blood or secretions of potentially infected people.

No vaccine is available to prevent infection with HIV.

Do not use or allow someone else to use contaminated, unsterilized syringes or needles when giving injections or performing skin-piercing procedures, including acupuncture, vitamin injections, medical or dental procedures, ear or body piercing, or tattooing.

HIV is not transmitted through casual contact: air, food, or water routes; contact with inanimate objects; or mosquitoes. The use of public transport by people with AIDS or HIV infection does not put you at risk.

If you are going to a country where AIDS is prevalent, find out what you should do in an emergency if you require an injection or a blood transfusion.

Some countries screen incoming travelers (primarily those planning extended visits, such as for work or study) and don't allow people with AIDS or whose test results indicate infection with HIV to enter the country. To find out the policies and requirements of a particular country, contact the consular officials of the country you're going to. You can get an unofficial list compiled by the U.S. Department of State at `http://travel.state.gov/// HIVtestingreqs.html`.

Hepatitis A

The hepatitis A (viral hepatitis) virus causes an inflammation of the liver and is transmitted by contaminated food or water or contact with the blood and other bodily fluids of a person who currently has the disease. Although both other hepatitis infections (B and C) can become chronic illnesses, hepatitis A doesn't — the virus does not remain in the body after the infection has resolved.

Symptoms of hepatitis A are similar to those of the flu: fatigue, loss of appetite, nausea and vomiting, and fever; however the skin and eyes may also become yellow (jaundiced).

Risk factors include having a family member who recently had hepatitis A, intravenous drug use, and recent travel in Asia, South, or Central America.

The best way to protect yourself is to avoid unclean food and water. Wash your hands! And avoid sharing plates, utensils, toothbrushes, and even a bathroom with someone who has active hepatitis A.

A vaccine, administered in two doses, guards against hepatitis A. The second dose is given 6 to 12 months after the first. The vaccine begins to protect four weeks after receiving the initial dose, but the 6- to 12-month vaccination is required for long-term protection. You may want to consider receiving the hepatitis A vaccine if you plan to travel to countries with high levels of hepatitis A.

If you do get hepatitis A or get flu-like symptoms after being exposed to hepatitis A, have a doctor test your liver function because hepatitis A attacks your liver. Rest is your best bet when the symptoms are most severe. Also, avoid fatty foods during the acute phase of the disease because fatty foods may cause vomiting.

Hepatitis B

The hepatitis B virus damages liver cells, causes liver inflammation, and in general, impairs liver function. Hepatitis B, like hepatitis A, is transmitted via blood and other body fluids. Symptoms include abdominal pain, dark urine, fatigue, jaundice, joint aches, loss of appetite, low-grade fever, malaise, nausea, and vomiting.

A safe and effective hepatitis B vaccine is given in a series of three doses over a six month period.

Hepatitis B never really goes away, but you can go into remission with a carefully managed diet and medications. The acute phase of the illness lasts about two to three weeks, and the liver returns to normal within 16 weeks.

People who develop a chronic hepatitis B infection (about 10 percent) may or may not display symptoms; those who do not show symptoms are considered carriers and can pass the disease on to others. Chronic hepatitis B increases chances of permanent liver damage and liver failure. If you know that you've been exposed to hepatitis B, you may want to get tested upon returning home.

Don't Drink the Water?!?

Chances are good that your diet will change while abroad. Most likely, this change will be for the better. People in countries outside of the U.S. don't usually eat or drink as much sugar, processed foods, or caffeine as Americans do. You will probably find more grains, fresh fish, fruits, and vegetables included in your diet while abroad.

Before you leave, try to learn more about the foods and eating habits of your host country. Be open to new cuisines: These are an integral part of the culture and your abroad experience.

Making water safe to drink

In areas with poor sanitation, you can contract hepatitis or cholera if the drinking water is untreated. Use your common sense — do you see people drinking tap water or bottled water. Ask your program director or students who have visited your host country whether the water is safe to drink. Remember that you as a foreigner may not have the resistance to certain bacteria that local people do. The following beverages are usually safe to drink:

- ✔ Boiled water
- ✔ Hot beverages (coffee or tea) made with boiled water
- ✔ Canned or bottled carbonated beverages
- ✔ Beer and wine

The following tips can help you steer clear of water-borne illnesses:

- ✔ Avoid ice. It may be made from unsafe water.
- ✔ Drinking from an unopened can or bottle is safer than drinking from a glass that you cannot ensure is clean and dry.
- ✔ Don't brush your teeth or wash vegetables with tap water.
- ✔ Purify water by boiling or chemical disinfection.

If you choose to boil the water, bring it to a vigorous boil and then allow it to cool. Do not add ice. At high altitudes, allow water to stay at a vigorous boil for a few minutes or use chemical disinfectants. Adding a pinch of salt or pouring water from one container to another improves the taste.

You can use iodine or chlorine to chemically disinfect water, although iodine provides better disinfection in a wider set of circumstances. Use either tincture of iodine or tetraglycine hydroperiodide tablets. You can find these disinfectants in sporting goods stores and pharmacies in the United States. If the water appears cloudy, first strain it through a clean cloth and then double the number of disinfectant tablets added. For cold water, warm it or allow increased time for the disinfectant to work.

Eating with care

Choose your foods carefully while abroad. Remember that raw foods in particular have the potential to be contaminated. Foods that require a bit of extra caution on your part include salads, uncooked vegetables and fruit, unpasteurized milk and milk products, raw meat, and shellfish. If you peel fruit yourself, it is generally safe. Cooked food that is still hot is also generally safe.

Even after cooking, some fish may not be safe because of the presence of toxins in the flesh. Tropical reef fish, red snapper, amber jack, grouper, and sea bass are occasionally toxic if they are caught on tropical reefs rather than in the open ocean. The barracuda and puffer fish are usually toxic, and you should try to avoid eating them. The highest risk areas for fish toxicity include the islands of the West Indies and the tropical Pacific and Indian Oceans.

Part V
Returning Home

The 5th Wave — By Rich Tennant

AFTER RETURNING FROM STUDYING ABROAD FOR SO LONG, ANTHONY FOUND HIS OLD FRIENDS STRANGE AND UNFAMILIAR.

In this part . . .

It may be hard to believe, but your time abroad will come to an end and you will have to return home. In this part, I cover all the details of concluding your abroad adventure: from taking exams to packing and saying good-byes to getting yourself through customs when you arrive back in the United States. I also talk about how you may feel like a Martian when you arrive home or back on campus. And for those of you who have fallen in love with traveling or living outside of the U.S., I give you a head start on ideas for going back abroad after you graduate from college.

Chapter 19

All Good Things Must End: Getting Ready to Go Home

*Y*our semester or year abroad has flown by. You're in the process of taking final exams, writing papers, and thinking about how you're going to get all your stuff into two pieces of luggage to go home. Maybe you're already feeling a little anxious about going home. Or you're in denial that this wonderful experience is quickly coming to an end. You feel like you just got here!

Sadly, you've got to go back home. You have things to do there — including finishing your undergraduate degree. For now, you need to close out this chapter of your life. And it isn't easy. As usual, the end of the semester is full of chaos and administrative details to take care of. You're probably more interested in spending your last days with your friends, wandering around the city you've lived in, and visiting all your favorite spots than you are in taking exams.

Don't book your plane ticket home for the day after you finish your exams. Give yourself a few extra days to say goodbyes and pack, so you're not stressed out about exams and packing all at once. If you need packing advice, check out Chapter 13.

Tying Up Loose Ends at School

At the end of your semester or year abroad, you must fulfill all your academic responsibilities, which include taking exams and making sure you collect all your academic materials (papers, textbooks, syllabi, and so on). You also need to take the time to say goodbye to people and places in your host country.

Make sure that you've returned all your outstanding library books, paid all the necessary fees, and completed any paperwork the international student office requires. You don't want your transcript, and therefore, the transfer of your credits, being held up because you forgot to pay a small library fine or turn in the keys to your dorm room!

Taking exams

You may find the end of a semester abroad very different than it is at home. Maybe at home you mostly write final papers or take-home exams. Maybe you're used to a flexible exam schedule, with professors letting you take exams early or late for various reasons; or you may even have self-scheduled exams! Don't expect this to happen while you're abroad.

Abroad universities tend to take final exams very seriously, primarily because they carry a much greater weight than they do in the U.S. Expect to sit through several three or four hour exams. (I took four exams in June, all of which counted somewhere between 85–100 percent of my final grade!) You have to take the exam on the day it is given — not earlier and not later, unless you have a catastrophe.

My younger sister graduated from high school on the same Saturday that I had my last exam. (Yes, exams may be given on Saturdays when you're abroad!) But there was no way for me to fly home for this. The department and course I had the exam in was just too large to accommodate special requests for exam changes. My only option was to take the make-up exam in late September; I would be in the middle of fall semester in the U.S. by then!

If you need to write final papers at the end of the semester, my best advice to you is to plan ahead. Chances are that you're at a big university where libraries are crowded and resources are a little harder to come by during finals. Many universities abroad do not have the same type of extended library hours during the regular semester or even during reading periods and finals that you may be accustomed to in the U.S. Additionally, if you don't have easy access to a computer, plan on spending time in computer labs and maybe waiting a little while to use a computer. If computer facilities allow you to book computers ahead of time, take advantage of this option.

Ensuring transfer of credit

Shortly after you return to your home university, you need to follow up with your registrar's office, dean, and major department to make sure all of your study abroad credits transferred correctly. As tempted as you are to throw out all your academic materials as you pack for home, don't! Although dragging textbooks, notebooks, syllabi, and papers home with you is a pain, it's the best way to guarantee that you receive credit for the work you've done. And if your course credit ever comes into question at your home university (for example, should a course count toward your major credits?), you can provide your home university professors with these materials. You can sometimes ship these things inexpensively at a book rate. If you want to avoid bringing textbooks home (unless you got attached to them), making note of the title, authors, publisher, and edition should be enough.

Keep copies of syllabi, notes, and graded papers. Always give papers directly to your professor, not to another student or a department secretary. If you turned in assignments (papers, projects, problem sets, and so on) that were to be graded and the professor has yet to hand them back, you must track these down! Professors aren't always the best at handing things back at the end of the semester, but you should be persistent, yet polite in your requests. If you leave before the professor has a chance to grade your assignment, provide him or her with a self-addressed, stamped envelope and ask that he or she mail it back to you when it is graded.

Goodbyes are never easy . . .

Goodbyes are hard. But maybe you'll return to your host country someday for a visit, volunteer work, or further academic study. So you may want to think of this not as goodbye, but rather "see you later." Before I left Dublin, I went to all my favorite local hangouts: coffee shops, bookstores, pubs, and restaurants. My Irish friends had a full week of goodbye events for me (they're always looking for an excuse for a party).

Taking the time to say goodbye to people, friends, places, and memories is important. Spend as much time as possible with your host family and friends. Attend all the going-away parties and allow friends or your host family to accompany you to the airport. Collect addresses, phone numbers, and e-mail addresses from your new friends.

Abruptly ending relationships and leaving a social and physical environment is much more stressful than slowly letting go.

Make sure to bring some of your host country home with you! Think about what you'll miss and try to collect reminders. Souvenirs, posters, clothing, favorite foods, and music are all excellent candidates. If you haven't faithfully used your camera during your stay, now is the time to take it out! Photographs of your friends and your experiences relieve some stress, just as photographs of your friends and family from home helped you adjust to your host country.

Adjusting to your new perspective

It would be impossible to spend months in a foreign country and emerge from the experience unchanged, as the same person who left the U.S. months ago. You have learned as much outside the university as you did in it, and coming home with all of this new knowledge can lead to something like the culture shock you experienced when you first arrived at your host university.

It may sound a little corny, but take some time to yourself to reflect on your abroad experience when preparing to go home. Think about who you were when you arrived in your host country and how this experience has affected your thinking and personality (politics, interpersonal relationships, priorities, view of time, community identification, and so on). Make sure you've done everything that you wanted to do.

Questions to start you thinking include:

✔ In what ways have I changed?

✔ In what ways may my friends and family have changed?

✔ What am I looking forward to most/least about going home?

✔ What lessons and skills have I learned that I do not want to forget?

✔ What can I do to make my transition at home easier?

✔ What are the important things about this study abroad experience that I want to share with family and friends?

✔ What do I want to do with the experience I've had (thesis, language study, go abroad again)?

✔ What experiences did I have that shocked and surprised me about the world?

✔ What stereotypes have I let go of? Kept? Modified?

✔ How did my experience make me think differently about the U.S.?

✔ What made me feel most "American" abroad?

Packing, Revisited: Clearing Customs

When you arrive back in the United States after enduring a long plane ride and the chaos of the luggage carousel, you have one thing left to do before you can greet your family and go home for a decent meal and some sleep: You need to clear U.S. Customs. Before landing, you fill out a Customs declaration form that declares everything you brought back that you did not take with you when you left the U.S. You then give this form to a U.S. Customs official, pass an inspection, and pay duties (if necessary) before you can leave the airport.

According to U.S. law, Customs inspectors are authorized to examine all luggage, cargo, and travelers that cross a U.S. border.

Check out the Web site www.state.gov/travel for the most up-to-date Customs info.

Determining what to declare

The basic rule on declarations is this: If you're bringing it back with you and you didn't have it when you left the U.S., you must declare it on your Customs form. If its total value is more than your Customs exemption, it is subject to duty.

Determining what you need to declare is much easier if you think about this while you're packing to leave your abroad country. Try to pack the things you need to declare separately and remember to keep sales slips throughout your time abroad so itemizing your Customs form is easy. On the Customs declaration you must state in U.S. currency what you actually paid for each item (including taxes). If you received an item as a gift, get an estimate of its retail value in the country where you received it. If you bought something on your trip and wore or used it on the trip (for example, clothing), it's still subject to duties.

U.S. Customs requires you to declare the following:

- ✔ Items you purchased and are carrying with you back to the U.S.
- ✔ Items you received as gifts (such as birthday presents).
- ✔ Items you bought in duty-free shops or on the plane.
- ✔ Items you brought home for someone else.

Register expensive items before you leave the U.S. or you may need to pay duty on them when you return to the U.S. For example, if your camera was made in Japan you may have to pay duty on it each time you bring it back into the U.S. unless you can prove that you owned it before you left on your trip. Documents that fully describe the item (such as sales receipts, insurance policies, jeweler's appraisals) are accepted as proof. You can also register items with Customs before you depart as long as they have serial numbers or other unique, permanent markings. Take the items to the nearest Customs Office and request a certificate of registration. This shows that you had the items with you before leaving the U.S. and all items listed on the form are allowed duty-free entry. Customs inspectors must see the item you are registering in order to certify the certificate of registration. You can register items with Customs at the international airport from which you're departing.

Bringing home food and medicine

Customs inspectors are required to enforce laws and requirements of other government agencies, such as the Drug Enforcement Administration (DEA) and the Food and Drug Administration (FDA), to protect community health and preserve domestic plant and animal life.

Food

Most fruits and vegetables either are prohibited from entering the United States or require an import permit (you most likely don't have one of these). Every fruit or vegetable must be declared to the Customs officer and be presented for inspection, no matter how free of pests it appears to be. Failure to declare all food products can result in civil penalties. Meats, livestock, poultry, and their by-products are either prohibited or restricted from entering the United States, depending on the animal disease condition in the country of origin. Importing fresh meat is generally prohibited and bringing in canned, cured, or dried meat is severely restricted from most countries.

Do yourself a favor and don't arrive home with fruits, vegetables, or meat! But feel free to bring home candies, chocolates, or other types of preserved foods.

Medication

By law, U.S. residents may import up to 50 doses of a controlled medication without a valid prescription at an international land border. You must declare that you have controlled medications in your possession upon arrival. Keep any medications you're bringing into the U.S. in their original containers.

It is against the law to not properly declare imported medications to U.S. Customs.

Be aware that you may not be able to import drug products that are not approved by the U.S. Food and Drug Administration. This is primarily because such drugs are often of unknown quality and could include addictive and dangerous substances.

Unapproved new drugs are any drugs, including foreign-made versions of U.S. approved drugs, that have not received FDA approval. It is your obligation, not the responsibility of U.S. Customs, to demonstrate that any drugs you want to bring in have been approved by the FDA. Unapproved, and therefore illegal, drugs for personal use may be refused entry or seized.

Do not assume that medications that are legal in foreign countries are also approved for use in the U.S. The FDA strongly discourages buying drugs sold in foreign countries. To find out if a drug has been approved by the FDA, check out www.fda.gov.

In addition to federal requirements, individual states may have additional requirements covering prescription or controlled medications. Travelers should check with state authorities to verify that a particular prescription does in fact comply with state regulations. In many areas, the local police department and pharmacies can provide additional information.

Try to finish all medications or have very few doses left when you go back to the U.S. You can always refill prescriptions there.

Sending things home

Inevitably, some of you out there just can't get everything that you've bought or collected while abroad in those two pieces of luggage (Remember that the airline imposes a luggage weight limit per bag of anywhere from 40-70 pounds). To save room in your luggage, consider donating old clothes, towels, or sheets to a charity shop in your host country or ask your host country friends if they could use such items. If you still can't fit everything in, you may need to ship some stuff. However, this can get expensive, so try to keep shipping items to a minimum. Don't mail home valuables, breakables, or anything sentimental because packages can be permanently lost. Consider mailing back old, unseasonable clothes, books, or other bulky items that don't have much value.

Items mailed to the U.S. are still subject to duty when they arrive. They can't be included in your Customs exemption when you get off the plane, and duty on them cannot be prepaid.

Shipping through the U.S. mail, including parcel post, is the most cost-efficient way to send things to the United States. The Postal Service sends all foreign mail shipments to Customs for examination. Customs then returns packages that don't require duty back to the Postal Service for delivery. If a package requires payment of duty, Customs attaches a form indicating how much duty is owed and charges a $5 processing fee as well. When the post office delivers the package, it also charges a handling fee.

You can send your personal belongings, like worn clothing, back to the United States duty-free if they are of U.S. origin. Just write the words "American Goods Returned" on the outside of the package and they will receive duty-free entry.

Duty on items you mail home to yourself will be waived if the value is $200 or less. So carry all your new stuff with you on the plane because your duty exemption is greater this way.

Doing Your Duty: Fees for the Stuff You Bring Home

If you bring items back with you that you didn't have when you left and their total value is more than your Customs exemption, then those items are subject to duty. *Duty* is the amount of money you pay on items coming from another country. It is similar to a tax, except that duty is collected only on imported goods. You most likely won't run into too many problems with paying duties, unless you exceed your exemption or try to import more alcohol and tobacco than you're legally allowed.

Understanding the duty-free exemption

The duty-free exemption, also called the *personal exemption*, is the total value of merchandise you may bring back to the United States without having to pay duty. If the cost of items you bring back exceeds your exemption, you have to pay duty on it. In most cases, the personal exemption is $800, but this rule has some exceptions. Additionally, you are limited on how much alcohol and tobacco you can bring back with you.

If you are returning from a Caribbean Basin country or a U.S. insular possession (U.S. Virgin Islands, American Samoa, or Guam) different exemption regulations apply.

You are entitled to duty-free exemptions if the items you bring back with you meet the following conditions:

- ✔ The items are for your personal use.

- ✔ The items accompany you when you return to the United States. You may not include shipped items in your duty-free exemption.

- ✔ You declare all items to Customs. If you do not declare something that should have been declared, you risk forfeiting it! If in doubt, declare it!

- ✔ The items aren't prohibited or restricted.

Don't be misled by the term "duty-free" shop — it does not mean that items purchased there aren't subject to duty when you return home. Items sold in duty-free shops are duty and tax exempt only in the country where the shop is located. Keep in mind that anything purchased in a duty-free shop is supposed to be taken out of the country; you're not supposed to use, wear, eat, or drink the item in the country where you purchased it.

Tobacco rules

The $800 exemption typically allows you to import not more than 200 cigarettes and 100 cigars.

You may import previously exported tobacco products as long as they do not exceed the amount indicated in your exemption allowance. If you bring back previously exported tobacco products not permitted by an exemption, they will be seized and destroyed.

Tobacco products of Cuban origin are prohibited unless you actually acquire them in Cuba and are returning directly or indirectly from that country. You may not, for example, bring in Cuban cigars purchased in Canada. Persons returning from Cuba may bring into the U.S. no more than $100 worth of goods.

Alcoholic beverage rules

You are allowed to include one liter of alcoholic beverages in your exemption as long as you are 21 years old, you are carrying it for your own consumption or as a gift, and it does not violate the laws of the state in which you arrive. State laws may limit the amount of alcohol you can bring in without the appropriate license. Customs officials enforce state law on importing alcohol even if it may be more restrictive than federal regulations.

If you bring back more than one liter of alcoholic beverage for personal use, you have to pay duty and Internal Revenue Service tax. Federal law prohibits shipping alcoholic beverages by mail within the United States.

While federal regulations do not specify a limit on the amount of alcohol you may bring back for personal use, importing unusual quantities of alcohol raise suspicion that you are importing the alcohol for other purposes, such as resale.

Unlike other kinds of merchandise, amounts of tobacco and alcohol beyond those that qualify as duty-free are taxed, even if you have not exceeded, or even met, your personal exemption. For example, if your exemption is $800 and you only bring back four liters of wine, three liters will incur duties.

Gifts

Gifts you bring back from a trip abroad fall under "personal use." Gifts worth up to $100 may be received, free of duty and tax, by friends and relatives in the U.S., as long as the same person does not receive more than $100 worth of gifts in a single day.

If you shipped gifts prior to your return to the U.S., you don't have to declare the gifts because you did not carry them on the plane with you. Know that if a package is subject to duty, the U.S. Postal Service will collect it from the addressee. The sender cannot prepay duty.

By federal law, alcoholic beverages, tobacco products, and perfume containing alcohol and worth more than $5 retail may not be included in the gift exemption.

Also, don't try to get creative and send a "gift" package to yourself. There's no reason to do this because the personal exemption for packages mailed from abroad is $200.

Duty-free or reduced rates

The United States gives duty preferences — that is, free or reduced rates — to certain countries. Check with Customs for details on these programs:

  ✔ Developing countries that fall under a trade program called the Generalized System of Preferences (GSP). Some products are not subject to duty when they come from a GSP country.

✔ Many products of Caribbean and Andean countries are exempt from duty under the Caribbean Basin Initiative, Caribbean Basin Trade Partnership Act, and Andean Trade Preference Act.

✔ Most products of certain sub-Saharan African countries are exempt from duty under the African Growth and Opportunity Act.

✔ Most products of Israel may also enter the United States either free of duty or at a reduced rate.

✔ If you're returning from Canada or Mexico, your items are eligible for free or reduced duty rates if they were grown, manufactured, or produced in Canada or Mexico, thanks to the North American Free Trade Agreement (NAFTA).

Paying duties

If you owe duty, you must pay it when you arrive in the U.S. You can pay it in any of the following ways:

✔ In U.S. currency.

✔ Personal check in the exact amount, drawn on a U.S. bank, made payable to the U.S. Customs Service. You must present identification, such as a passport or driver's license.

✔ Government check, money order, or traveler's check if it does not exceed the duty owed by more than $50.

✔ In some locations, you may pay with credit cards, either MasterCard or VISA.

Chapter 20

Bracing Yourself for Re-entry Shock

*Y*ou'll probably find many aspects of studying abroad tedious, annoying, or inconvenient. You may find your academic work or new cultural living environment challenging. But nothing is as outright difficult or next to impossible as returning home. How can coming home be hard, you ask. You're coming back to a place you know! Ah, but you're coming back as a different person than the one who left 12 weeks or 8 months ago.

Returning home comes with a mix of happiness and sadness. While on one hand you're returning to all you love in the States (and if you start referring to the U.S. as "the States," then you know you adjusted very well to your abroad home!), at the same time, you're leaving everything you learned to love in your abroad country, including new friends.

When you come home, you go through a period of reverse culture shock. *Reverse culture shock* consists of feeling out of place in your own country or experiencing a sense of disorientation. While everything is familiar, you feel different. This chapter helps you identify reverse culture shock, understand it, and then work your way through it, so that you're not jumping on the next plane out of the U.S.

Feeling Strange? It's Reverse Culture Shock

Cross-cultural adjustment doesn't end when you set foot back on U.S. soil. The bad news: Reverse culture shock can be more stressful, start earlier, and last longer than the stress of adapting abroad. In fact, chances are that the more you immersed yourself in the host culture, the more you will experience re-entry stress when you return home. A successful adjustment abroad tends to increase your self-confidence and you fail to anticipate difficulties in coming home and end up getting blindsided by reverse culture shock.

You know you're experiencing reverse culture shock when you feel disoriented and out of place in your own home, town, and country. For example, you get off the plane and make your way to the baggage carousel and hearing everyone speak English feels slightly surreal. Many things feel distinctly different than when you left — something is just not quite right.

So, what is different? YOU ARE! You may not realize that you've changed until you come home. Most students return home more self-confident, flexible, tolerant, creative, and worldly. Your behavior and communication patterns have changed and most likely, so have your values.

Be aware of how your behaviors and values shifted while you were abroad because these differences can lead to awkwardness or conflict between you and your friends or family.

You probably return with a greater awareness of your U.S. culture. In fact, you may find yourself outright disgruntled or annoyed with your home culture. Remember when you were abroad and thought host nationals did not "do things right" or do things "the American way." Eventually, you probably lost most of these feelings and even began to believe that your host culture did things better than we do in the U.S. Now that you're home, you're wondering why Americans don't do things the right way!

Wait, I have to go back home?

For me, coming home was the most challenging part of studying abroad. I knew I didn't want to come home long before final exams started and planned to stay in Dublin through the summer. My parents were afraid I was never coming home. I returned to the U.S. in mid-August, two weeks before I was due back at school. Initially, coming home was bittersweet — I missed my Irish friends, living in a city, and the mild Dublin summer. But I was looking forward to the things I had missed while abroad, like ice cream shops, chocolate chips, my sisters, as well as my final year of college.

I think I was home all of two days before I was ready to hop on the next plane to Dublin. Nothing was as I had left it, and it seemed like my life was in another country — not in Boston. When I went back to college, the shock became even more obvious. This may seem like a very elementary observation, but everyone's life went on without me! I mean, I expected life to continue on without me, but I didn't expect to feel so out of the loop. Even to this day, my sister occasionally says, "Remember when . . . oh, wait, you were in Dublin when that happened." I'm still catching up on that year I was away.

Realize that reverse culture shock is normal. You learn and grow from it, even if it seems a bit painful at times. You cannot avoid reverse culture shock — it is an inevitable part of study abroad. And, if you find yourself experiencing it, don't hide from it! I give you some tips on effective ways to cope with culture shock later in this chapter.

Examining the Stages of Reverse Culture Shock

Just like culture shock, which I discuss in Chapter 15, reverse culture shock progresses in four stages. The amount of time you spend in each stage varies. The first stage starts before you even leave your host country and the last stage is completed as you are happily re-settled in at home.

Stage 1: Disengagement

While you're still abroad, you start to think about returning to the U.S. You think about leaving the new home you've made for yourself and saying good-bye not only to your friends, but also the place you now call home. You may even start to feel anxious about the transition. The stress of finals, goodbye parties, and packing can make you feel sad and frustrated. You haven't even left and you already miss the friends you've made and are starting to feel reluctant about leaving.

Stage 2: Euphoria

You're excited to be home, your parents and siblings are excited that you've returned, and your friends can't wait to see you. Everyone is so excited to have you back — the phone calls and social plans can get overwhelming! People say how nice it is that you're home and ask about your abroad experience, which you can't help talking about, but it's not long before they're obviously no longer paying attention and are interested in something else (usually talking about themselves).

Stage 3: Alienation

The thrill of being home or back at school has worn off. You feel alienated, frustrated, and maybe even a little angry. Everything may seem different from how you remember it. You find yourself getting easily irritated and impatient with others — your friends and family don't seem to have grown as much as you have. You grow frustrated with yourself and the struggle you're having readjusting. You may feel lonely, resentful, helpless, "out of it," or sad (all these feelings are normal!).

Stage 4: Gradual readjustment

You start to readjust to life at home. You get your "groove" back. You're used to U.S. traffic patterns and having a million cable channels at your fingertips once again. You're biting your tongue when you want to make a comment about how things in your abroad country were better. Your study abroad experience is becoming an integrated part of your life.

Dealing with the Feelings

When you return home, feeling slightly depressed, uncertain, confused, or restless is normal. You may want to be alone. You may realize that your priorities have changed, as well as your future career goals. Or maybe you hate the U.S. all of a sudden and are homesick for your abroad country. You may also feel extremely bored. You probably lived in an environment with a high activity and anticipation level. You could hop a plane or a train and go to Paris for the weekend and now there are no exotic destinations suitable for a weekend trip.

You wonder why your friends and family don't seem to understand the importance of your experience abroad. They all ask questions about your experience, but don't pay any attention to your answers or just don't understand what was so special about living somewhere else. Or maybe you just can't seem to explain all you saw and did while you were away. You have trouble talking about your experience with people who haven't had similar studies or travels abroad.

You also may feel trapped in pre-abroad roles that now no longer fit because of your experience. Maybe you developed new interests while you were away. Maybe before you left you were a little quieter and more of a listener when you found yourself in a group setting. Now, you're more outgoing, talkative, and an active participant.

Many students fear that they're going to "lose" their study abroad experience upon returning home. It will just fade away and become a distant memory. Once you get involved in your busy day-to-day activities here, you may feel like you were never abroad and that semester or year is increasingly seeming like a souvenir or photo album that you only occasionally revisit.

All these feelings are okay — and you should deal with them in the way that is most comfortable for you. You may just want to be left alone or you may only be interested in hanging out with other students who studied abroad on your same program or other programs. You may be unable to stop talking about your time abroad. For suggestions on how to deal with these reverse culture shock feelings, check out the next section on surviving reverse culture shock.

If you're experiencing an extraordinary amount of emotional stress, or it is taking a long time for you to readjust, you may want to consider individual counseling through your campus health center.

If you persistently feel physically ill, don't hesitate to make an appointment with your primary care physician. You should not expect problems adjusting back to the foods you eat in the U.S. And you shouldn't get sick with more than a cold.

Surviving Reverse Culture Shock

One of the best ways to get through reverse culture shock is to anticipate it. Don't think "it will never happen to me." You're going to go through a process of making your new life mesh with your old life. Maintain your perspective here. Every country has a different approach to life, and adjusting can be difficult if you're used to a different set of social norms. Integrate the best aspects of your abroad culture with your old culture. College libraries were not open on the weekends while I was in Dublin; when I returned home, I decided that I would continue to stay out of the libraries on the weekend. I had adopted the Irish sentiment that visiting a library on a weekend was a ridiculous idea!

You may have internalized some of your abroad country's philosophies, which could conflict with U.S. ways of life. When I returned from abroad, I had the hardest time being on time for anything! I was always five, ten, or fifteen minutes late. In Ireland, this was never a problem. In fact, it was expected. I was slightly puzzled as to why my American friends were upset with my lateness. I had forgotten that in the U.S. being on time is highly important. Americans are obsessed with their wristwatches.

While anticipating reverse culture shock gets you well on your way to conquering it, I give you a few other ways that can help you win this battle.

Avoid the "grass is always greener" syndrome

Don't become a victim of the "grass is always greener" syndrome. Everything is better over there. Nothing is good here. Remember that every country has its flaws and its strengths. It is easy to dramatize how wonderful your return home will be. It is similarly easy, when you've returned home, to over-romanticize your experience abroad. Be careful not to make a habit of scape-goating: blaming others for your readjustment problems. Neither life here nor there is ever perfect. So if home isn't quite the paradise you remember, know that life would probably not be perfect in your abroad country either.

Revive relationships

You've been away for a semester or a year. Realize that the friends you were close with when you left, even if you kept in touch with them, will seem differ-ent when you return. You and your friends have had unique experiences during the time you were apart. Maybe she was studying abroad, too. Or maybe he met the love of his life in the university library while you were gone. You have all changed, and you may need to adjust to interacting in different ways. The distance you feel from your friends isn't permanent. And your new experiences can make for some very interesting conversations.

If parents, siblings, or friends express bewilderment or annoyance with your behavior after you've returned home, this could be a signal that you're either experiencing reverse culture shock or that your personality has changed as a result of being abroad. The best thing you can do is explain what reverse culture shock is and tell them this is what you're experiencing. If they know what is hap-pening to you and that you're simply in the middle of the readjustment process, they can be more supportive and understanding of what you're going through. Good communication with family and friends reduces reverse culture shock.

Maintain language proficiency

One of students' biggest fears when returning home after spending time in a non-English speaking country is that they will lose their newly acquired for-eign language skills. Because you spent time and effort developing language skills that are difficult to acquire in a college classroom, try the following sug-gestions for maintaining your language proficiency.

- ✔ Keep up your language studies by registering for a language class.
- ✔ Ask the international student adviser or dean whether any students are on campus from your host country/region. You may be able to practice your language skills with them — and make a new friend.
- ✔ See whether any residents from your host country are in your local area and looking to learn English. You can make arrangements for a language exchange — you tutor them in English in exchange for having conversa-tions in their native tongue.

✔ Stay in touch with your friends and host-family abroad. Periodically call or e-mail them so you can practice your language skills.

✔ Tune into news broadcasts in your foreign language by using a short wave radio or the Internet. Read newspapers and books in your host language. Rent movies or watch TV in this language.

Take these additional hints to ease the transition

If you're experiencing a bout of reverse culture shock, here are some helpful hints to minimize the amount and length of stress you're feeling so that you can readjust to your U.S. life.

✔ Remember the coping strategies you developed overseas and use them! You increased your self-reliance while abroad and probably developed a few coping skills as you went through culture shock.

✔ Keep your sense of humor; be flexible and open-minded.

✔ Focus on the positive aspects of returning home. You can talk to family and friends without running up a huge phone bill! You can eat at your favorite restaurant! You can function in a language you're completely comfortable with and everyone understands you. You no longer get lost when trying to find the library.

✔ Practice patience with yourself and others. Appreciate the rare privilege of having two "homes."

✔ Refrain from bombarding your friends and family with nonstop pictures, anecdotes, or perspectives of your host country. They simply may not be interested in hearing endless stories about your host country, and their boredom will only frustrate you more.

✔ Don't try to do too much. Take good care of yourself and ease back into life here. In particular, realize that you need time to adjust to the hectic pace and pressures of university life. Gradually increase your day-to-day academic and extracurricular pace. You may find that you tire easily, both physically and mentally, if you take on too much too soon.

✔ Your old time and stress management tricks may no longer work, so explore other options. Even if you can now roll out of bed and go to class, you may find yourself missing your walk to school each day. So get up and go for a walk before your day begins. Or are you used to not doing work on the weekends because the libraries at your host university closed? Try to plan your schedule so you don't have to spend the weekends in the libraries here either.

✔ If your values and beliefs have changed, learn to incorporate your new way of thinking into your life.

✔ You may discover that you're frustrated by the lack of opportunities to apply the new skills you learned while abroad. I, for example, was unable to find a trampoline team that I could bounce with and so my trampoline skills went undeveloped after I returned home. Maybe while you were away, you learned to cook and made your own dinner every night. Now you're back at the mercy of the dining hall. While it may not be possible to have your own kitchen or show off other newly acquired talents, change what is possible and use your creativity!

✔ Find someone who is willing to update you on the university, local, and national changes and events that may have happened while you were away.

✔ Talk to others who have studied abroad and have already successfully readapted. They can suggest ways of dealing with reverse culture shock and they will understand how you feel.

✔ Seek out fellow study abroad returnees. They may be experiencing the exact same feelings, so communicating with them may be very easy. They can also provide you with support as you readjust. Don't be afraid to make a few new friends with whom you can share your international experiences. However, while these returnees can be a good support group, be careful that they don't become your only friends.

✔ Stay in touch with your abroad experience by taking a course with international flavor; try a history, political science, or literature course that covers your host country. Use your experience as a starting point for a thesis or independent research project; stay informed about international events and events in your abroad country.

✔ Get involved with international students; join international or multicultural clubs; go to foreign language tables at lunch. International students typically enjoy making new friends who know a little about their culture or how it feels to live abroad.

✔ Become a peer adviser or volunteer for your home university study abroad office. This allows you to stay in touch with the international world, while sharing your fantastic experience with potential study abroad students.

Never forget how lucky you were to study abroad in the first place. Most people in the world do not have the time or money to simply pack up and live in another country, and this perspective may make you less hostile to people who just don't "get" living abroad.

If you need more information

If you're struggling with reverse culture shock or just want to learn more about it, the following four books provide a more in depth discussion of the transition from life abroad to life at home.

✔ *The Art of Coming Home*, by Craig Sorti. Yarmouth, ME: Intercultural Press, 1997.

✔ *So You're Coming Home*, by J. Stewart Black and Hal Gregersen. Global Business Publisher, 1999.

✔ *Students Abroad: Strangers at Home*, by Norman Kauffman, Judith Martin, and Henry Weaver. Yarmouth, ME: Intercultural Press, 1992.

✔ *Strangers at Home: Essays on the Effects of Living Overseas and Coming "Home" to a Strange Land*, ed. by Carolyn Smith. Aletheia Publishers, 1996.

Chapter 21

Going Abroad Again!

Many of you have fallen in love with being abroad. You want to go back as soon as possible. After you graduate from college is a wonderful time to do this, if you can afford it and aren't swimming in student loans. Most college grads depart the U.S. to continue their studies, work, teach, volunteer, or just travel for fun. You may find that, for some countries, acquiring a visa to work or volunteer abroad is not as easy as getting a student visa. If you have secured employment or a volunteer position before leaving the U.S., the organization you're working with may help guide you through this process. Because going abroad the second time around is a little trickier because you're planning everything yourself, keep in touch with those you met abroad — those connections may come in handy.

Going Back for More

Quite often, the easiest way to live in a foreign country for an extended period of time is through a student visa. From the perspective of another country's government, you can stay in the country for a specific period of time to study at one of their universities because you are a paying student (unless you luck out and receive a fellowship or grant). In most countries, education for citizens is either free or costs very little, so the university makes money by having students from other countries pay higher fees to study. By the same token, you are expected to support yourself while you're studying abroad, so you contribute money to the country's economy by paying for housing, food, travel, and so on.

So if you have the motivation and the finances to spend another year studying abroad, it is a good option. You don't necessarily have to be working towards a graduate degree either. You can spend a year at a university doing post-baccalaureate work as well. A *post-bac* (as they're commonly called) consists of academic study undertaken after earning a bachelor's degree. Post-bac work can be toward a degree (such as another bachelor's degree — maybe you want to take some classes to turn your college minor into a major), toward a certification in some specialty, or just extra course work that doesn't result in a certificate or a degree. Some college graduates want to improve their academic credentials before applying to graduate schools.

The one difficult thing about embarking on studying abroad after finishing your undergrad degree is that you have to plan it all on your own. You most likely won't have the aid of a study abroad office or U.S.-based program to sort out details of what to take or where to live.

In most cases, you need to apply directly to the foreign university and deal with their international student office or the department you're accepted into to make your plans. You can also use a lot of the information in this book to assist you in studying abroad for a graduate degree. Check out Chapter 25 for ten good reasons to complete graduate study abroad.

Volunteers Anyone?

If you have the luxury of being able to spend time volunteering after you complete your undergraduate education, you can usually find a volunteer position almost anywhere in the world for varying lengths of time (from as little as three months to as long as three years). Many volunteer programs require you to commit for a specific period of time, while other agencies are always looking for volunteers and accept you for whatever time you can give them.

The number of volunteer opportunities that fully cover volunteer expenses (room, board, transportation, and a stipend) are limited. Most positions usually do provide room and board, while a few expect volunteers to cover their own expenses. If you can commit to volunteering for a year, you have a better chance of getting your organization to share a substantial portion of your expenses.

Be wary of organizations that charge fees in exchange for securing a volunteer placement for you! However, a fee may be reasonable if you apply to a short-term volunteer program that provides training, on-site support, and academic credit.

When looking for volunteer opportunities abroad, do your research. Use your home university's career center or study abroad office as a starting point. Career counselors usually keep track of alumni who volunteer abroad, so perhaps they can give you contact information or recommend a program. You also may want to check out these offices at your home university to see whether they have information on grants and fellowships for service work abroad. Volunteering abroad is financially easier for you if you obtain some level of funding!

After you identify the volunteer programs you find interesting, get the application materials if they have a formal application procedure. Otherwise, try making contact with the organization via phone or e-mail. You can also go ahead and send a cover letter and resume. Volunteer organizations are often understaffed and very busy, so follow-up on information you send to ensure that your materials have been received or to find out whether you need to provide additional information.

Volunteer organizations run the gamut from U.S. government-sponsored organizations (such as the Peace Corps), large international multigovernment-sponsored organizations (like the United Nations), smaller non-governmental–sponsored organizations (NGOs), and religious-sponsored organizations.

U.S. Government: The Peace Corps

The Peace Corps is an independent volunteer agency within the executive branch of the U.S. government. It travels and works only in countries where it is invited and attempts to provide the services requested by the inviting country. Peace Corps volunteers work with people in developing countries on a wide range of projects involving education, protection of local environments, economic opportunities, and public health initiatives (just to name a few). Thus, the Peace Corps welcomes volunteers with skills in areas such as math and science, health and nutrition, skilled trades, business, education and special education, forestry, fisheries, and agriculture. You must also be a U.S. citizen.

A benefit of joining the Peace Corps is the amount of training and support you receive as a volunteer, including intensive language and cross-cultural training so that you can become part of the community where you live. You're expected to speak the local language and adapt to the cultures and customs of the people with whom you work. The Peace Corps also covers all your expenses and transportation, extensive training, a "resettlement allowance" of approximately $5,400 at the end of the two-year assignment, and in some cases, partial cancellation of educational loans and tuition assistance for future study.

For more information, check out `www.peacecorps.gov`.

Multigovernment organizations: The UNV

The United Nations Volunteer Program (UNV) is the volunteer arm of the UN that supports sustainable human development globally by mobilizing volunteers. It works towards peace and development by creating or improving opportunities for people and communities around the world. Benefits include a settling-in grant paid at the beginning of an assignment that lasts more than three months, a monthly volunteer living allowance, travel to and from your assignment location, life and health insurance, and a resettlement allowance when you complete at least a three month assignment.

The UNV is for experienced professionals only, so if you're interested, you need to get some practical experience in your career first. The UNV is particularly interested in recruiting professionals who can share their expertise with developing countries: such as humanitarian aid specialists, senior business leaders or retired executives to work on private sector development in developing countries, and information technology professionals to employ technologies that will help human development. Go to `www.unv.org` for more info.

Non-governmental organizations (NGOs)

Non-governmental organizations can be split into two categories: those that hire only experienced professionals and those that hire volunteers without special skills (like college graduates). The NGOs that only hire experienced professionals do sometimes accept graduate school interns. NGOs seeking experienced help include Doctors without Borders, OXFAM, and Save the Children.

A sampling of NGOs that consider applicants without specific skills (a college graduate like yourself) include the following:

- ✔ Conservation Volunteers in Australia: `www.atcv.com.au`
- ✔ Food for the Hungry: `www.fh.org`
- ✔ Volunteers for Peace: `www.vfp.org`
- ✔ Visions in Action: `www.visionsinaction.org`

You may also want to check out the following Web sites for more information on NGO volunteer opportunities:

- ✔ `www.idealist.org`: A Web site that is a project of Action Without Borders. Provides searchable lists of over 33,000 nonprofit and community organizations in over 165 countries. Good starting point for those looking for international service opportunities.
- ✔ `www.charity.org`: Web site for Global Impact, which represents 50 U.S.-based international charities. Provides links to international charity organizations.
- ✔ `www.oneworld.net`: Links you with organizations that offer volunteer positions throughout the world.

Religious-affiliated organizations

Religious-affiliated organizations typically offer extensive volunteer support. These organizations also break-down into two categories: those who work for social change and those who focus on missionary work and converting others to their faith. If you're an active member of a particular faith, you may want to start your search for volunteer work abroad at your local church/temple or consult the office of religious life on your home university campus.

Religious organizations who are willing to consider applicants "open to (religious) values" even though they may not currently practice the organization's faith include Jesuit Volunteers International, United Methodist Volunteers in Mission, Christian Foundation for Children and Aging, and Brethren Volunteer Service.

Hello, My Name Is John: Teaching English Abroad

Teaching English abroad bridges the volunteer/work abroad categories. English as a Second Language (ESL) programs are all over the world and in some cases, you can get paid for this (but don't expect to become a millionaire this way!). Other programs are unpaid volunteer positions.

Don't get confused by the variety of acronyms out there that describe programs that use native English speakers to teach others to speak English as a second language. Here's what they all mean:

- EFL: English as a Foreign Language
- ESL: English as a Second Language
- TEFL: Teaching English as a Foreign Language
- TESL: Teaching English as a Second Language
- TESOL: Teachers of English to Speakers of Other Languages

While some ESL programs accept you as long as you're a native English speaker and have a bachelor's degree, other programs may require you to get certified to teach English as a foreign language before becoming an employee or volunteer. Some universities have ESL certification programs, so you may want to investigate whether your university or a nearby university has such a program. However, speak with an ESL certification program's alums before forking over the money to obtain an ESL teaching certificate. Not all programs are the same.

You can often start looking for ESL teaching opportunities at your home university's career office, as some ESL organizations actively advertise and recruit on college campuses. You can also get information on ESL programs via the Internet, using the following links as a starting point:

- ✔ www.eslmag.com: Here you can find links for job openings, ESL instructional materials, information on ESL associations, and a variety of dictionaries.

- ✔ www.eslworldwide.com: View job postings, post your resume, and research ESL organizations.

- ✔ www.eslcafe.com: Good place to access ESL resources and job opportunities. Chat with other instructors and read about other teachers' experiences.

- ✔ http://exchanges.state.gov/education/engteaching/: The State Department maintains a Web site for the Office of English Language Programs. Reliable information, answers to frequently asked questions, and information on State Department EFL programs in different regions of the world.

- ✔ www.jetprogramme.org: The Japan Exchange and Teaching Program (JET) is a well-established program for teaching English in Japan. JET Program participants are placed in organizations throughout Japan, including city governments, town and village governments, and some private schools. Program provides orientations, seminars, and a stipend to cover living expenses. Initial contracts are for one year of service.

- ✔ www.worldteach.org: WorldTeach is a non-profit, non-governmental organization based at the Center for International Development at Harvard University. It provides volunteer opportunities in developing countries such as Costa Rica, Ecuador, Namibia, the Marshall Islands, and Poland. Because WorldTeach receives no government or outside funding, volunteers are expected to pay for most of the expenses associated with their placement, travel, training, and support (You can fundraise to help cover costs). When you get to your host country, your host school, community, or government provides a living allowance.

Treat your search and application process for an ESL teaching position just like any other professional job search. Research programs, fill out applications, send cover letters/resumes when appropriate, and follow-up on your applications.

Whipping Up Work Abroad

I start off with the bad news: Starting a career abroad is difficult — but it isn't impossible. U.S. companies who have overseas offices often require you to spend a certain amount of time in a U.S. office before you're able to work in their abroad office. And you often have to prove that you have a special skill, which is why they're sending you abroad and not hiring someone native to that country. Foreign companies also have to justify why they're hiring you as opposed to a national.

If you're looking to work abroad, you have to give your job search your best effort, so set aside lots of time. Start by using your home university's career center counselors to point you in the right direction. (You're probably not the first student who has arrived in the career office wanting to work abroad.)

 Do your research! Lots of programs out there offer bogus work opportunities in exchange for a hefty fee. Or they may charge you a fee and find you an undesirable job placement. See whether any alums from your home university have had success with such services before forking out any money.

Hints for finding work abroad

To get you off on the right foot in your work abroad job search, try these tips:

✔ Determine the region, country, or field in which you want to work and then research opportunities and employers accordingly.

✔ Organize and prioritize! Request applications and application deadline information. Prioritize your program choices and develop a timeline for completing applications. Keep all of your job search materials organized and in a safe place. Take notes when you speak with representatives from potential employers.

✔ If an international employer has no formal application process, you should aim to contact them at least six months before your desired start date. (Have a cover letter and resume available.)

✔ Avoid generic application materials as much as possible. Tailor your cover letter, resume, and writing sample to the organization to which you are applying.

✔ Keep electronic or paper copies of all your application materials (in case they get lost in the mail).

✔ Follow-up with all the organizations you apply to. Allow ten days to two weeks for materials to reach the organization and give them a chance to review them. If you haven't been contacted by the programs, don't hesitate to follow-up with a phone call or e-mail! In a follow-up message, reiterate what school you are graduating from, that you forwarded materials to their attention, and if they need any additional information, they should feel free to contact you.

Short-term international employment

If your goal is to work abroad for just three months to a year, the number of options available to you are greater than if you're seeking long-term employment abroad. Most of these opportunities exist in the areas of teaching English as a second language (see the section on teaching English abroad earlier in this chapter) and hospitality or recreation jobs (such as summer camps). These particular options usually have established application procedures (that can take awhile) and provide you with the appropriate and mandatory working papers if you're hired. In these short-term situations, you don't have to struggle to acquire a work visa. The only document you need to provide is your passport.

Another bonus of short-term work abroad: You usually don't have to write a resume tailored to the conventions of the country you want to work in.

Many short-term work abroad opportunities can't be easily categorized. Most of the organizations I mention here usually actively recruit on U.S. college campuses. So keep your eyes open for career office announcements regarding employers that visit campus. The following resources also take the hassle out of obtaining working papers — which is helpful because an endless number of international employers make you responsible for getting your working papers. In this section, I also include programs that help you get working papers in a foreign country, but do not guarantee you a job. Usually, they can help you look for a job after you have your working papers.

- ✔ **BUNAC (British Universities North America Club):** Sponsors work/travel programs to Britain, Ireland, Australia, New Zealand, Canada, and South Africa that range from two to twelve months. See www.bunac.org.

- ✔ **Club Med:** Actively recruits college graduates to work in their world-wide operations (particularly the Bahamas, Mexico, or the Caribbean). Includes opportunities in food service, customer service, recreation, and much more. You must have a valid passport and be able to relocate for a minimum of six months. Check out www.clubmed.com.

- ✔ **STA Travel:** Assists participants with temporary working permits for Australia, New Zealand, Canada, Ireland, and Great Britain. They help you find work and housing and provide an in-country orientation. Finding a professional position related to your career path may take more time. Go to www.statravel.com.

- ✔ **OverseasJobs.com:** Provides excellent information on international jobs. Search for jobs by location or keywords and browse company profiles. Although many of the jobs listed on this site are more long-term, many jobs make ideal short-term opportunities. See www.overseasjobs.com.

Searching outside the box

If you're having a tough time or getting particularly discouraged with the search for a job abroad, you may want to investigate the possibility of exploring international search companies or recruiting services. Before getting too involved with this option, carefully research a company's professional credentials. It also may help to check out these books, written specifically for anyone searching for a job abroad:

✔ *Work Abroad: The Complete Guide to Finding a Job Overseas* (4th edition) by Clayton A. Hubbs (ed.), Transitions Abroad Publishing, 2002. Available at `www.transitionsabroad.com`. A guide to all aspects of international work, including work permits, short-term jobs, teaching English, volunteer opportunities, and planning out an international career.

✔ *Work Worldwide: International Career Strategies for the Adventurous Job Seeker* by Nancy Mueller, Avalon Travel Publishing, 2000.

Long-term international employment

If international travel and work are a part of your long-term career plans, you can choose from a variety of government, not-for-profit, and corporate jobs that afford you the opportunity to live and work abroad for significant periods of time throughout your career. (Note: You may not immediately be working and living overseas.) A great way to learn about careers with an international twist is through your home university's alumni network. See whether you can contact alumni who have (or had) international careers.

Have you ever considered working for a university's study abroad program? U.S. schools typically need staff to coordinate their programs in various countries. You may be based in the country where the program is as a resource to its abroad program participants. Or you may be based in the U.S. but visit the program in its abroad location several times per year. You can usually stay in this job for several years and it may lead to other employment opportunities abroad.

Conducting your search

Finding a job that provides you with opportunities to live or travel abroad throughout your career is challenging. Don't get discouraged. Remind yourself why you like being abroad and focus on your long-term career goals. Be patient and diligent in your search.

The actual mechanics of searching for an international job are not that much different from searching for a job here in the U.S. (be sure to check out the hints for finding work abroad earlier in this chapter). Employers with international opportunities are more interested in your specific skills and competencies (such as whether you know Javascript) than in what languages you speak. Although language skills could be as important as your job skills and competencies in some international jobs, focusing on how to become competitive for a specific job or field (for example, complete an internship or take specific courses) betters your chances for a successful long-term international job search.

Understand the visa requirements for working in a particular country before you begin talking to employers. Consult the country's embassy Web site to start researching working visa information.

Making your search effective

I've put together some tips for finding work abroad that are particularly helpful if you're looking for a long-term job or career opportunity.

- ✔ Do your homework! After you identify the field that interests you, research companies and organizations that have the type of job you want and an international presence.

- ✔ Network, network, network! Discuss your career plans with your professors, family, and a career counselor. Ask them for help contacting people who may already work in your areas of interest and then interview these people.

- ✔ Pay attention to career center programs and events. Companies in which you are interested may conduct informational sessions at your home university. Meet with recruiters and get information about who to contact regarding your specific interests, including options to work abroad for their company.

- ✔ Understand that the competition for positions abroad is tough. Spend extra time polishing cover letters and resumes. Make sure to highlight your relevant skills and experience for that particular employer or job. If you really care about getting the job, take the time to get a second opinion on cover letters and resumes before you send them out. Career counselors usually have time to review job search correspondence.

Part VI
The Part of Tens

The 5th Wave   By Rich Tennant

In this part . . .

*E*very *For Dummies* book ends with a part devoted to top-ten lists. I include four lists on the more practical side, which cover why going to graduate school abroad is such a great idea, some unusual study abroad options, and exciting getaways in all corners of the globe.

Chapter 22

Ten Unique Study Abroad Programs

*H*ow cool would it be to spend an entire semester on a sailboat and get academic credit for it? In this part of tens, I investigate study abroad programs that are slightly off the beaten path. My criteria for inclusion: There has to be something about the program that makes it stand out, whether it is the guarantee of an internship, a service learning opportunity, or a program that provides a study abroad experience based in more than one country. Also, for those of you who are artistically inclined, I've included study abroad programs that provide hands-on experience in the performing or visual arts.

Field Experience/Internship Programs

There are several study abroad programs out there that provide an opportunity to observe or get involved with a culture through volunteer work or internships. This is a great way to make friends, improve your language skills, and learn about a working world outside of the U.S. Also, many programs offer opportunities for independent field research projects while abroad, which can be a great way to start a senior or master's thesis.

Arcadia University internship programs

Arcadia University's Center for Education Abroad offers five fall or spring semester internship programs, as well as summer internship programs, for academic credit. These include the Australian, Dublin, or Scotland Parliamentary Internship programs, the London Internship program, and the Sydney

Internship program. For each program, extensive coursework in the subject area or prior internship or professional experience is preferred. Because internships are for academic credit, they are unpaid. The Australian Parliamentary internship offers an internship with the Australian Parliament or in a public service agency, an industry or community organization, or a lobby group. In addition, you are responsible for completing coursework in Australian politics and government at the Australian National University (ANU).

The Dublin Parliamentary internship pairs you with a member of Parliament and requires that you take courses at the Institute of Public Administration with other North American students.

The Scottish Parliamentary internship also pairs you with a member of Parliament and expects you to pursue some coursework at the University of Edinburgh in British and Scottish politics and government, as well as Scottish society and culture.

Both the Sydney and London internship programs offer the opportunity to earn academic credit while working side-by-side with Australian/British professionals in areas such as arts, business, communications, public policy, or the social sciences. You'll also need to participate in and receive credit for courses that complement your professional and academic interests.

Arcadia University's Center for Education Abroad, 450 S. Easton Road, Glenside, PA 19038; phone 866-927-2234; Web site www.arcadia.edu/cea.

Consortium for Overseas Teaching

The Consortium for Overseas Teaching (COST) is a student teaching program that sends college seniors overseas to fulfill their student teaching requirements in American-sponsored overseas schools or in overseas schools under the supervision of institutions with which COST has an agreement. Placements are available in Australia, Bahamas, Canada, Costa Rica, Ecuador, England, Greece, Ireland, Japan, Mexico, New Zealand, Scotland, South Africa, and Switzerland.

COST strives to arrange student teaching experiences that help prospective teachers not only develop the skills associated with teaching, but also teach in a bilingual setting and learn how to bring an international perspective back to their classrooms in the U.S. Some of the student teachers who participate in this program accept full-time jobs abroad after finishing. Students typically live in homes of local citizens during their stay abroad.

COST is a voluntary pact among a group of U.S. colleges and universities working together on student teaching placements in a setting outside the U.S. The COST offices are located at the University of Alabama.

Office of Clinical Experiences, College of Education, University of Alabama, 105 Graves Hall, Box 870231, Tuscaloosa, AL 35487; phone 205-348-1153; Web site www.teachabroad.ua.edu.

International Partnership for Service Learning

The International Partnership for Service-Learning (IPSL) offers a study abroad program that combines academics with volunteer service and homestays, which immerse you in the host country culture in many different ways. IPSL has programs in the Czech Republic, Ecuador, England, France, India, Israel, Jamaica, Mexico, the Philippines, Russia, Scotland, South Africa, Thailand, and on a Native American reservation in South Dakota.

The program's courses are designed to increase your fluency in the host country's language, provide a thorough understanding of the local culture, and integrate your volunteer experience with classroom learning. Undergraduates take 12-18 credits per semester, 24-36 credits for a year-long program, and 6-12 credits if participating in a summer program.

IPSL students are not housed as a group with other Americans. They live with host families or in university housing where they can interact with students from the host nation and speak the local language.

Your IPSL program director secures a volunteer placement for you that hopefully fits with your interests and skills, as well as the community needs in the area you plan to visit. You spend approximately 15-20 hours per week volunteering. You study with other IPSL students, but you may be the only IPSL student in your volunteer placement. At most, you work with only one or two other IPSL students, which maximizes your contact with and contribution to the agency. Service projects usually fall into three categories: teaching and tutoring, health care, and community development. Examples include serving at schools, orphanages, healthcare institutions, or recreational centers. For example, at a school in Jamaica, volunteers provide one-on-one tutoring. Healthcare volunteers have assisted at a trauma center in Scotland and distributed pharmaceuticals for Medicine without Frontiers in France.

You don't receive credit for just showing up to your volunteer placement and working the requisite 15-20 hours per week. That fulfills your service requirement, but your school credit comes from the courses connected to your service project, in which you demonstrate what you've learned in papers, presentations, and examinations that are evaluated by the professors of the host university.

A transcript is issued by the host university at the conclusion of the program, and The International Partnership forwards it to you and to your home college or university.

The International Partnership for Service-Learning, 815 Second Ave, Suite 315, New York, NY 10017; phone 212-986-0989; Web site www.ipsl.org.

Lexia

Lexia offers more than 12 different semester-long international study abroad programs in locations all over the globe. Lexia's semester starts out with highly structured coursework and concludes with weeks of independent study and field work.

In all non-English-speaking sites, students must take an intensive language course taught by faculty associated with the Lexia program at the local affiliated university or a specialized language institution. All students also take an interdisciplinary civilization seminar, which covers the history, society, politics, art, economics, geography, and cultural aspects of the host country and is led by professors from the host institution.

The less structured portion of the semester begins with a research methods seminar that introduces students to fieldwork methods (observation, participation, surveying, interviewing, analysis, and so on) and how to report knowledge gained in the field in academic writing. Finally, students are expected to complete an independent field research project on a topic of their choice that relates to the host country's culture.

Lexia also offers the option of completing an internship in addition to required coursework. Internships must be requested in advance, are unpaid, and require only ten hours per week. Lexia students have completed internships in government, the arts, health care, business, media and non-profit organizations.

Lexia International, 25 South Main Street, Hanover, NH 03755; phone 800-77-LEXIA; Web site www.lexiaintl.org.

School for Field Studies

The School for Field Studies (SFS) focuses on environmental studies and research. SFS offers fall and spring semester programs as well as shorter summer courses. Their field study centers are located in Australia, Canada, the British West Indies, Costa Rica, Kenya, and Mexico. While the SFS program is particularly attractive to students interested in environment-related fields, students from a wide variety of academic backgrounds study with them. SFS uses an interdisciplinary case study approach to solve environmental problems.

Each SFS Center has a director and three full-time faculty members (usually an ecologist, a resource manager, and an ecological economist) who live on-site. SFS programs incorporate lectures with hands-on field work and directed research projects. The research projects are designed based on the requests of local residents or organizations. The results of students' projects are put to use by local clients for helping to improve conditions or direct progress on environmental issues.

All SFS participants are registered at and receive credit from Boston University, which accredits SFS programs, unless students are from SFS Affiliate and Consortium schools, in which case they receive credit directly from their home institutions.

The School for Field Studies, 10 Federal Street, Salem, MA, 01970; phone 800-989-4418; Web site www.fieldstudies.org.

School for International Training

The School for International Training (SIT) offers 55 experiential, field-based-learning study abroad programs. SIT, which is accredited by the New England Association of Schools and Colleges, Inc., aims to advance international under-standing, help students work and learn in multicultural environments, and aid community and country development. Most programs include an orientation, intensive language studies, an extended homestay, coursework, a field study seminar, an independent study project, and field trips.

SIT constructs programs around a theme related to the host country's culture: environmental studies, development studies, arts, gender studies, multicultural studies, peace and conflict resolution, or social justice. Each theme-based pro-gram has an interdisciplinary curriculum taught by local professors, experts, and professionals.

SIT offers language study coordinated through universities, language institutes, or qualified private teachers. The field study seminar teaches you research methods for independent fieldwork. Your independent study project (which makes a nice springboard for a senior thesis) is conducted on the topic of your choice and supervised by your academic director and a local professor. SIT arranges field trips to the region's major cultural, natural, and historical sites related to your course of study.

School for International Training, Kipling Road, P.O. Box 676, Brattleboro, VT, 05302; phone 800-257-7751; Web site www.sit.edu.

Programs with Multiple Locations

Can't decide where to study? Would you like to see more than one city during your abroad experience? Then maybe choosing a program that allows you to sail down the Atlantic coast or check out locales along the route from the U.S. to Europe to Asia to South America is for you.

International Honors Program

The International Honors Program (IHP) allows students to study abroad in multiple countries for either a semester or a year. IHP focuses on interdisciplinary study and cross-cultural comparison. IHP offers four different programs, each with its own theme and itinerary: Global Ecology (England, India, the Philippines, New Zealand, Mexico, and the United States), Challenges of a Global Culture (Nepal and Tibet), Indigenous Perspectives (United States, India, New Zealand, and Mexico), and Cities in the 21st Century (New York; Chennai and Bangalore, India; Cape Town, South Africa; Rio de Janeiro and Curitiba, Brazil; Boston).

IHP programs are relatively small, with about 30 participants in each one, and major fields of participants vary. Students are expected to take a full course load, and courses are taught by traveling IHP faculty and coordinators from each country visited. Course work includes traditional classroom meetings as well as guest lecturers, fieldwork, case studies, and frequent field trips. Students typically live with host families.

IHP partners with Boston University, Bard College, and Trinity College.

International Honors Program, Boston University, 232 Bay State Road, 5th Floor, Boston, MA 02215; phone 617-353-9888; Web site www.ihp.edu.

Sea Education Association

The Sea Education Association (SEA) offers both a twelve-week semester program and an eight-week summer program for undergraduate credit. Located on Cape Cod in Woods Hole, Massachusetts, the program combines coursework, research, and hands-on experience. The first half of the program, or "shore component," is spent on coursework in which students study maritime history and literature, ship navigation, oceanography, and technology. Students also design the research projects that they will conduct at sea during this part of the program. The second half of the program, or "sea component," is spent at sea, where students have a chance to apply what they learned during the first six weeks, complete their research projects, and develop sailing skills.

The SEA program emphasizes critical thinking, problem-solving, team-building, and leadership skills. This experience is most suitable for marine biology, geology and physical science, or environmental studies majors, although participants come from all areas within the liberal arts and sciences. SEA has partnered with Boston University to grant academic credit for the semester.

Sea Education Association, P.O. Box 6, Woods Hole, MA, 02543; phone 800-552-3633; Web site www.sea.edu.

Programs for the Artistically Inclined

How amazing would it be to study sculpture in the same city where Michelangelo walked the streets more than 400 years ago? Or what about learning to perform Shakespeare's works just yards from his favorite stage at the Globe Theater? All of you artists out there will be happy to know there are programs where you can do exactly that — and more.

Studio Art Centers International

Studio Art Centers International's (SACI) study abroad program in Florence, the epicenter of the Italian Renaissance, offers a multitude of courses in studio art, art history, and art conservation. The program takes advantage of Italy's rich resources for both field trips and class assignments.

All SACI students enroll in full-time course work. Most SACI courses award three semester hours of credit. During the school year (fall and spring), students typically take four or five courses. SACI also offers a late spring and summer session, in which students usually take two courses. The academic year program includes a series of student exhibitions and ends with a major student art show that gives students an opportunity to display their work. Students are housed in SACI apartments with two to six other students; apartments are usually no more than thirty minutes' walking distance from the school.

SACI is administered through the Institute of International Education (IIE, www.iie.org). SACI is accredited by the North Central Association of Colleges and Schools and Bowling Green State University.

Studio Art Centers International, c/o Institute of International Education, 809 United Nations Plaza, New York, NY 10017; phone 212-984-5548; Web site www.saci-florence.org.

Tisch Performing Arts Programs, NYU

New York University's (NYU) Tisch School of Arts offers semester-long programs focused on the performing arts in London, Dublin, South Africa, and Prague. Students can expect to register for 16-18 undergraduate credits; all courses are fully accredited NYU courses. Non-NYU students should apply as non-matriculated or visiting students. Qualified students need to participate in an interview and audition (if applicable).

The London program, based at the Institute of Contemporary Arts (ICA), is designed to expose students to all facets of London's performing arts culture. Courses are taught by instructors at the Royal Academy of Dramatic Art, the British Broadcasting Corporation, the Writers' Guild of Great Britain, and Trinity College of Music. Students may study in any of the following programs: Advanced Directed Projects in Photography; Musical Theatre; Shakespeare in Performance with the Royal Academy of Dramatic Art (RADA); Television Production with the British Broadcasting Corporation (BBC); British Literary, Visual, and Performing Arts; Writing with the Writers' Guild of Great Britain; Playwriting; and Screenwriting.

The Dublin program is run in collaboration with faculty from University College Dublin, the Irish Film Centre (IFC), and several theatre companies including The Abbey and The Gate Theatres. Students may study documentary, dramatic, and cinematic arts as well as take courses on contemporary Ireland. Field trips and cultural activities supplement coursework. Students receive associate membership to the IFC with access to all of its resources, including the Irish Film Archives, Ireland's largest public archive collection.

NYU offers a spring semester program in Johannesburg, South Africa, in conjunction with the University of Witwatersrand. Since 1994 when Nelson Mandela was inaugurated, there has been tremendous development of arts programs and institutions, which represent South Africa's rich history and multicultural heritage. Students earn credits toward their degrees by participating in one of three programs: Theatre-Making, The Arts and Culture of South Africa, and Media Arts: The Picture as Truth.

The newest international study program at the Tisch School is a fall directing semester in Prague (considered the emerging film capital of Europe). Hosted at FAMU (The Prague Film and Television Academy of the Performing Arts), the program is essentially an intense semester of filmmaking with instruction in directing, cinematography, writing, and editing.

Tisch School of Arts, 721 Broadway, 12th floor, New York, NY 10003; phone 212-998-1500; Web site www.nyu.edu/tisch.

Chapter 23

Ten Fun Adventures

Although I am not a *Frommer's* guide, I would be remiss in not letting you know about some fun places you can visit — if you happen to be in the area. Some of my favorite abroad memories are from my travels, and many of the places I visited were recommendations from friends.

The really bizarre or challenging things that happened during my travels are the memories that remain particularly vivid to this day. During the week I visited Rome, I drank Dunkin' Donuts coffee at the Trevi fountain every morning. When my program took us all to an adventure center in Connemara (Ireland), I went kayaking in the freezing cold Atlantic (in November) and body-surfed down a river (wearing a helmet and wetsuit) with a few very turbulent white-water areas.

For this chapter, I solicited ideas from well-traveled friends who studied abroad in various parts of the globe. I picked places that not only sound interesting, but provide the opportunity for some unusual thrill-seeking outdoor adventures, if the weather cooperates and you feel so inclined.

European Escapades

Traditionally, the majority of American study abroad students head to Europe and so most of the nominations I received for fun abroad adventures were for European destinations. The great thing about Europe is that it is extremely accessible: Once you get over there, all you have to do is hop on a train or a plane and you can be in another country in as little as an hour! And chances are you have plenty of friends abroad whom you can stay with (free accommodation, even if it is on a floor, is always good!) and persuade to go exploring with you. Here are some places you shouldn't miss if you're studying on or near "the Continent."

The wild west of Ireland

Not only is the west of Ireland gorgeous with its mountains, lakes, rivers, castles and stone walls, quaint villages, and traditional pubs, but in sunny to mildly rainy weather, there are millions of things to do: water sports; diving (scuba or cliff); sea, game, and coarse angling (in other words, fishing); golfing (including mini golf, or "pitch and putt"); caving; dolphin watching; horse riding; and walking, hiking, and cycling.

Start north of Galway in Connemara National Park to enjoy over 2,000 hectares of scenic mountains, expanses of bogs, heaths, and grasslands. Work your way down to the seaside town of Westport and use it as a base of operations for cliff jumping off Old Head beach or hiking Croagh Patrick (8km west of Westport). Croagh Patrick, rising to 762 meters on the southern shore of Clew Bay, is where St. Patrick is said to have spent 40 days and nights fasting and praying for the people of Ireland around the middle of the fifth century. Since early Christian times, a national pilgrimage to Croagh Patrick has taken place on the last Sunday in July each year. Thousands of devout pilgrims, many barefoot, climb the mountain in the footsteps of St. Patrick.

Drive or take a bus south to the city of Galway to take in some of the best traditional Irish music as well as wander around a variety of pubs, restaurants, and shops. County Clare, directly south of Galway, is another "must see" with the Burren National Park, Ailwee Caves, and the Cliffs of Moher. Spend a night at O'Connors in Doolin, which has the second best pint of Guinness in the world and a wicked seafood chowder, before ferrying over to the Aran Islands for a day of cycling and exploring the cliffs (you can rent bikes when you get off the ferry). Dún Aonghasa, located on Inishmore (the largest of the three Aran Islands), is the largest and most spectacular of the prehistoric stone forts of the Aran Islands, set on a cliff overlooking the Atlantic Ocean. Don't be alarmed if you don't understand the language you hear while cycling around the islands; they still speak Irish (Gaelic) here.

Idyllic Italy

Italy is a wonderful place for art, food, wine, and history — although I recommend visiting in the fall or spring when the pace of tourist season is a little slower. Here are some not-so-touristy highlights:

Cinque Terre

In Italian, *cinque terre* means five villages. Located about an hour's train ride south of Milan on the Italian Riviera, these five towns — Riomaggiore, Manarola, Corniglia, Vernazza, and Monterosso — are built into the mountainous coastline. Peace and quiet reigns here, as the towns are car-free. Some of the best hiking I did while abroad were the two days I spent hiking between the five villages on scenic pathways speckled with olive groves and vineyards, overlooking a perfectly blue-green Mediterranean Sea. Manarola is perhaps the most picturesque of the five villages. Corniglia sits high above the water and is reached by a set of seemingly endless steps. Vernazza has gorgeous sea views from the piazza, which looks out onto the water (I saw one of my favorite sunsets of all time while staying in Vernazza). Monterosso sits above the only beach in Cinque Terre — look out for the huge statues carved into the rocks facing the beach.

Norcia

A small out-of-the-way Umbrian hill town where the twins Saints Benedict and Scholastica were born. The remnants of their Roman house can be seen beneath the Benedictine church. This town is also renowned for its varieties of sausages and cured meat. In the warm weather, take advantage of some great outdoor sports and horsebackriding, hiking, camping, and kayaking.

Sicily

Sicily is underrated. The Greek ruins here are better preserved than in Greece, particularly the Valley of the Temples in Agrigento. Sicily's heritage is extremely diverse: Phoenician, Arab, Greek, Roman, Norman, and Bourbon — to name a few. One of my favorite places is Syracuse: amazing ruins of the Greek amphitheater and the "ear of Dionysus" (a quarry with freaky acoustics, which an ancient tyrant used as a prison so he could spy on his captives). Syracuse is also home to Ortegia Island, a really cool place with St. Lucy's Basilica and the "fountain of Arethusa." Taormina, also worth seeing despite being a bit touristy, is located above Naxos. The highlight of this place is the Roman theater, which uses the stunning natural backdrop of Mt. Etna sloping into the sea. Other reasons to go see Sicily are the great beaches, sunny weather, and delectable food.

Sperlonga

"More Greek than Greece," this town in Lazio (Latium) is a terraced, white-washed town with an amazing beach and the ruins of the villa of the Emperor Tiberius. Archeologists once found life-sized Hellenistic Baroque sculptures that depict scenes from the Odyssey in Tiberius' grotto on the beach. Also worth checking out is the ten foot tall statue of Cyclops about to be blinded.

Switzerland: Skis and spas

In Switzerland, like in Italy, a great time to visit is spring (April and May) or fall (September and October). If skiing or snowboarding is your preferred sport, ski resorts in the Alps open in late November and stay open until the snow starts to melt in April.

Konstanz

Technically belonging to Germany, Konstanz is half in Switzerland, half in Germany. It's an historical town with buildings from the 15th century and earlier; lots of museums and cute shops here. Near Insel Mainau, a tiny island that's one big botanical garden (absolutely breathtaking in May!), check out my favorite pub, the Klosterkeller. The Klosterkeller resides in a very old building with a variety of religious and historical decor. You have to whisper in the pub and it's rumored that the bouncer is a monk. Konstanz is also a university town and only about one hour from Zurich.

Lausanne

Lausanne, located in southwest Switzerland on the edge of Lake Geneva, is known as the Swiss Riviera (all the wealthy Swiss people come here in the summer). It has nice beaches, decent clubs and bars, and a plethora of indoor and outdoor spas not haunted by millions of tourists — all with the scenic Alps and Lake Geneva nearby. You can also take a boat across the lake to Evian (where the water comes from). Nestlé Chocolate headquarters are in the nearby town of Vevey.

San Bernardino Pass

If you want to see some of the most beautiful mountains in the world, you should visit the San Bernardino pass in Switzerland. It begins on the southern side of Thusis, passes the Via Mala, and follows the Rhine River into a valley where you find wild countryside and small villages. As you start to climb a mountain again, you have a spectacular view over the entire Rhine valley. As you begin the narrow descent down the pass towards Bernardino village, you notice a distinct increase in the temperature and you cruise into Bellinzona, where in the summer the temperature rises over 95° Fahrenheit (35° Celsius)!

Sojourning near the Equator

Australia, New Zealand, and the islands of the South Pacific are great destinations for those of you who love the outdoors. This part of the world has amazing landscapes and outdoor activities that will dazzle and amaze you. Where else can you climb to the summit of a glacier, skydive, snuggle up to a crocodile, and go snorkeling in an ancient coral reef? The options are endless! Why not try scuba diving in crystal clear water, white-water rafting, deep sea fishing, whale watching, sailing, or surfing? And don't forget the national sport in this part of the world: rugby. So, what are you waiting for? Get out your pack and choose an adventure if you're studying in this part of the world!

Koh Tao, Thailand

The smallest in a chain of three islands in the Gulf of Thailand Koh Tao is the forgotten neighbor. The three islands, which include Koh Samui and Koh Phangnan, are separated by about an hour's ride on a speedboat. The island next to Koh Tao, Koh Smaui, is famous for its long beaches, expensive resorts, and full moon parties that attract many backpackers, but Koh Tao is the real gem.

An adorable, serene island somewhat hidden in the Gulf of Thailand, Koh Tao translates as "Turtle Island" and for a very good reason: Sea turtles dominate its shores. With beautiful beaches (gorgeous sunsets) and many coral reefs, you get a big bang for your buck here if you're looking to scuba dive. And if you want to get certified, the prices here are a fraction of U.S. prices, and the instruction is just as good. Furthermore, the weather is generally great all year around. February and March are usually the warmest months with very little rainfall, while November is probably the most rainy.

You can get a beachfront bungalow here for as little as $5–$10 a night.

North Sulawesi Island, Indonesia

You can fly to North Sulawesi Island from Singapore or Jakarta. The island is not insane with tourists like Ibiza or Bali and the people are great. North Sulawesi is one of the 32 provinces in the Republic of Indonesia. The terrain on the island is extremely mountainous and hilly (good for hiking!) but also has quite a few lakes. North Sulawesi has a typical equatorial climate with two seasons: rainy (November to March) and dry (April to October).

The highland town of Tondano comes highly recommended. Located above a lake, it's surrounded by oceans, world-class off-shore snorkeling, and jungles. Here you can also explore the rice paddies, clove or coconut plantations, and flower gardens. And you can easily spend a day hiking to a mountain waterfall or soaking in a hot spring.

The island has an endless amount of scuba diving options, as well. You can dive to see the coral gardens of Bunaken Marine Park or view the whales, manta rays, and other ocean creatures at Bangka Strait. After a short sail to the Sangihe Islands, you can explore the fish and underwater volcanoes or go in search of a sunken city. Divers can also investigate World War II shipwrecks or the unusual and rarely seen marine life at Lembeh Strait.

If you're not into scuba diving, go for a hike in the rain forest of the Tangkoko Nature Reserve (home to the largest concentration of black crested macaques and the world's smallest primate, the tarsier) and the Dumoga Bone National

Park (home to the fabled babirusa pig deer). The extremely adventurous may opt for a three-day overland trip to the rainforests of Central Sulawesi. Other popular activities include climbing to the rim of a volcano (the island has both active and extinct volcanoes) or rafting down a white-water river.

Kaiteriteri, New Zealand

Kaiteriteri is an area in the northern part of the South Island of New Zealand (just 13 km from the town of Motueka, 5 km from Marahau) and is the main gateway to Abel Tasman National Park. Kaiteriteri is one of the best beaches in the South Island with very colorful sands. You can hike, kayak, or just stroll. The hikes take you through unbelievable tropical terrain, over wooden bridges, and next to an astounding view of turquoise water and little islands and inlets. You can also visit Abel Tasman National Park where the Tonga Island Marine Reserve has a famous fur seal colony, seabirds, and plentiful fish. A little further inland, you can explore the Ngarua Caves or Harwood's Hole (a vertical shaft 183 meters deep).

Paihia, Bay of Islands, New Zealand

The Bay of Islands is a maritime park created by the great melt that ended the last Ice Age. The rising sea drowned many river valleys, which produced a series of islands in a harbor. Many travelers choose this as a favorite destination because you can swim with dolphins here! What you need to do is take a guided boat trip, which brings you out into the bay to look for schools of wild dolphins. If the dolphins are in a playful mood, you can go swimming and snorkeling with them. Dolphins love playing with you, reply to your calls, and perform all kinds of jumps to amuse you. And after that, you get to spend the day on a beautiful island before the boat comes back to pick you up. Or you can stay in the town of Paihia, which has plenty of cafes, restaurants, and craft shops and museums. It is the base for cruises, bus tours, and visits to the Waitangi Treaty House and grounds (historic site).

Blue Mountains, Australia

The Blue Mountains, located about one hour west of Sydney (get there by car, train, or bus), have plenty for all ages and ability levels: hiking, bush walking, mountain biking, horseback riding, rock climbing, and repelling (or as the Aussies say, abseiling or canyoning). You can go camping on your own or take a guided camping tour. The area has a few adorable towns and lots of indigenous sights, like the "Three Sisters" rock formation, an aboriginal landmark.

Odysseus Never Had It So Good:
Other Odysseys

If you choose to stay on this side of the globe and study in the Americas during your year or semester abroad, believe it or not, there are exotic sun and ski adventures here, too! Even if you don't go abroad, but are at school in the United States, why not head to Canada or South America for spring break? Both places have very affordable adventure options.

Cachagua, Chile

Cachagua, a beautiful seashore town located along the central coast in Chile, is a great place to see some penguins! On Cachagua Island, the Santuario de la Naturaleza protects Humboldt and Magellanic penguins, which are warm-weather penguins about a foot tall.

Las Cujas is a small beach next to Cachagua, made out of crushed shells and surrounded by rock. The rocks close to the beach are not good for climbing, but two trails lead north and south of the beach along the rocks. The south path goes all the way to the sand beach at the south end of Cachagua and has some climbing close to the ocean. At the end of the north path is a climbing wall with many different kinds of rock. If you want to climb here, take along a brush because the rock is covered in sand and salt.

Vancouver, British Columbia

Vancouver, located in the southwest corner of British Columbia, boasts the mildest weather in Canada and is an outdoor adventure haven. Spring arrives in early March and warm sunny days stay through the end of October; winter is generally the rainy season. Vancouver is an extremely bicycle friendly city with many bike paths and routes, so one of the best ways to explore this city is on a bike! You can hike or bike through some of Vancouver's mountains: The Lions, Mount Hollyburn, Grouse Mountain, Mount Seymour, Golden Ears, Cypress Mountain, and Garibaldi Provincial Park. Rent rollerblades to cruise through Stanley Park or the Lower Seymour Conservation Reserve.

A few sports that may not immediately spring to mind when thinking of Vancouver include white-water rafting, windsurfing, and scuba diving. The Thompson, the Nahatlatch, the Squamish, the Elaho, and the Chilliwack Rivers are all perfect for white-water rafting. Vancouver is a great place to learn how to windsurf because it doesn't have consistent winds. At English Bay or on Jericho beaches beginners can rent windsurfers and take lessons. Experienced windsurfers looking for high-wind sailing can head to Squamish. While Vancouver is located far away from the tropics, it does have some amazing cold water scuba diving between Vancouver Island and the mainland. Or try the Sunshine Coast, where near the jagged coastal fjord of Jervis Inlet you can find a sunken mermaid that has been submerged by local divers.

Vancouver rarely sees snow, but there is fabulous downhill and cross country skiing minutes from downtown Vancouver at Grouse Mountain, Cypress Bowl, and Mount Seymour. If you have the time, make the two hour trek north to Whistler and Blackcomb ski resorts. You can downhill ski, helicopter ski, or for the really adventurous, hire a guide and climb up the mountains before skiing back down.

Chapter 24

Ten Considerations for Nontraditional Destinations

Students often overlook Africa, Asia, and Latin America as destinations for study abroad experiences, but the majority of the world's population lives in these three places. Studying in a nontraditional area is a great way to understand some of the less developed parts of the globe and a good way to make your study abroad experience stand out from the average student who spends time in Europe. Although exploring one of these off-the-beaten-track locations is much the same as studying in more popular foreign locales, gaining knowledge about a particular subject area, culture, or language outside the typical destination gives you an unusual and unique experience — just consider the following places.

Satisfying the Thrill-seeker in You

Studying in Africa, Asia, or Latin America is not for everyone. You need to be a little more adventurous, flexible, and open-minded than the average study abroad student. Living in a non-Western area often means fewer advancements in infrastructure and communications systems than you're probably accustomed to. If you don't like dealing with surprises or uncertainty, then you're probably better suited to a more Westernized and stable study abroad experience.

Quelling Health and Safety Anxieties

If the only thing holding you back from choosing a program in Africa, Asia, or Latin America is health and safety concerns, check out all the helpful health and safety advice I provide in Chapter 18. Whether you're going camping in the Amazon for a semester, living in Beijing, or staying home, your safety *never* is guaranteed.

The Centers for Disease Control (CDC, www.cdc.gov) report that the biggest health concern in these nontraditional destinations is traveler's diarrhea, which is transmitted through food and water. You can get traveler's diarrhea in Europe, too. Another common health concern in these areas is malaria, which is serious, but preventable. Your risk of malaria may be higher in some countries than in others. You can prevent contracting malaria by seeing your health care provider for a prescription antimalarial drug and by protecting yourself against mosquito bites.

Exploring Alternative Locations with Familiar Languages

You may want to practice a language you've learned at college, like French, Spanish, or Portuguese. Keep in mind that France, Spain, and Portugal aren't the only places to work on these languages!

Remember that many countries in Africa are former British colonies, so the language of university instruction is English. Likewise, former French colonies often use French as an official instruction language. Consider former colonies particularly if you want to be fully immersed into an African university.

Overcoming Language Barriers

Africa, Asia, and Latin America all offer opportunities to either hone or develop new language skills. In this case, plenty of English-based programs are available with language emersion components. Or if you're not ready to tackle Chinese, plenty of U.S.-based programs require little or no language training and offer courses taught in English.

Studying in Asia: Not just for experts anymore

Many students make two incorrect assumptions about studying in Asia in particular. The first is that Asian languages are difficult or impossible to learn. Not true! Just because Asian languages lack the familiar Roman alphabet doesn't mean you're incapable of learning them. The second assumption is that you must speak an Asian language to study in Asia. Many universities have forged partnerships with American universities or specifically created English-taught programs to cater to foreign students. These programs usually are taught by faculty members who earned their degrees in the U.S. and spent time teaching at U.S. universities. Additionally, at universities in Hong Kong and Singapore, English is the main language of instruction. English also is widely used in Taiwan, Malaysia, Korea, and the Philippines.

Discovering the Wonders of the World

Six out of the seven ancient wonders of the world did not survive to this present day. The one wonder that's still standing, the Pyramids of Egypt, is found just outside of Cairo. Poets, writers, and historians have all sought to create a new list of wonders, but no single list has won unanimous approval. However, the list of forgotten, modern, and natural wonders is long in Africa, Asia, and Latin America. To name just a few, I've made the following list:

- The Great Wall of China
- Taj Mahal (Agra, India)
- Mount Everest (Nepal)
- The High Dam (Aswan, Egypt)
- Mount Kilimanjaro (Tanzania)
- The Panama Canal
- Angel Falls (Venezuela)
- The Aztec Temple in Tenochtitlan (Mexico City, Mexico)

Studying outside of Europe (because that is pretty much what nontraditional means) allows you to see some pretty cool stuff. Check out www.studyabroadlinks.com for links to study abroad programs in many countries of Africa, Asia, and Latin America.

Alfresco African Adventures

Tropical rain forests, massive expanses of desert, plains that go on forever, and modern metropolises are all great reasons to visit Africa. When studying in Africa, many students opt to go on a safari organized by a safari tour operator. You can focus on experiencing nature and observing wildlife or choose a safari more geared toward adventure-seekers who want to scuba dive, hike, kayak, or white-water raft. If this appeals to you, you may want to check out the Kenya Wildlands Study Program at www.kenyawilds.com.

Uncle Sam Wants You — To Study in Asia

Roughly 6 percent of American undergrads who study abroad choose Asia, but the U.S. actually needs more students to study in Asia because it's an area of the world that is increasingly important to the economic well-being of the U.S. and to global security. Even though American businesses are deeply involved in Asia, not enough American professionals can truly understand Asia or communicate in East and Southeast Asian languages. Ironically, American familiarity with Asian cultures is severely lacking in comparison with Asian familiarity with American culture. The evidence: Approximately 5,000 Americans are studying in East and Southeast Asia, but more than 250,000 students from East and Southeast Asia are studying in the U.S.

Coping with Congestion

Imagine walking down a city street and the smog is so thick you're having problems breathing. The sidewalks overflow with people and the road is crowded by cars as well as bicycles. You try to seek some relief underground, but find subway cars bursting at their seams with travelers. Welcome to cities in Asia. Industrial pollution and high population densities tend to be problems in most Asian metropolises. If you anticipate that either of these factors may be a problem for you, do your research, consult your study abroad adviser, and look for study-abroad programs in a smaller city or rural village.

Another tip to keep in mind is that these bustling metropolises beget increased crime rates. Theft, the most common crime that affects visitors, occurs more frequently in crowded public areas, such as hotel lobbies, bars, restaurants, and tourist and transportation sites. Thieves are particularly interested in stealing a U.S. passport. The loss or theft of a U.S. passport needs to be reported immediately to local police and to the nearest U.S. Embassy.

Capybaras Don't Bite

Latin America is a unique study abroad destination for students interested in biology or ecology. The Amazon River area contains the world's largest tropical forest and has an amazingly diverse plant and animal population. It offers an opportunity for students to come alongside scientists studying the balance between finite ecological resources and the demands humans place on these resources. The Galápagos Islands, also located in this region, are home to plant and animal species found nowhere else on earth and perhaps the world's most renowned environmental destination.

Belém, located at the mouth of the Amazon, has a lush, tropical atmosphere and is a principal center for Amazonian research. Students gain insight into studies conducted in rain-forest villages and at research laboratories, extractive industry locations, and archeological sites. Ecuador is another great place to study a tropical environment; it contains an Amazonian rain forest, the highlands at Páramo, and indigenous cultures diligently developing conservation strategies. Quito, Ecuador's capital city, is located at the foot of the Pichincha Volcano and serves as a great home base for exploring the Andes.

Latin America: An Overnight Sensation

Latin American studies is quickly becoming a subject area worthy of its own major at many universities in the U.S. One of the world's foremost developing regions, Latin America is attracting students who want to investigate its accelerating political and economic systems, the cultural issues that arise in times of dramatic change, and environmental degradation issues.

Study abroad programs in this region often offer opportunities to intern or complete independent studies with grass-roots organizations and social movements that deal with the issues facing the region. You can greatly increase your understanding of the issues that face the region by examining a specific culture and theme. Examples of research topics include:

- Analyzing the dynamics of early indigenous civilizations
- Investigating the conquest and domination by European powers
- Sorting through the struggle and negotiation between social and political groups
- Examining the return of democracy and the challenges of democratization
- Studying military involvement and social revolution
- Calculating African, Judaic, and Asian cultural retention
- Dissecting the emergence and legacy of authoritarian regimes

Chapter 25

Ten Reasons to Do Grad School Abroad

In This Chapter

▶ Taking advantage of the time, quality, and economics of grad school abroad

▶ Missing out on going abroad as an undergrad

▶ Studying abroad again!

▶ Getting noticed because of global education

*T*he United States is not the end all and be all of higher education. There are some fabulous graduate schools and study opportunities around the globe that you can take advantage of if you're willing to move away from home for a few years.

Many reasons for pursuing graduate school abroad are the same as the reasons for spending a semester or a year of your undergraduate education somewhere else. (See Chapter 1 for convincing arguments on why to study abroad.) However, the unique reasons for going to graduate school abroad deserve some discussion.

If you studied abroad in college, realize that going abroad this time around will be different. You are applying directly to a university abroad. No undergraduate institution or U.S.-based program is going to look after you. You're on your own this time. Going abroad for grad school may be slightly more stressful because you have to find your own housing, budget down to the last detail, and chart your own academic course in a foreign place (with the help of an adviser, of course). But, if you're serious enough to pursue graduate studies, you're probably quite capable of handling all those relocation details.

Most American graduate students who study abroad obtain their full graduate degrees at a university abroad. However, a growing number of U.S. universities and study abroad programs are organizing short-term study abroad for graduate students. These programs are as short as a few weeks or as long as a year.

Taking Advantage of a Quick Finish

Graduate degrees earned here in the U.S. tend to take longer than those earned abroad. A taught master's (classroom-based) program abroad usually takes about one year while the U.S. equivalent takes about an average of two years. You also have an option abroad that isn't as popular here: a master's by research instead of coursework. A research master's may keep you in school anywhere from 12 to 18 months. PhDs earned abroad generally take less time as well. Earning a PhD in the U.S. hovers at about six years and can extend up to eight. Receiving a PhD outside the U.S. works out on average to be four years.

One reason for shorter PhDs in some countries is that students enter undergraduate universities at a higher level than Americans do, so they're doing U.S graduate level work by the end of their undergraduate degrees — they're a little bit ahead of us.

Realize that a MA or a PhD will be respected regardless of where you end up after school. No one can take a degree you worked so hard for away from you!

If you come back to the U.S. after earning a PhD abroad in three or four years, you may need to spend a year or two doing a post-doc to make yourself more marketable.

Attending professional schools (business, law, and medical) abroad tends to work a little differently. In the U.S., students earn these degrees after completing four year bachelor's programs: MBAs take two years, JDs take three years, and MDs take a whopping eight years to complete. In some countries, students start these degrees directly after secondary school, so they take fewer years off their lives in the grand scheme of things. However, choosing to do an MBA program abroad isn't a big savings in tuition. Foreign business universities tend to charge rates that are nearly equivalent to U.S. business school rates for U.S. nationals. Furthermore, depending on the country where the degree was granted, law and medical degrees in particular are not likely to be recognized by many U.S. institutions.

Experiencing Excellence

Many foreign universities have incredibly strong reputations and world-renowned post-graduate studies. If you research your particular subject area, you're sure to discover a school or two outside the U.S. that does excellent research and produces top quality graduates in your field. Why not go there?

A note of caution about the quality of graduate school programs: Here in the U.S. we tend to get caught up in rankings. Which graduate school is ranked highest for business? Psychology? English? These rankings are all rather arbitrary. You could go to one of these so-called top schools and have a miserable experience or get a lousy education because your program has too many PhDs and you fail to get any personal attention. What, to you, characterizes a high quality program? A small PhD program in Canada may be just as good, if not better for you, than a program on one of those top U.S. graduate school lists.

Making Economical Sense

Well, if your graduate degree takes less time if you do it abroad, then it follows that it costs you less money. Like they say, time is money. Schools abroad, in general, have tuitions much lower than their U.S. counterparts. If you couple that with a really good exchange rate in U.S. to local currency and a lower cost of living than here in the U.S. — you could have yourself the bargain of a lifetime! Not only that, but applying to a foreign university as an international student can give you an advantage: You're different, you add variety to the program, therefore, the school may want to give you money (in the form of merit scholarships or stipends) to study at their university.

Two caveats to keep in mind when considering the economics of grad school abroad:

- ✔ Many places abroad, especially big cities, are much more expensive than where you currently live in the U.S. So check the cost of living in areas where you're looking at programs.

- ✔ Don't expect to pay the low tuition of citizens in your host country. Like state universities in the U.S., most universities abroad charge much higher fees for non-citizens. (These fees, however, could still work out to be less than what you'd pay in the U.S.)

Trying Something New

The number one regret of college graduates I know is that "I didn't go abroad." Well, just because you didn't do it as an undergrad doesn't mean it is too late! Consider having your abroad adventure a little later in life and go abroad for grad school! It's never too late to take advantage of all that study abroad has to offer: personal growth, opportunities to travel, and continuing the quest for knowledge, to name a few.

Going abroad for grad school becomes an especially attractive offer if your current life is as, if not more, commitment free than it was as an undergrad. If you don't own a car, an apartment/house, a dog, have a child or a significant other — then what is stopping you from packing up and studying abroad now? I guarantee this becomes immensely more challenging when and if you acquire any of the aforementioned commitment-laden objects.

Going Again Because You Loved It the First Time

If you went abroad in college and wished you could have stayed longer, or if you went abroad and traveled to a really neat place where you want to live one day, or if you promised yourself you'd somehow get back to your abroad location for another extended stay someday — then grad school abroad can satisfy some of these wishes. If you found a second home on your first abroad adventure, then why not go back? Remember, studying is one of the easiest ways to get a visa to live in a foreign country! You still may have very good friends there or have established a great working relationship with a professor you want to have advise your graduate work.

However, a note of caution on returning to the same study abroad location: It will never be exactly the same as your first time around. It may still be great, it may even be better, but remember, you're not the same person as before. Time has passed and you're probably at a different place in your life when you get on that plane for foreign lands this time around. Be sure you're going abroad for the right reason — to further your education in a subject you're passionate about. Don't go back to chase some mysterious foreigner you fell in love with but couldn't do anything about because you were only there for eight weeks.

Getting a Global Education: The Wave of the Future

With globalization, the advancements in technology, and the ease of jetting off to a foreign land, education has become more international in nature. Exploring the big world outside the U.S. and discovering how the rest of the world views us is important. Understanding the histories, religious beliefs, ethical philosophies, artistic traditions, and world views of others can help us decide how to make a difference in the world.

As a graduate student at an abroad university, you are embracing this wave of global education. You bring a unique perspective to a classroom and this perspective will probably be questioned and challenged, but it will make life interesting. Not only are your own studies enriched by those around you, but through graduate seminars, presentations, and conferences, you also enrich the world of your fellow students. You may be able to acquire unique internships or gain access to some of the most radical or popular thinkers in your field by studying outside the U.S. The possibilities are endless — and surprising — when you pursue your education elsewhere.

Getting Accepted to Grad School in the U.S.

Doing a master's degree or post-baccalaureate outside the U.S. is also a good way to propel yourself into graduate programs in the U.S. Spending a year working on post-graduate study abroad can strengthen your application before an admissions committee, particularly if you do extremely well in your studies abroad. Not only is this an economical option to bolster your C.V. (resume), but it makes your application stand out. You bring something different to a grad program than candidates who have been in the U.S. for their entire academic career. Plus, getting accepted to do a year of post-graduate study abroad can be relatively easy — not only are you international, but some abroad schools will see you as a source of income because they can charge higher fees to students from outside their country.

Studying French in France

Where better to study Celtic civilization than Ireland or Scotland? Or get your master's in French literature in France? Earn your PhD in Chinese culture in Beijing! Don't these suggestions seem to make sense? As long as you speak the native language, then go to the country in question if you're looking to do graduate work on a specific cultural or regional subject. In doing so, you'll probably rub elbows with more than one expert in the field. Furthermore, the opportunity to do field research or take field trips to locations pertinent to your studies is not to be missed!

Avoiding Pesky Grad School Admissions Tests

Fear of standardized tests? Are you just a poor test taker? Well, if any of the College Board's graduate admissions tests have got you down or are proving to be a large obstacle to attaining your grad school goals, consider going to a school that does not require any of these tests. Your best bet of finding a school that doesn't care about U.S. grad school test scores is going to be outside the U.S. Other countries don't have a college board equivalent. Many abroad graduate programs place a heavy emphasis on your undergraduate academic record, references, and completed research in your proposed field (For example, did you write a senior thesis in college?).

Some schools are on to this little trick and may ask for your test scores (business schools are the worst offenders and often ask U.S. applicants for their GMAT scores), so this isn't a foolproof strategy.

Opening Doors for Working Abroad

If your ultimate goal is to permanently live or work abroad, then graduate school is a good avenue to getting your foot in the door. Looking for a job abroad is exceedingly difficult if you're living in the U.S. Going to grad school in the country of your dreams is one way to get into the country so that eventually you can apply for permanent residence. Graduate school in another country also helps you make connections for when you finish your degree. Another option that you may have the luxury to pursue as a graduate student is unpaid internships. Spending ten hours a week working for free in a company could eventually lead to a permanent job.

Index

• D •

• E •

• Z •

FOR DUMMIES®

The easy way to get more done and have more fun

PERSONAL FINANCE & BUSINESS

Investing FOR DUMMIES

0-7645-2431-3

Home Buying FOR DUMMIES

0-7645-5331-3

Grant Writing FOR DUMMIES

0-7645-5307-0

Also available:

Accounting For Dummies
(0-7645-5314-3)

Business Plans Kit For Dummies
(0-7645-5365-8)

Managing For Dummies
(1-5688-4858-7)

Mutual Funds For Dummies
(0-7645-5329-1)

QuickBooks All-in-One Desk Reference For Dummies
(0-7645-1963-8)

Resumes For Dummies
(0-7645-5471-9)

Small Business Kit For Dummies
(0-7645-5093-4)

Starting an eBay Business For Dummies
(0-7645-1547-0)

Taxes For Dummies 2003
(0-7645-5475-1)

HOME, GARDEN, FOOD & WINE

Feng Shui FOR DUMMIES

0-7645-5295-3

Gardening FOR DUMMIES

0-7645-5130-2

Cooking FOR DUMMIES

0-7645-5250-3

Also available:

Bartending For Dummies
(0-7645-5051-9)

Christmas Cooking For Dummies
(0-7645-5407-7)

Cookies For Dummies
(0-7645-5390-9)

Diabetes Cookbook For Dummies
(0-7645-5230-9)

Grilling For Dummies
(0-7645-5076-4)

Home Maintenance For Dummies
(0-7645-5215-5)

Slow Cookers For Dummies
(0-7645-5240-6)

Wine For Dummies
(0-7645-5114-0)

FITNESS, SPORTS, HOBBIES & PETS

Fitness FOR DUMMIES

0-7645-5167-1

Golf FOR DUMMIES

0-7645-5146-9

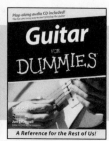

Guitar FOR DUMMIES

0-7645-5106-X

Also available:

Cats For Dummies
(0-7645-5275-9)

Chess For Dummies
(0-7645-5003-9)

Dog Training For Dummies
(0-7645-5286-4)

Labrador Retrievers For Dummies
(0-7645-5281-3)

Martial Arts For Dummies
(0-7645-5358-5)

Piano For Dummies
(0-7645-5105-1)

Pilates For Dummies
(0-7645-5397-6)

Power Yoga For Dummies
(0-7645-5342-9)

Puppies For Dummies
(0-7645-5255-4)

Quilting For Dummies
(0-7645-5118-3)

Rock Guitar For Dummies
(0-7645-5356-9)

Weight Training For Dummies
(0-7645-5168-X)

Available wherever books are sold.
Go to www.dummies.com or call 1-877-762-2974 to order direct

WIL

FOR DUMMIES®

A world of resources to help you grow

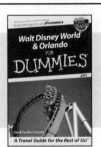

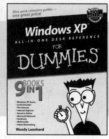